Self-Presentation

Self-Presentation
Impression Management and Interpersonal Behavior

Mark R. Leary
Wake Forest University

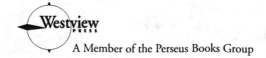

Westview Press
A Member of the Perseus Books Group

Social Psychology Series
John Harvey, Series Editor

Empathy: A Social Psychological Approach, Mark H. Davis

Violence Within the Family: Social Psychological Perspectives, Sharon D. Herzberger

Social Dilemmas, Samuel S. Komorita and Craig D. Parks

Self-Presentation: Impression Management and Interpersonal Behavior, Mark R. Leary

Experimental and Nonexperimental Designs in Social Psychology, Abraham S. Ross and Malcolm Grant

Intergroup Relations, Walter G. Stephan and Cookie White Stephan

Published in 1996 in the United States of America by Westview Press, Inc., 5500 Central Avenue, Boulder, Colorado 80301-2877, and in the United Kingdom by Westview Press, 12 Hid's Copse Road, Cumnor Hill, Oxford OX2 9JJ

Leary, Mark R.
Self-presentation : impression management and interpersonal behavior / by Mark R. Leary.
p. cm.
Madison, Wis. : Brown & Benchmark Publishers, c1995.
Includes bibliographical references and index.
ISBN 0-8133-3004-1 (pbk.)
1. Self-presentation 2. Interpersonal relations. 3. Social interactions. I. Title.
BF697.5.S44L43 1996
158'.2—dc20 96-1276
CIP

The paper used in this publication meets the requirements of the American National Standard for Permanence of Paper for Printed Library Materials Z39.48-1984.

10 9 8

To the students who have also been my teachers—
especially Robin, James, Kelly, Tom, and Susan.

CONTENTS

PREFACE

This book is about the ways in which human behavior is affected by people's concerns with their public impressions. No matter what else people may be doing, they typically prefer that other people perceive them in certain desired ways and not perceive them in other, undesired ways. Put simply, human beings have a pervasive and ongoing concern with their **self-presentations.** Sometimes they act in certain ways just to make a particular impression on someone else—as when a job applicant responds in ways that will satisfactorily impress the interviewer. But more often, people's concerns with others' impressions simply constrain their behavioral options. Most of the time we are not inclined to do things that will lead others to see us as incompetent, immoral, maladjusted, or otherwise socially undesirable. As a result, our concerns with others' impressions limit what we are willing to do. Self-presentational motives underlie and pervade nearly every corner of interpersonal life.

Herein lies an interesting paradox. Virtually everyone is attentive to, if not explicitly concerned about how he or she is perceived and evaluated by other people. Yet most people try to deny that they are personally bothered by such superficial concerns with public appearances. We sometimes suspect that *other people* are "putting on a show"—they are not as smart/wealthy/competent/ethical/connected/etc. as they try to appear. But, with a few exceptions, most of us deny that *we* put on similar shows for the various audiences we encounter throughout the day. Of course, such denials are, themselves, often self-presentational. To achieve our goals in social life, we must assure that others take our public impressions at face value—that they do not doubt that we are who and what we appear to be. (This is one hazard of doing self-presentational research; people assume that a psychologist who studies self-presentation must be a particularly fervid impression manager.)

One theme of this book is that, far from being a sign of insecurity, vanity, or shallowness, a certain degree of concern for one's public impressions is essential for smooth and successful social interaction. That's not to say that such concerns aren't sometimes inappropriate, excessive, or even dangerous. But self-presentational excesses should not blind us to the fact that a certain degree of attention to the impressions we are making is often a good thing. Because the course of social interaction is strongly affected by the impressions the interactants have of one another, something would be amiss if people *weren't* concerned about being perceived in ways that facilitate their goals. Indeed, people who show no concern for others' impressions of them are generally derogated and ostracized. We label such people as rude, inconsiderate, socially unskilled, boorish, or even mentally disturbed.

This book is organized around four general issues or themes regarding the functions, causes, and effects of self-presentation in everyday life. The first two chapters provide us with a background for understanding self-presentation, with an emphasis on the tactics people use to manage their impressions. As we will see, virtually any behavior can be used for self-presentational purposes. Don't infer from this that all behavior is self-presentational; it certainly is not. I'm simply saying that almost any behavior can be motivated by self-presentational concerns on some occasions.

The second issue we will address involves the question of *why* people are motivated to manage their impressions. This is, in fact, two questions, one asking why people should *ever* be motivated to manage their impressions, and the other asking why people are more motivated to impression-manage in some situations than in others and why some people are generally more motivated to impression-manage than other people.

The largest portion of the book, Chapters 4–8, examines the myriad of factors that affect the kinds of impressions people try to convey in a particular situation. As we will see, some of these factors involve features of the social setting, whereas others involve the person's own personal characteristics.

Finally, the book concludes with a look at what happens, both behaviorally and emotionally, when people think they are making undesired impressions on other people. Self-presentational worries can seriously disrupt social interactions and the behavior of people in them.

In writing the book, I've tried to walk the very fine line between writing a relatively comprehensive, integrative review of the literature that will be of use to behavioral researchers interested in self-presentational processes and a readable, "user-friendly" text that will provide interesting and educational reading for undergraduate and graduate students. The book would serve nicely as a supplemental text in undergraduate and graduate courses in social psychology and personality. I hope I've successfully walked that line but, in the end, that's for you, the reader, to judge.

Many people have contributed indirectly to this book by facilitating my thinking, research, and writing on self-presentational processes over the past 15 years. Most notably, I extend my thanks to Barry Schlenker, my graduate school advisor and mentor, who has had a profound impact on my professional development generally and my interest in self-presentation more specifically. The many graduate and undergraduate students who have collaborated on my research over the years also deserve my deepest gratitude. Their ideas, questions, criticisms, and hard work have enhanced my understanding of self-presentation and related topics immeasurably. Similarly, the feedback of several colleagues at Wake Forest University have also facilitated my thinking about self-presentation.

I'd also like to thank my colleagues at other schools, who reviewed this book in manuscript form, for their valuable comments and contributions. Thanks to Robert A. Giacalone of the E. C. Robins School of Business at the University of Richmond, James A. Shepperd of the University of Florida, and to John A. Harvey of the University of Iowa, the consulting editor for the Brown and Benchmark Social Psychology Series.

As this book was going to press, psychologists around the world were saddened to learn of the death of Dr. Edward E. Jones of Princeton University. Ned Jones was a social psychologist *par excellence* who left indelible marks on several areas of social psychology, including self-presentation. Not only did he contribute extensively to our understanding of self-presentational processes, but he was responsible for initiating the study of self-presentation in psychology. We will encounter Jones' important work repeatedly throughout the book.

This book might have never been written without the support provided by a Reynolds Research Leave from Wake Forest University, to which I am indebted. I also appreciate the help of Edward Jones, James Tedeschi, Barry Schlenker, and Roy Baumeister who generously provided reminiscences about their own self-presentational research and answered my questions about their personal views of the history and current state of research on self-presentation. Finally, I'd like to thank Rowland Miller, Donelson Forsyth, and Tedra Walden—three graduate school cronies whose personal friendships are a source of continuing professional support and personal pleasure.

Mark R. Leary
Winston-Salem, NC

CHAPTER

1

Introduction

CHAPTER OUTLINE

If you were raised like many Americans, I suspect that your parents tried to teach you not to worry about what other people thought of you. Americans have a maxim that says that we should rarely be concerned about others' opinions of us. "Just be yourself. March to your own drummer. Don't worry about what other people will think."

In spite of widespread lip service to this view, you probably grew up realizing that people are, in fact, often very concerned about how other people perceive and evaluate them. Virtually everyone thinks about other people's impressions of him or her from time to time, and some people worry a great deal about how others regard them. Furthermore, just about everybody occasionally behaves in ways that he or she hopes will lead others to form particular impressions of him or her. The reason is clear: despite what our parents told us, most of us realize that the impressions we make on other people *do* make a difference.

When people interact, they are responding to the impressions they have of one another. Sometimes those impressions are accurate; sometimes they are not. Either way, the impressions people form strongly affect how they respond to one another. As a result, few social situations exist in which people can afford to disregard totally how others are perceiving and evaluating them.

The Nature of Self-Presentation

Given the importance of others' perceptions in social interaction, we should not be surprised that people keep an eye on how others regard them and, from time to time, try to control the impressions people have of them. The process of controlling how one is perceived by other people is called **self-presentation** or **impression management** (Leary & Kowalski, 1990; Schneider, 1981; Schlenker, 1980).

Contrary to what our parents tried to teach us, self-presentation is not always a bad thing. Rather than reflecting manipulativeness, vanity, or insecurity, paying an appropriate degree of attention to others' impressions is healthy and adaptive. Think for a moment about what the world would be like if no one ever cared about what other people thought of him or her. Think about how people might act if they didn't care what others thought. Think how they would look, what they might say, how they'd probably smell!

If people showed no regard for others' perceptions of them, they would fare quite poorly in life. Because our concern with others' impressions helps keep our behavior within socially appropriate limits, people who were unconcerned with others' impressions would often behave inappropriately, resulting in negative reactions ranging from disparagement to ostracism. They might laugh at funerals, wear swimwear to the office, or never bathe. They certainly wouldn't try to put their best foot forward when the situation called for it. As a result, they would have serious difficulties in job interviews and on first dates. Even if initially successful, the tactless person who never impression-managed would have trouble keeping jobs, friends, and lovers.

Furthermore, a certain degree of attention to one's self-disclosures to other people is essential for the formation of close relationships (Derlega, Metts, Petronio, & Margulis, 1993). People who don't convey an appropriate amount and type of information about themselves to other people have difficulty developing and maintaining friendships and romantic relationships.

That's not to say that self-presentation is never problematic. Although it's an essential component of social interaction, concerns with others' impressions can create difficulties. For example, people are sometimes too concerned about what others think of them, or they are concerned about their impressions in situations that are inappropriate. As we'll discuss in later chapters, people's self-presentational concerns can also interfere with their performance on important tasks, cause them to feel anxious, and lead them to do things that are harmful to themselves or to other people. Yet, despite these problems, there is nothing inherently bad or sleazy about self-presentation.

Few aspects of people's behavior are unaffected by self-presentational motives. Sometimes people act in certain ways primarily and explicitly to foster a certain impression. When a man tells his date about his glory days as a college athlete, a student cleans up his apartment when his parents are coming to visit, or a woman chooses the clothes she will wear on a job interview, their behavior is affected primarily by their desire to make certain impressions.

At other times, self-presentation is a secondary concern. But even when people's behavior is motivated by other goals, they typically pursue those goals in ways that do not jeopardize their image in others' eyes. As a student eats with friends in the cafeteria, her primary goal is to eat (and perhaps to enjoy the company of her friends), and self-presentational concerns are secondary. Even so, the student does not take food off others' plates without asking, wipe her mouth on her blouse, or belch loudly. When I am walking through a music store to buy a new compact disk, my primary goal is to buy the CD. But I pursue my goal in a way that doesn't create bad impressions. I walk—not run—through the store; I don't shout at people who get in my way; and I don't criticize other shoppers' choices of music, no matter how stupid I might think they are.

Thus, even when we are doing other things and impression management is not our primary goal, our behavior is usually constrained by our concerns with others' impressions. No matter what else we might be doing, we rarely intentionally do things that will make us appear incompetent, immoral, unattractive, or otherwise socially undesirable. (Of course, some of us may accidentally present such negative images of ourselves more often than we would like.) Self-presentation provides a constraint within which most other behaviors occur.

Self-Presentation and Deception

You don't need a psychologist to tell you that people sometimes lie about themselves. In extreme cases, people may con others into thinking they are someone or something they are not. More commonly, people may try to get others to form impressions that, although not completely false, are more positive than is warranted—that they are wealthier or more intelligent than they really are, for example.

Although some self-presentations are exaggerations and others are downright lies, most of the time the impressions people try to make on others are not deceptive. We are all multifaceted individuals, and in any given situation, we could convey many different impressions of ourselves, all of which are true. Rather than lying, people typically select the images they want others to form from their repertoire of true self-images. This selection is often tactical in the sense that it is based on their goals in the situation and on their assumptions about which impressions will best achieve those goals. But the impressions they ultimately try to create in others' minds are more often accurate rather than deceptive (Schlenker, 1980; Schlenker & Weigold, 1992).

If you and I met, what would we disclose about ourselves to one another? Would I tell you that I am a university professor and specifically a social psychologist? Would I mention that I run regularly, or that I once played in rock and jazz bands? Do I tell you that I enjoy football more than baseball, or confess that I know as little about cars as anybody else I know? Would I describe my childhood, my successes and failures, my goals in life?

I could convey any one of these impressions of myself to you, all of them truthful, but (as you would) I would be selective in the images I created. I'd probably be more likely to mention that I'm a psychologist if I knew you were a psychology student because I've found that nonpsychologists seem to think I'm going to analyze everything they say. I'm probably more likely to mention running if you look physically fit than if you look like you've never exercised a moment in your life. Unless I intentionally wanted to argue with you, I might not mention my musical interests if you enjoyed only classical music and were on a tirade about the decadence of popular music. If we're just talking about sports, I might mention my preference for football, but if you were a member of the university baseball team, I probably wouldn't. If you're a mechanic who's working on my car, I'm not likely to profess my ignorance about cars; if you get the impression I'm an automotive illiterate, who knows what you might try to pull off on me?

My point is that, although people sometimes present images of themselves that are not true, impression management usually involves accurate impressions colored by tactical changes in emphasis, tone, and omission. Sometimes the selection is completely self-serving (as when I fail to mention that I'm a psychologist because you might think I'm weird), but sometimes it's also for others' benefit (as when I don't brag about running a marathon to someone who's a couch potato).

Schlenker and Weigold (1992) suggested that believability is a very important consideration when people construct their social identities. If others do not regard the images that people project as reasonably accurate constructions of reality, they will be dismissed as manipulative, deceptive, or deluded. Furthermore, most people find it anxiety producing to project and maintain public images that they know are not true. Because of these considerations, people project truly deceptive self-presentations only in rare instances.

Unflattering Self-Presentations

Think for a moment of a specific instance in which you wanted other people to form a certain impression of you. Chances are the situation you imagined was one in which you wanted to make a positive or favorable impression. In most cases, we want others to perceive us in socially desirable ways. We would usually rather be regarded as competent than incompetent, as moral than immoral, and as attractive than as unattractive, and so on.

However, not all self-presentations are positive. In some cases, the impressions people try to convey are far from socially desirable. For example, people sometimes want to be seen as threatening or intimidating because such impressions will help them achieve their interpersonal goals. Perhaps you've had a boss who made sure his employees perceived him as gruff and intolerant to keep them in line. Similarly, a member of a street gang may dress and act in threatening ways so that people will be scared of him. Closer to home, most of us have tried to get rid of a bore by conveying an impression of hostility or disinterest (Schneider, 1981). In other cases, people may want to be seen as incompetent or weak because such impressions will lead others to help or support them. People will even try to be seen as unlikable if doing so helps them achieve their goals (Jellison & Gentry, 1978).

The primary goal of self-presentation is not to be perceived positively per se, but to influence other people to respond in desired ways

(Jones & Pittman, 1982). In most cases, people are more likely to treat us as we want them to when they have positive impressions of us—that we are friendly, competent, ethical, and attractive, for example. Because of this, the impressions people usually try to make are positive, socially desirable ones.

In other cases, however, people are more likely to be treated as they desire if they foster undesirable impressions in others' eyes. As we'll explore in detail later in the book, people sometimes think their interests will be best served if they can get others to perceive them as violent, incompetent, ill, or even mentally disturbed (Braginsky, Braginsky, & Ring, 1969; Jones & Pittman, 1982; Kowalski & Leary, 1990).

A Brief History of Self-Presentation Research

As a student, I cringed whenever the author of a book launched into a discussion of the history of his or her topic. But I see now that understanding something about the development of an area helps us understand the area itself—its emphases, biases, controversies, blind spots, and so on. So, please bear with me. I'll make this history as brief and as painless as possible.

Interest in self-presentation emerged somewhat independently at about the same time in psychology and sociology. Although it may seem that sociologists and psychologists (especially social psychologists) would have many things in common, connections between the disciplines have traditionally been weak, and sociologists and psychologists have typically relied little on each other's work. However, researchers interested in self-presentation would find it nearly impossible to carry out their work without relying on concepts, theories, and research from both sociology and psychology.

Goffman and the Sociological Approach

The systematic study of self-presentation began with the work of sociologist Erving Goffman. Although he wrote many essays relevant to the study of human interaction, Goffman's major contribution was *The Presentation of Self in Everyday Life,* published in 1959. Goffman's basic premise was that many of the most revealing insights about social behavior are to be found not in analyzing people's inner motives or personalities, but in studying the surface appearances people create for one another. Whereas psychologists often look beyond people's overt behavior to understand their "true" underlying motives and characteristics, Goffman insisted that much can be gained by focusing on public behavior.

In the course of social life, people's responses to one another are heavily based on these surface appearances. Contrary to the advice we receive, we *do* judge books (and people) by their covers. And, because of this, people often present images of themselves that affect others' judgments and reactions. According to Goffman, a full understanding of human behavior requires that we pay attention to these public images. His view was consistent with Cooley's (1902) claim that "the imaginations which people have of one another are the solid facts of society" (p. 87).

For Goffman, people control how other people treat them by influencing others' definition of the situation. They influence others' definition of the situation by giving others the kind of impression that will lead them to act voluntarily in accordance with their objectives. "Thus, when an individual appears in the presence of others, there will usually be some reason for him to mobilize his activity so that it will convey an impression to others which it is in his interests to convey" (Goffman, 1959, p. 4).

According to Goffman, self-presentation is not only functional for the individual, but it is essential for smooth interaction. Effective social interaction requires that the interactants know a little about one another—about one another's socioeconomic status, attitudes, trustworthiness, competence, and so on. Yet, interactants often find it difficult to learn much about other people. Here's where self-presentation helps. The public images people convey give other interactants some idea of how they expect to be treated and how they should expect to treat others.

Goffman seemed particularly interested in what happens when self-presentation goes awry. When the impressions people project are contradicted or discredited, the interaction is disrupted. In fact, the interaction often grinds to a halt until the person's public image is successfully restored (Goffman, 1955, 1959, 1967). Goffman wrote extensively about embarrassment and face-work, topics we explore in later chapters.

Goffman has been associated with what is known as the "dramaturgical approach" because he made great use of metaphors of the theater, complete with acts, roles, props, audiences, and backstage areas. However, nowhere in his writings does Goffman argue that life is nothing but a stage or that men and women are merely actors. Rather, he used the idea of life as drama as an analogy or metaphor to elucidate certain facts about social life (Brissett & Edgley, 1990).

Goffman's work was more akin to social anthropology than sociology (indeed, his Master's degree was in anthropology). His articles and books were essentially anthropological descriptions of everyday interactions in Western society. Rather than recording the habits of the natives in some far-off land, he watched the interactions of people in the

British Isles and United States. Goffman was an astute observer of human behavior with the ability to see processes of social life in new ways and to describe them in an engaging fashion.

Jones and Social Psychology

At about the same time Goffman published *The Presentation of Self in Everyday Life,* Edward Jones, a social psychologist, began a program of work on flattery. At the time, Jones was unfamiliar with Goffman's work but became involved with self-presentation because of his interest in how people figure out what other people are like. Jones realized that our perceptions of other people are determined in part by their attempts to convey particular impressions of themselves. As Jones (1990) put it, "the study of impression management and self-presentation is an integral part of the study of interpersonal perception. We cannot understand how people perceive each other without at the same time understanding the dynamics of self-presentation" (p. 170). Thus, from early work on how people ingratiate themselves to others (Jones, 1964; Jones & Wortman, 1973), Jones moved on to study many facets of the self-presentation process.

Jones' approach to research on self-presentation was quite different from Goffman's. Whereas Goffman reported what were essentially anthropological field observations in narrative essays, Jones and his students designed laboratory experiments to investigate specific factors that affect self-presentation. Goffman tried to *persuade* his readers of his insights through observations and anecdotes, whereas Jones tried to confirm and disconfirm particular theoretical ideas through controlled experimentation.

Jones' contribution to the study of self-presentation cannot be overestimated. Not only did he produce a wealth of empirical studies on the topic and offered important theoretical advances, but he trained several social psychologists who went on to make contributions to the area of self-presentation in their own right. We'll encounter the contributions of Jones and his students throughout this book.

Resistance to Self-Presentation

From the beginning, some social psychologists, as well as many lay people, were extremely interested in self-presentation. Many realized that a great deal of social behavior is affected by people's concerns with others' impressions of them. However, self-presentation did not begin to emerge as a mainline area of interest among behavioral researchers for many years, and some researchers initially displayed outright resistance to self-presentational approaches. Jones noted that, when he first became interested in self-presentation in the early 1960s, some of his colleagues seemed to feel that he had entered a domain of investigation that was "as unsettling and almost as disreputable as parapsychology" (personal communication, March 17, 1992). One manifestation of this disinterest in self-presentation was that, until recently, it was difficult to find the terms "self-presentation" or "impression management" in the indexes of most textbooks on social psychology.

The reasons for this resistance to the topic are not entirely clear, particularly when one considers how much of human behavior is affected by self-presentational motives. I recently asked four of the most productive researchers in the area of self-presentation—Edward Jones, James Tedeschi, Barry Schlenker, and Roy Baumeister—why they thought self-presentation had remained on the periphery of social psychology for so long. They offered four basic explanations.

Part of the resistance may have come from the fact that many psychologists initially viewed self-presentation as inherently manipulative and deceptive, the ugly underbelly of interpersonal life. As we have seen, self-presentation is not necessarily inauthentic, but this view may have led some to regard the topic as unsavory or unnecessarily narrow (see, for example, Buss & Briggs, 1984).

Furthermore, during the past 20 years, social psychology has been dominated by an interest in cognitive processes—attribution, person perception, social cognition, and the like—and motivational processes have taken a back seat. Because the study of self-presentation focused on people's interpersonal motives, it attracted less attention than certain other topics.

Third, during the 1970s, some researchers became frustrated by the fact that self-presentation theorists offered impression management as an alternative to accepted explanations of many interpersonal phenomena. It seemed to some that the self-presentation perspective could explain almost anything. Punching holes in a lot of other people's theoretical balloons didn't win the self-presentational perspective many allies. As Baumeister (1986) colorfully described it:

> Many psychologists had spent their lives and staked their careers on theories about inner motives. They were less than delighted to be told that their theories were egregiously mistaken, that they had overlooked a (or even *the*) main cause. They could not dismiss self-presentation, but they did not have to like it. Self-presentation grew up as an all-purpose alternative explanation for many other theories. It was greeted and treated like a rude bastard relative at a family gathering (p. vi).

Finally, although researchers interested in the topic approached self-presentation scientifically, discussion of self-presentational strategies often sounded too much like the how-to-manipulate-others vein of "pop psychology." Many viewed impression management as an inherently applied topic more appropriately studied by politicians, advertisers, and business executives than by psychologists.

Interest in Self-Presentation Spreads

Over time, however, interest in self-presentation became more widespread. Initially, research focused primarily on identifying factors that affect the kinds of impressions people try to convey. In early studies, researchers studied variables such as the effects of status, interpersonal goals, expected interaction, other people's evaluations, and social feedback on people's self-presentations. Soon afterwards, however, researchers began to apply self-presentational perspectives to the study of other psychological phenomena, thereby demonstrating that a great deal of behavior is affected by people's concerns with what other people think of them. One of the first examples of the application of self-presentational concepts to other areas examined how hospitalized schizophrenics manage their impressions to appear either more or less mentally disturbed depending on the immediate social context (Braginsky, Braginsky, & Ring, 1969); we'll examine this fascinating line of work in detail in Chapter 6.

During the 1970s, researchers began to offer self-presentational explanations of many behaviors. For example, James Tedeschi and his students proposed that many behaviors that were originally explained as reactions to cognitive dissonance may actually reflect self-presentational strategies (Tedeschi, Schlenker, & Bonoma, 1971). Self-presentational perspectives were also applied to understanding aspects of aggression, helping, conformity, attribution, resource allocation, group decision-making processes, task performance, voting, exercise behavior, and leadership. More recently, self-presentational explanations have also been offered for an array of emotional and behavioral problems such as social anxiety, shyness, depression, hypochondriasis, anorexia, and underachievement. With the application of self-presentational perspectives to the study of psychological problems, interest in self-presentation spread into clinical and counseling psychology (Leary & Miller, 1986).

Over time, evidence for the viability of self-presentational explanations accumulated. Study after study showed that behavior was affected by people's desires for others to perceive them in particular ways. Furthermore, such findings were obtained for a wide variety of behaviors that spanned much of the content not only of social psychology, but of other areas of psychology as well. By the mid-1980s, it was difficult to find an interpersonal behavior in which self-presentation was not occasionally involved (Baumeister, 1982a).

Along the way, the self-presentational perspective was expanded in such a way that it became more useful and palatable to a larger number of behavioral researchers. In his book, *Impression Management,* and other writings, Barry Schlenker (1980, 1985; Schlenker & Weigold, 1992) showed that self-presentation involves far more than attempts to gain approval and, thus, was applicable to understanding a great deal more about interpersonal behavior than simply how people get others to like them. As researchers began to apply self-presentational explanations to real-world problems, many people began to realize that it was not just a laboratory curiosity, but a potent human motive that pervades everyday life. Recent applications of self-presentational approaches to business and organizational settings have further demonstrated their usefulness (Giacalone & Rosenfeld, 1989, 1991).

Judging the Impact of One's Impressions

As we'll see throughout the book, impression management is a complicated psychological process. People who want others to form a particular impression of them cannot simply push a button or flick a switch to produce the desired effect. Many things can go wrong as people try to assess the most desirable impression to convey to particular targets in a given situation, adjust their behavior to foster the desired impression, and assess whether others have formed the impression they intended. Two considerations in particular complicate the impression-management process.

Because a given behavior can usually be interpreted in more than one way, people run the risk of conveying images other than those they wanted to make. For example, a person trying to be seen as intelligent may offer some esoteric information during a conversation only to come across as pompous, egg-headed, vain, or boring. Thus, we must distinguish between the impression that a person wanted others to form (the *calculated impression*) and the impressions that the person did not intend others to form (the *secondary impression*) (Schneider, 1981). Although unintended, the secondary impression is not always an undesirable one. For example, the person trying to appear intelligent may also come across as a good conversationalist. However, quite often, the secondary impression is inconsistent with how the person wants to be perceived.

Unfortunately for the person who is motivated to impression-manage, secondary impressions are difficult to anticipate and control because they rely as much on the style and appropriateness of a person's self-presentation as on its content (Schneider, 1981). For example, people sometimes find it difficult to determine whether other people will accept a particular self-disclosure at face value or whether something will make others suspicious of its accuracy. I'm sure you've sometimes been surprised when other people questioned the truthfulness of something you said about yourself even if your self-presentation was, in fact, honest. In such cases, your effort to create a particular calculated impression resulted in an undesired secondary impression (that you were being untruthful).

People may also be unable to anticipate all of the secondary inferences that others may draw from the calculated impression they intended. You may try to express your heartfelt thanks to a teacher or boss but realize that he or she interpreted your appreciation as crass ingratiation. Or, you may understate your accomplishments to a job interviewer so as not to be seen as braggardly, only to find that she inferred that you lack self-confidence.

The self-presentational difficulties created by undesired and unanticipated secondary impressions are compounded by the fact that people aren't always good judges of the impressions they are making. For people to make a desired impression, they obviously need to know how others perceive them; yet, research suggests that people do not always know the kinds of impressions they convey. People seem to have some idea of the kinds of impressions they generally make on others but are less accurate at determining how they are perceived by specific other people (DePaulo, Kenny, Hoover, Webb, & Oliver, 1987). In part, this is because how a particular other person responds to us depends not only on how that person perceives us, but also on that person's own personality (for example, how openly he or she expresses feelings about others). Thus, we sometimes find it difficult to determine what a particular other person thinks of us. However, as we look at our social interactions as a whole, we can get a better sense of how people in general regard us on particular dimensions.

Furthermore, research suggests that people overestimate how consistently other people perceive them. People seem to assume that most other people have similar impressions of them when, in fact, others' impressions may differ greatly (DePaulo et al., 1987). People tend to see themselves as relatively constant and unchangeable even when their behavior differs a great deal across different situations. As a result, they tend to think they come across similarly much of the time when, in reality, their behaviors may vary markedly from situation to situation.

Taken together, the fact that people are not perfect judges of others' impressions of them accounts for many of their self-presentational difficulties. Although events beyond their control sometimes damage their public images, people often fall victim to self-presentational miscalculations because of erroneous assumptions about how others perceive them. Of course, in many instances, people accurately judge how they are coming across, yet are nonetheless unable to convey the impressions they desire. Even so, knowing how one is being perceived is generally a prerequisite for successful impression management.

The Person and the Situation

Which is most important in understanding people's behavior—their personal characteristics (such as their personality, intelligence, genetic makeup, and life history) or the nature of the situation in which they find themselves (such as the characteristics of others who are present, the physical layout of the room, or the social norms that are operating)? Although much has been written over the years about this "person-situation debate," most psychologists today would agree that the question is a silly one.

Most behavior is a function of both the person and the situation. On one hand, the nature of the situation exerts a strong influence on our behavior. For example, we act differently at funerals than at weddings; we sometimes respond differently to superiors than to subordinates; we often interact differently with men than with women, and we react differently in crowded than uncrowded environments.

Even so, each person brings to the situation his or her unique personality, background, and physiological makeup so that two people in precisely the same situation may not respond in exactly the same way. Some people are typically outgoing, whereas others are introverted; some people are more argumentative than others; and some people try harder to please.

As we discuss self-presentation, we will repeatedly see that the impressions people try to create on others are a function of both the situation and the individual. Sometimes, the situation exerts considerable pressure on people to present themselves in particular ways; we must *appear* solemn at a funeral no matter how good we really feel. At the same time, however, people differ in the degree to which they are concerned about others' impressions of them and, thus, the degree to which they impression-manage at all. They also differ, as we will see, in how they want other people to see them.

An Overarching Framework

After many years of research, behavioral scientists have compiled a large amount of information about self-presentation. The difficult task has been to organize all of these findings into a coherent framework. If we step back and take a broad view of the entire research literature, we can see that most studies of self-presentation deal with one of four topics.

First, some research is designed simply to demonstrate that a particular behavior is affected by people's concerns with others' impressions. Virtually any behavior can be used for self-presentational purposes, and much research has documented the variety of self-presentational tactics that people use. Thus, to begin, we take a look in Chapter 2 at the wide array of tactics that people use to convey impressions of themselves to other people. You are likely to be surprised by how much of your behavior seems designed for public consumption.

A second body of research has investigated factors that motivate self-presentational behaviors. The degree to which people manage their impressions differs across situations and time. Chapter 3 will focus on the question of *why* people manage their impressions. As it turns out, there is more than one answer to this question, which we'll address from a number of perspectives, including evolution.

The third and largest body of self-presentational research has dealt with factors that affect the kinds of impressions people try to make on others. Chapters 4 through 8 will examine five primary sets of factors that affect the images people try to convey of themselves. People's self-presentations are affected by the norms of the immediate situation and the roles they play in social life (Chapter 4), the values of the targets they want to impress (Chapter 5), their current social image in other people's eyes (Chapter 6), the instrumental usefulness of the impression (Chapter 7), and aspects of their private selves (Chapter 8).

A fourth body of research has dealt with the emotional and behavioral consequences that occur when people begin to worry about the impressions others are forming of them. Not only do self-presentational concerns result in aversive emotions, but people tend to behave differently when they're worried about how they're coming across than when they are confident about their self-presentations. The book concludes in Chapter 9 with a look at how people respond when they become particularly worried about their impressions.

Summary

Self-presentation (or impression management) refers to the process of controlling how one is perceived by other people. Although some people seem to regard concerns with others' impressions as a sign of vanity, manipulativeness, or insecurity, self-presentation is an essential and unavoidable aspect of everyday interaction. People's outcomes in life depend heavily on how they are perceived and evaluated by other people. As a result, they often monitor and regulate the impressions others have of them. Most of the time, the images people present of themselves are reasonably accurate, although they tend to tactically select the kinds of information they will reveal about themselves. Because people tend to be rewarded for making "good" impressions, they usually present favorable images of themselves. However, when they think undesirable images will help them obtain their goals, people sometimes foster unflattering impressions.

The scientific study of self-presentation began with the work of sociologist Erving Goffman, followed shortly afterward by social psychologist Edward Jones. The study of self-presentation was initially viewed as a topic of secondary importance in social psychology, but interest in the topic has increased notably in recent years.

Successful self-presentation requires that people accurately assess the impact of their behavior on others' impressions of them, but people do not always know the kinds of impressions they convey. Not only may their behavior lead to unexpected secondary impressions, but they sometimes have trouble determining how specific other people perceive them.

Self-presentational behaviors are a function of both the person and the situation. The kinds of impressions people try to convey are guided by the individual's motives and personality, as well as by the immediate social setting.

CHAPTER

2

Tactics

CHAPTER OUTLINE

Virtually every aspect of our behavior provides information from which other people draw inferences about us. Whenever we are in the presence of other people, they have ready access to a wealth of information from which they can form impressions of our personalities, abilities, attitudes, moods, and so on.

We typically go about our daily affairs with only passing attention to what our behavior says about us. And, in most situations, we do not do things simply to make impressions on others. In other instances, however, we are quite aware of the fact that others are forming impressions of us. We are in a state of **dramaturgical awareness** in which we realize that our behavior is expressing things about us to others (Brissett & Edgley,

1990). And, in many situations, we may not only be aware of the impressions others are forming but act in ways that we hope will lead others to form certain impressions of us.

Self-presentation is usually viewed as the process by which people convey to others that they are a certain kind of person or possess certain characteristics. Self-presentational tactics that attempt to convey that a person possesses particular characteristics or is a particular kind of person are called **attributive tactics.** Often, however, people are more interested in conveying that they *aren't* a certain kind of person. Tactics that deny that the person possesses particular characteristics or is a particular kind of person are called **repudiative tactics** (Roth, Harris, & Snyder, 1988; Roth, Snyder, & Pace, 1986). When the movie starlet of the 1950s stops the leading man's romantic advances with a slap and says "I'm not that kind of woman," she's indicating to him the kind of woman she's *not* (that is, she's using a repudiative tactic), but not telling him much about the kind of woman she *is*.

Nearly any aspect of behavior can be controlled for self-presentational purposes. One's clothing, the recounting of a particular personal experience, a well-timed laugh, or even one's choice of food at a restaurant can all be used to create certain impressions in others' minds. This chapter will present a broad overview of the kinds of behaviors that people use for self-presentational purposes. The staggering variety of behaviors that can serve self-presentational goals prevents us from creating an exhaustive list of self-presentational tactics in this chapter, but it should be sufficient to demonstrate how virtually any behavior can be used for impression management on certain occasions. Throughout the book, we'll examine many other examples of ways in which ordinary, everyday behavior is affected by people's concerns with others' impressions of them.

Self-Descriptions

The most straightforward way for people to convey information about themselves involves verbal descriptions. By telling others about their personalities, likes and dislikes, previous experiences, accomplishments, families, occupations, emotional reactions, fears, and so on, people can create particular impressions in others' eyes. Although self-descriptive self-presentations usually occur in face-to-face interactions, people often describe themselves to others in writing. For example, job applicants engage in self-presentation when they write a letter of application or prepare their resume (Feldman & Klich, 1991). Likewise, the personal ads that people place in newspapers to attract dating partners are essentially self-presentational advertisements ("Intelligent, attractive, affectionate man seeks committed professional woman. . . .") (Gonzales & Meyers, 1993).

As we noted earlier, for many people, the concept of impression management implies that people go through their days lying about themselves for their own social gain. In the case of self-descriptions, however, people are more likely to selectively present true information about themselves than they are to lie. In a given interaction, you have a nearly infinite variety of facts you could reveal about yourself—all of which are absolutely true. When you have the opportunity to tell someone about yourself, what you choose to say is heavily influenced by the kind of impression you would like the other person to have of you.

Self-descriptions differ along a continuum of explicitness. On one hand, people may make explicit claims about themselves, as when Richard Nixon announced to the country, "I am not a crook." As a self-presentational tactic, such explicit claims are risky, however. Because people rarely reveal information about themselves so directly, listeners may be alerted to the possibility that the person's claim is tactical, if not deceptive.

For this reason, people's self-descriptions are often more indirect or tacit. In making an indirect claim, people state a fact about themselves that they believe will lead others either to make a particular inference or to ask a question that calls for a self-presentational claim. For example, rather than baldly claiming, "You know, I was a football player in college—and a damn good one at that," a man discussing sports with a new colleague might simply note that "football sure has changed—the big money and all—since I played the game." At minimum, such an indirect tactic conveys that he played football; at maximum, the colleague may be enticed to ask for more information, allowing the man to legitimately talk about his glory days on the gridiron.

Just as important as what people say about themselves to others is what they could say about themselves, but don't. People manage their impressions not only by describing themselves in particular ways, but by excluding certain information from their self-descriptions. As Goffman (1959, p. 141) put it, self-presentation involves "the over-communication of some facts and the under-communication of others." As you might imagine, people use these **exclusionary self-presentation tactics** when they think that accurate self-descriptions will make an undesired impression. How many times have you withheld information about yourself because you thought others would react negatively to it?

Although real life self-presentation often involves exclusion and editing, if not downright evasion, most psychological research on self-presentation has failed to investigate these kinds of self-descriptive tactics. In the typical experiment, self-presentation is measured by asking subjects to rate themselves on a questionnaire that will subsequently be seen by another person (usually the researcher or another subject). Because the subject completes the questionnaire knowing that his or her answers will be seen by others, these ratings can be regarded as self-presentations.

The shortcoming of this standard approach to measuring self-presentation is that it more or less forces subjects to disclose information about themselves on the dimensions specified by the questionnaire items; leaving certain ratings blank is usually not an option. When subjects are told they may leave certain items blank or that they can choose which self-ratings they will show to another person, they tactically exclude information from their self-descriptions that will create an undesired impression (Leary, 1993).

Attitude Statements

Traditionally, psychologists have regarded attitudes as internal feelings of liking or disliking based on a set of beliefs about a person, object, or event. This traditional view stresses the psychological, intrapersonal nature of attitudes and the effects that attitudes have on people's individual actions.

Such cognitive-affective structures as attitudes undoubtedly exist. However, this emphasis on the psychological nature of attitudes has neglected their importance in interpersonal relationships. From the standpoint of the study of social behavior, people's *expressions* of their attitudes are as interesting and important as their "real" attitudes. When people express attitudes to others, those expressions have clear interpersonal implications.

In particular, the attitudes we express influence the impressions other people have of us. To the extent this is so, we should not be surprised that people use their attitude expressions as self-presentational tactics. By expressing certain attitudes, people convey particular impressions of themselves. For example, if a woman says she supports capital punishment, you probably form an impression of her that goes far beyond simply her attitudes toward the death penalty. As a result, she could tactically express, misrepresent, or hide her attitudes to lead others to form certain impressions about her.

Often people convey their attitudes nonverbally rather than verbally, but the self-presentational implications are the same. For example, we smile and nod when speakers express opinions we share, even though we would be unlikely to do so if we were alone listening to the speaker on videotape. When I taught a course in human sexuality, students sometimes expressed their reactions to topics they found offensive (such as sadomasochism) by groaning, rolling their eyes, or grimacing as I described certain sexual practices. Such displays are as much a way of conveying one's views to others as they are an automatic expression of one's own attitudes.

The tactical use of attitude statements is probably nowhere more obvious than in politics. Politicians talk about different attitude domains to different audiences (expressing attitudes about day-care to an audience of professional women, but attitudes about the military to a meeting of veterans), and avoid talking about attitudes that a particular audience may find objectionable. They also modify or construe their attitude statements in a single domain depending on the attitude position of the audience. Although we find it easy to criticize politicians' tactical, self-presentational use of attitudes, we should remember that, in many ways, we are all "intuitive politicians" (Tetlock, 1985).

This is not to say that people are trying to manage their impressions each time they express an attitude. However, their expressions have clear self-presentational implications, and people sometimes express certain attitudes for the purpose of creating an impression. In most instances, the attitude that is expressed is truly held by the individual. Even so, the fact that the person chooses to express the attitude to a particular audience at a particular time may reflect an attempt to create a particular image. After all, we all hold many, many attitudes. Why do we express them only occasionally?

When viewed from a self-presentational standpoint, much of past behavioral research on attitudes and attitude change is cast in a different light. Once we acknowledge that attitude expressions are often self-presentations, we must consider the possibility that what appears to be a change in a person's attitude may actually be only a change in the attitudes the person *claims* to have (Hass, 1981; Tedeschi et al., 1971). We return to this important point in Chapter 4.

Public Attributions

An **attribution** is a causal inference or explanation a person makes about the cause of a particular event. We make attributions about many of the events in our lives: Why did I fail the exam even though I studied? Was the test too hard? Did I study the wrong material? Was the professor unfair? Am I just downright stupid? Whatever conclusion I ultimately reach, I have made an attribution about my failure.

The recognition that people's reactions to events are affected by their explanations of them spurred tremendous interest in attributions during the 1970s and 1980s. In fact, attribution was the most widely studied topic in social psychology for over a decade. Throughout this area of research, the focus has been on the attributions that people make about themselves and others, and the effects of those attributions on people's behavior. Like research on attitudes, the study of attributions emphasized the cognitive, intrapsychic causes and effects of attributions.

However, people often share their attributions with others. We explain *to others* why we failed on the test, why we were late for class, or why we lost our temper. And when people make attributional statements to others, their attributions clearly affect the kinds of impressions others form of them. We have a very different impression of a coach who blames himself for a disappointing loss than we have of a coach who blames the members of the team. Thus, attributions serve not only to explain one's outcomes to oneself, but may have interpersonal functions, including self-presentation (Forsyth, 1980).

People often recognize the tactical possibilities in their attributions, and, not surprisingly, make attributional statements that portray them in the best possible light. For example, people tend to claim that they were personally more responsible for their successes than for their failures (Schlenker & Miller, 1977; Sicoly & Ross, 1977). Similarly, members of groups tend to say that they had greater influence over the group's performance when the group did well than when it performed poorly (Leary & Forsyth, 1987). People also try to convince others that their behavior was due to positive motives (such as wanting to help another person) rather than to nonpositive motives (such as trying to make a good impression) (Doherty, Weigold, & Schlenker, in press).

Initially, researchers regarded these **self-serving attributions** as ways in which people protect and enhance their personal self-esteem. By attributing successes to oneself but failures to outside forces, people can maintain a positive view of themselves. However, whatever benefits these self-serving attributions have for one's personal ego, they have social benefits as well. The explanations we offer to others can affect how they perceive and evaluate us. As a result, people sometimes use attributional statements for self-presentational purposes (Bradley, 1978; Schlenker, 1980; Weary & Arkin, 1981).

I should note that self-presentational motives don't always lead people to attribute more responsibility to themselves for success than for failure. Under some circumstances, people publicly accept responsibility for failure. However, even these attributions may reflect tactical self-presentations. In some situations, one will make a better impression—of being magnanimous, courageous, modest, or fair, for example—by accepting responsibility for failure (Bradley, 1978; Miller & Schlenker,

1985). Attorney General Janet Reno received a great deal of praise for straightforwardly accepting responsibility for the FBI's raid on the Branch Davidian compound in Waco, Texas that led to the deaths of over 80 cult members.

Remembering and Forgetting

Comedian Steve Martin once recommended in one of his routines that people can get out of many difficult situations in life with two simple words: "I forgot." You can be a millionaire yet never pay taxes, he said, simply by telling the I.R.S. that you "forgot." You can even hold up banks, then claim that you "forgot" that armed robbery was illegal.

This bit of humor contains more than a grain of truth. People can manage their impressions through strategic remembering and forgetting. For example, people sometimes show off their memory by publicly recalling things. We all know people who make a habit out of remembering sports statistics, song lyrics, and other trivia. When students speak up in class, their motive is as often to demonstrate their knowledge or insight to the teacher or other students as to educate those who are present.

One special type of self-presentational remembering involves **memory contrivances**—acts in which people "distort, reconstruct, or fabricate memory performances as they interact with others in order to achieve social goals" (Gentry & Herrman, 1990, p. 242). All of us have used memory contrivances to cover up our own forgetfulness. For example, people may pretend to recall meeting someone they don't really remember or act like their failure to meet some obligation was due to factors other than that they simply forgot it. At other times, people pretend to have forgotten certain things that they really didn't forget. For instance, it's sometimes better to seem to have forgotten to do something (such as not paying the rent) than to admit you remembered, but purposefully didn't do it. In addition, appearing to forget something can sometimes make a person look magnanimous ("Oh, I had forgotten you owed me $10").

Research has shown that people who behave in a manner that is inconsistent with their existing attitudes sometimes "forget" what their initial attitudes really were (Bem & McConnell, 1970). Having performed a counterattitudinal behavior, they seem to believe that they *always* agreed with what they did. Early explanations of this effect emphasized people's need for cognitive consistency (e.g., people forget their original attitude so they won't feel inconsistent) or explained that people simply inferred their attitude from their behavior (e.g., they infer that they must have always believed in what they did since they did it).

However, recent data suggest that this effect is sometimes due to self-presentational motives. People who have acted inconsistently with their attitudes may want other people to think that they always believed in what they did so as not to look inconsistent, hypocritical, or unstable (Rosenfeld, Melburg, & Tedeschi, 1981). People seem to be more concerned about *appearing* inconsistent to others than they are with *feeling* inconsistent.

Nonverbal Behavior

So far, the tactics we have discussed have involved what people *say* about themselves. Nonverbal behaviors are also used for impression management. Through their nonverbal behaviors—such as expressions, appearance, gaze, body position, and gestures—people can express information regarding their personalities, moods, opinions, and physical and psychological states (DePaulo, 1992). Of course, much of the time, nonverbal behaviors occur naturally and do not reflect an attempt to make impressions. Yet, in many situations, people use their nonverbal behaviors as self-presentational tactics.

Emotional Expressions

Most people think of emotions as something we *feel,* and psychologists have tended to emphasize the subjective, affective nature of emotional experience. Yet, quite often, we don't just experience emotions, but express them to other people. Researchers have increasingly recognized that emotions are not only internal responses but also social acts involving interactions with other people. Not only do many of our emotions spring from social sources, but they influence the behavior of other people and may even exist because of their social impact (Denzin, 1984; Frijda, 1986; Miller & Leary, 1992).

Although some emotional expressions are involuntary, we have a great deal of control over the degree to which we reveal our emotional reactions to other people. Sometimes we hide our emotions, sometimes we exaggerate them, and sometimes we even feign emotions we are not feeling. In each case, the goal is often to convey information about ourselves to other people—that is, to present ourselves in certain ways (Patterson, 1987). Laux and Weber (1991) introduced the term **emotion presentation** to refer to expressive reactions that are used to project images of oneself to others.

Have you ever wanted another person to know how angry you were, or that you felt hurt, or that you weren't going to tolerate his or her abuse any longer? Have you ever showed certain emotions to convey that you cared for someone, were happy with a gift he or she gave you, or were going to miss him or her while he or she was gone? Are there other times in which you've hidden feelings such as these because you didn't want others to know you were angry, hurt, happy, or vulnerable? Have you ever tried to get other people to think you were experiencing emotions you really weren't feeling?

For example, although we often think of smiling as an expression of a person's internal emotion, smiling is as likely to reflect self-presentational motives as it does a feeling of happiness. We often smile to convey friendliness or acceptance to others whether or not we actually feel like smiling. Research shows that people smile more when they ask another person for help (Lefebvre, 1975) or when they are trying to get another person to like them (Rosenfeld, 1966). People are also more likely to smile after bowling a strike if their faces are visible to other people (Fridlund, 1991). In everyday language, we use the term "polite smile" to refer to smiles that aren't really felt; research shows that polite smiles can be distinguished from smiles of happiness or pleasure (Bugental, 1986). Such findings suggest that we sometimes smile not because we are happy but because we want to convey an impression of friendliness or happiness to other people. On the other hand, we sometimes adopt unsmiling expressions to purposefully convey to others that we are angry, bored, or tired.

In many instances, people try to show they are feeling an *appropriate* emotion. People tend to make better impressions on others when they express emotions that are appropriate for the situation than when they express inappropriate emotions (Graham, Gentry, & Green, 1981; Heise, 1989). As a result, they may want to seem concerned about another person's misfortune or happy at another's success, whether or not they really feel that way. (Are the losers at the Academy, Grammy, Emmy, or Tony Awards really as pleased as they appear when another person is announced as the winner?)

Furthermore, because people who express positive emotions are perceived more favorably than those who express negative emotions (Sommers, 1984), people may try to give others the impression that they feel better than they really do. Not surprisingly, then, people who are particularly motivated to impression-manage are more likely to deny that they experience negative emotions, such as anger, than people who are less concerned with others' impressions of them (Flett, Blankstein, Pliner, & Bator, 1988). In brief, far from being spontaneous expressions of inner feelings, emotional expressions can serve as self-presentations.

People also use their nonverbal expressions to convey information about the nature or quality of their relationships with other people—to present an image of the relationship so to speak (Patterson, 1987).

Parents may adopt an attentive, caring expression to convey involvement and interest to their children, even though the child is rambling inane nonsense at the time. Similarly, people may use expressive behaviors to convey interest to their partners or friends or, conversely, to convey that they are disinterested or fed up. A couple may even use nonverbal behaviors (smiling, eye contact, touching) to convey to others that their relationship is stable when, in fact, it is not. Even couples who are in the midst of dissolving their relationship may want others to think they are still happy.

Physical Appearance

Personal appearance is perhaps the most apparent nonverbal channel of self-expression. Others rapidly form impressions of us based on what we look like. Much research has shown that one's level of physical attractiveness has a profound effect on the inferences others draw. Attractive people tend to be viewed as possessing more desirable characteristics than less attractive people (Dion, Berscheid, & Walster, 1972; Miller, 1970). Compared to less attractive persons, attractive people are perceived as more sociable, dominant, intelligent, socially skilled, and adjusted (Feingold, 1992). Is it any wonder, then, that people invest so much time, effort, money, and worry in trying to look good?

Of course, what it means to "look good" differs markedly across groups. For some, it means being preened and prim, whereas in others it means being disheveled. In either case, people typically strive to meet minimal standards of attractiveness for their comparison groups.

Viewed in this way, the things that people do to affect their personal appearance are self-presentational tactics. Many of these are quite conscious and deliberate. For example, when trying to decide whether or not to change her hairstyle, a woman is, in effect, considering the self-presentational implications of her choice—what will other people think? Similarly, a man trying to decide whether or not to have a face-lift typically considers how he will be regarded *by others*. These decisions are seldom made on the basis of one's personal preferences alone.

Other things we do to improve our appearances are less consciously self-presentational. Each time we comb our hair, put on makeup, or iron our clothes, we are not consciously thinking about doing so to make an impression on others. Nevertheless, we have to admit that, if our motivation to make impressions suddenly disappeared, we would be less likely to use combs, makeup, and ironing boards.

One's clothing also conveys clear impressions to others (Burroughs, Drews, & Hallman, 1991). The cliche that "clothes make the man (or woman)" is a truism. People's impressions of others are heavily influenced by the clothes they wear. A man will be regarded quite differently if he is dressed in a three-piece business suit than if he is dressed in greasy, kneeless jeans, a dirty Grateful Dead T-shirt, and bikers' boots. A woman will make different impressions if she wears a blouse and dress slacks than if she dons a baggy, sleeveless shirt and miniskirt. Depending on the situation, each of these outfits may be either appropriate or inappropriate (the well-dressed man will be as out-of-place at a Dead concert as the shabbily dressed one is at a business meeting). But, we cannot doubt that others' impressions are strongly affected by the clothes people wear.

Many people in business are particularly attuned to what they wear, as evidenced by the popularity of books such as *Dress for Success* and *The Women's Dress for Success Book.* Although I personally find it hard to fathom, apparently people are sometimes hired, promoted, demoted, and fired based on nuances such as the kind of shoes or socks they wear (Riordan, 1989). Isn't it curious that some people devote so much attention to how to dress, when their time would be better spent working on being more effective managers, lawyers, bankers, or whatever?

Gestures and Movement

People also use gestures and bodily movements to convey impressions of themselves. For example, people use nonverbal self-presentations to be perceived as powerful. If you think for a moment about how a "powerful" person looks, I think you'll see the importance of body position and gestures in connoting power and leadership (Henley, 1977). Is the person standing erect or slouched? Do they gaze at others directly or do they have trouble maintaining eye contact? Are their hands and feet steady or shaking? Are their movements forceful and purposeful or are they sluggish? Given that we associate certain nonverbal behaviors with power, we should not be surprised that some people tactically control their nonverbal behavior to convey an impression of being a powerful individual (Korda, 1976; Schlenker, 1980).

Social Associations

People are truly known by the company they keep. People's choices of whom they associate with, at least publicly, can enhance or detract from their public images. Self-presentation by association is an indirect form of impression management in the sense that people strategically manage information about the people and things with which they are connected rather than managing information about themselves directly (Cialdini & Richardson, 1980).

Basking in Reflected Glory

People want to be associated with those who are successful, powerful, attractive, popular, or otherwise esteemed in others' eyes. By connecting themselves with those whom others admire, they can **bask in reflected glory** (BIRG). Sometimes, people tout their associations with noted others verbally, such as when they "drop names" or tell about their connections to movie stars, historical figures, or other famous people. Sometimes the linkages are quite loose, such as when a person recounts seeing a rock star on a New York City street or brags that a sports hero was born in his or her hometown.

At other times, people connect themselves to others symbolically. One common way in which people bask in reflected glory involves highlighting their connection to successful athletic teams. By wearing team-identifying apparel, fans can associate themselves with successful teams. Of course, people wear team shirts and jackets for many different reasons. Yet, research shows that university students are more likely to wear apparel that identifies their school after the football team has won a game than after the team has lost. Furthermore, the larger the margin of victory, the more students are likely to wear school-identifying apparel (Cialdini, Borden, Thorne, Walker, Freeman, & Sloan, 1976).

Experimental research shows that people are more likely to tout their connections to successful others when their own public images have been threatened, and those others are successful in an area in which they themselves are deficient. They are far less likely to mention their connections to those who are deficient on the same dimensions as themselves (Cialdini et al., 1976; Cialdini & DeNicholas, 1989).

People also do the opposite of basking in reflected glory—they **cut off reflected failure** (CORF) by disassociating themselves from people of disrepute, particularly when the disreputable person's reactions may reflect personally on them (Snyder, Higgins, & Stucky, 1983; Snyder, Lassegard, & Ford, 1986). My grandfather is the family genealogist, but I've always suspected that he only tells us about ancestors who were notable in some way; I have yet to hear about a single horse thief, murderer, or other reprobate in my family tree. Another common example of CORFing occurs after political elections. People who display candidates' signs in their yards are more likely to take the sign down if the candidate they support loses the election than if their candidate wins (Bernhardt, 1993). Few people want to be publicly associated with a loser.

In an extreme case of CORFing, Giovanna Portapuglia, an Italian countess, was kept locked up in a room not much larger than a broom closet for nearly 50 years because her family wanted to preserve the family's honor and dignity in the eyes of other people. When she was discovered by police in 1980, the 65-year-old woman was emaciated, mute, and mentally disturbed. The family decided to hide her from public view after an illness she had as a teenager left her "different" ("Countess was Chained," 1980).

BIRGing at the State and City Level

People sometimes bask in reflected glory simply by mentioning that a famous person was born in, lived in, or was otherwise associated with their town. Occasionally, entire cities or states get in on the action as they try to bask in the reflected glory of their native sons and daughters. Most commonly, states and cities advertise the fact that a prominent person was born there—even though where famous people were born may have little to do with what they ultimately achieve.

I read recently that North and South Carolina have been arguing for over a century about whether Andrew Jackson, the seventh president, was born in their state. Jackson was born a few days after his mother left her home in North Carolina for her brother's plantation in South Carolina, but experts disagree about precisely where she was when Andrew was born. South Carolina claims that she made it to her brother's home before the baby was born, but North Carolina offers evidence that Andrew was born along the way in another uncle's cabin in North Carolina. The fact that North Carolina has spent hundreds of thousands of dollars to strengthen its claim that Jackson was born there attests to the importance to the state's image of being associated with a U.S. President ("Native Son?," 1991).

Although both individuals and entities such as states and cities BIRG, there seems to be one difference. Individuals sometimes BIRG with well-known people regardless of whether the reason the person is well-known is for being good or bad. We seem to take nearly as much pleasure in telling others that a mass murderer lived on our street as a sports hero. In contrast, cities and states only advertise their connections with those whose claim to fame is socially desirable. For example, I doubt that New Orleans will ever erect a sign at the city limits proclaiming "Birthplace of Lee Harvey Oswald."

Burnishing and Boosting

In a slight twist on the basking effect, people also increase the apparent value of people, places, and institutions with which they are already connected (**burnishing**) and minimize the unfavorable features of things with which they are associated (**boosting**) (Cialdini, 1989). We brag about people to whom we are related or who we otherwise know. We often extol the virtues of our neighborhoods, hometowns, and states. We point out to others the positive aspects of the groups and organizations to which we belong—our churches, colleges, and civic groups, for example. Our strong ties of affection to such things spring from many sources, but among them is our desire to be associated in other people's eyes with valued things.

In an interesting demonstration of boosting, Finch and Cialdini (1989) had subjects read about Rasputin—the mad monk of Russia. As you may know, Rasputin was not a particularly desirable character. He was always filthy, his greasy hair and beard encrusted with debris. He drank heavily, fought often, and sexually assaulted women. At banquets held at the royal court of Russia, Rasputin ate food from the serving bowls with his dirty, bare hands. At one point, it was revealed that he was not a monk at all but was married and had three children. Given that he was one of the best-known crude and debauched people who ever lived, we shouldn't be surprised that people don't go around bragging about their connections to Rasputin. What would people do, however, if they thought they were already associated with Rasputin, even in some relatively trivial way? In this experiment, subjects were led to believe that they either did or did not share a birthday with Rasputin. Subjects who thought they and Rasputin were born on the same day of the year subsequently engaged in burnishing and boosting. They described Rasputin more favorably than subjects who did not think they shared his birthday!

Although the self-presentational associations people make are often tenuous and remote, evidence suggests that such seemingly trivial associations *do* affect people's impressions of others (Cialdini & DeNicholas, 1989). As balance theory (Heider, 1958) suggests, people tend to perceive things similarly that are associated with one another in order to maintain a sense of cognitive balance or harmony. Thus, as silly and superficial as it may seem, social associations can be effective self-presentation tactics.

The MUM Effect

Just as people associate and disassociate themselves from other people, they associate and disassociate themselves from events that may reflect on how others feel about them. For example, people try to be associated with good news, but try to disassociate themselves from bad news—a phenomenon known as the **MUM effect** (Rosen & Tesser, 1970; Tesser, Rosen, & Batchelor, 1972).

People prefer not to communicate bad news to others not so much because they feel uncomfortable about it but because they are worried that the recipient of the bad news will evaluate them negatively (Bond & Anderson, 1987; Johnson, Conlee, & Tesser, 1974). Their concerns are not entirely misplaced. People like those who communicate favorable information better than those who tell them unfavorable things even when the recipient of the information understands that the conveyer neither caused nor endorsed the unfavorable information (Manis, Cornell, & Moore, 1974).

Conformity and Compliance

People often go along with the crowd because they're afraid of how others will regard them if they don't. Because people who do not conform to group norms are often rejected (Festinger, Schachter, & Back, 1950; Schachter, 1951), people may try to convey that they share other group members' attitudes and values. Of course, self-presentation is not the only reason people conform. Sometimes we do what others are doing because their behavior provides us with information about the most effective course of action. If the bridge is washed out and I see other cars detouring down a side road, I'm likely to follow not because of social pressure but because I assume other people know where they're going. Often, however, we conform because we want others to form certain impressions of us (Baumeister, 1982a).

One example of impression-induced conformity involves tipping in restaurants. I suspect that many diners regularly leave a tip not because they really *want* to, but because they'll be perceived as stingy if they don't. The pressure to tip is so strong that many people feel compelled to leave a tip even if the service was quite poor. They are unwilling to be seen as stingy or as breaking a social norm even when they truly desire not to leave a tip.

In addition, people sometimes comply with others' direct requests for self-presentational reasons. Have you ever given money to a so-called "good cause" not because you really wanted to but because you didn't want to seem unconcerned or stingy? Have you ever shared your class notes with another student so as to appear friendly and helpful even though you resented it?

One example of the effect of self-presentation on compliance involves the door-in-the-face effect. The door-in-the-face effect works like this: By first making a large request that is sure to be rejected, a person increases the likelihood that a second, smaller request will be granted. If my students want me to postpone the next test for one week, they increase their chances if they first ask me to postpone it *two* weeks, then retreat to the smaller request after I have turned the first one down. Although various explanations of the door-in-the-face effect have been offered, Pendleton and Batson (1979) suggested that the person who has turned down one request ultimately complies with the second, smaller one "to avoid being perceived as an unhelpful, inconsiderate person" (p. 77).

The Physical Environment

People commonly form impressions of what others are like from their possessions and physical surroundings (Burroughs et al., 1991). We make different inferences about a professor whose office is cluttered than one whose office is well-organized. We form different impressions of a new acquaintance who drives a late model BMW than one who drives an old pick-up truck. We perceive a person reading a *Wall Street Journal* differently from one reading the *National Enquirer*. Because the impressions people make are affected by their possessions, they sometimes use the physical environment for impression management.

To draw an analogy to the theater, we may distinguish three aspects of the physical environment that are used for self-presentational purposes: sets, props, and lighting. Just as theatrical stages have sets, so do the "stages" on which people play out their daily lives. **Sets** include relatively immovable aspects of the physical environment, such as the size of the spaces in which people live and work (e.g., large offices make different impressions than small ones), the style of furnishings (e.g., colonial versus contemporary), finishings (e.g., wallpaper, carpeting, light fixtures), and even color scheme (e.g., off-white versus shocking pink paint) (Ornstein, 1989).

Props include moveable and temporary aspects of the environment. Virtually any object can be used as a prop as long as the user believes that the possession or display of the prop will affect others' impressions of him or her. For example, the magazines one leaves on the living room table, the artwork and diplomas hung on an office wall, and the display of trinkets and bric-a-brac can all be used to convey certain impressions of oneself.

Just as **lighting** sets the mood in a theater, it can set the mood in a home or office. The type and intensity of lighting can be used to convey impressions of the occupant. For example, diffuse, peripheral lighting conveys a greater sense of warmth and openness than harsh, overhead lighting (Ornstein, 1989).

Homes and Offices

Because others glean a great deal about us from seeing the places where we live and work, most people take a certain amount of care that their homes and offices are fitted in a way that is consistent with the image they want to project to others. To the extent possible, they choose living accommodations that are consistent with the impressions they want to create, then outfit and care for their residences in ways that are consistent with those images. One's choice of furnishings, artwork, magazines lying on the table, degree of clutter, and even knickknacks can reflect self-presentational tactics. (Why do some people display *National Geographic* in their living rooms, but hide their copies of *Playboy* and *True Confessions?*)

I am not suggesting for a moment that people choose their furniture, artwork, reading material, or knickknacks purely to make an impression. But, their choices are often partly affected by the impressions they want to create. For example, people's choices in furniture are related to both their aesthetic preferences (the style of furniture they personally like) and the symbolic value of the furniture—the kind of impression it conveys of them (Bell, Holbrook, & Solomon, 1991).

The same holds true for people's offices and other work spaces. Of course, the importance of appearances has not been lost on the business world. In offices, many aspects of the physical environment are used to convey the impression of power to others in the organization. For example, a large, imposing, wooden desk is a sign of power in many companies; the larger the desk, the more power is connoted (Ornstein, 1989).

Other aspects of the physical environment are meant to convey an impression of competence or credibility to one's co-workers or to the public. Image consultants recommend that people in business use props to manage others' impressions of their competence and importance, and many companies invest large sums of money so that their offices and facilities give clients the right impression, whatever that may be for a certain business and location. Korda (1976) described one business that displayed several clocks in its lobby, each prominently labeled with the name of a different world city: New York, London, Tokyo, New Delhi, and so on. The intended impression is clear: this is a business with an international scope. Of course, the walls of many offices are peppered with framed diplomas and awards. The self-presentational purpose of such items is obvious. Korda also suggested that managers should use a small appointment calendar rather than a large one so that their schedules always look crammed full of endless frenetic activity.

Still other aspects of the environment can be used to convey an impression of the person's warmth and approachability. People who want to convey an impression of being open and warm tend to arrange their offices so that visitors sit beside their desks. Office visitors report that such arrangements convey a sense of friendliness, openness, and warmth, compared to the arrangement where the office occupant and visitor sit across the desk from one another (Ornstein, 1989). Similarly, people who want to be seen as "human" sometimes display pictures of family members or other personal memorabilia.

The self-presentational use of props continues even after death. Many people select the headstones for their graves long before they plan to die. Sometimes this is to spare their loved ones from having to do so after they are gone, but often it is to assure that the headstone's size, appearance, and message is consistent with the image of themselves they want to leave behind.

Seating Preferences

People also manage their impressions by where in a room they sit (Reiss, 1982). Although this may at first seem trivial, think for a moment of how your impressions of other people are affected by where they sit. In class, for example, don't you have a different impression of a student who chooses to sit in the front center of the classroom than one who takes a seat in a rear corner? I know that teachers do. Similarly, when people are seated around a rectangular table, people form different impressions of those who sit at the head of the table than those who sit along the sides (Lott & Sommer, 1967; Russo, 1966). Furthermore, people form different impressions of those who sit directly beside them as opposed to across from them; side-by-side seating connotes more friendliness (Russo, 1966).

Because people are aware of the connotations associated with various seating positions, they can purposefully sit in places that will convey the desired impression. People who want to be seen as leaders of a group tend to choose to sit at the head of the table, for example, whereas those who want to convey their disinterest in participating choose more peripheral seats (Reiss & Rosenfeld, 1980).

Other Tactics

The self-presentational tactics described above reflect rather direct means of conveying impressions of oneself to other people. It is easy to see the self-presentational implications of behaviors involving self-descriptions, attitude expressions, or props, for example. Many other self-presentational tactics are more subtle, however, involving behaviors, such as helping or eating, that we normally do not think of as being performed for self-presentational reasons. In this section, we briefly examine five such behaviors: helping, aggression, sport and exercise activities, eating, and risk-taking.

Prosocial Behavior

Although we might like to believe that people help one another because they are truly concerned about one another's well-being, many acts of helpfulness are actually motivated by the helper's own self-interest. We often help other people not because we are good-hearted but because we have something to gain by being helpful. If nothing else, being helpful makes us feel better and avoids the guilt we would experience if we didn't help (Cialdini & Kenrick, 1976).

From a self-presentational perspective, one of the benefits of helping is that it generally makes a good impression on others. Thus, people sometimes do favors, give gifts, and help in other ways to make a positive impression or to gain approval (Baumeister, 1982a; Deutsch & Lamberti, 1986; Jones, 1964; Satow, 1975). For example, Satow (1975) showed that people donated *seven times* more money when others would be aware of how much they donated than when their donations were private. People are also more likely to help other people after they've made a bad impression because doing so helps to repair their tarnished images (Tedeschi & Riordan, 1981). I'm not suggesting that all helping is motivated by self-presentation, but some clearly is.

At the same time, people sometimes fail to help when help is needed because they're worried about the impression they might make (Latané & Darley, 1968; Schwartz & Gottlieb, 1976, 1980). People are sometimes afraid that they'll look silly if they rush to help another person only to find that they had misinterpreted the situation, and the person didn't need help after all. As a result, they may refrain from helping unless they are absolutely sure help is needed. Of course, it is sometimes difficult to tell whether a person really needs help, so people may sometimes fail to help even when the emergency is real (Latané & Darley, 1970; McGovern, 1976).

Aggression

Much aggressive behavior is motivated by self-presentation. First, some people behave aggressively to establish an image of being threatening so that others will do their bidding (Felson, 1978; Tedeschi, Smith, & Brown, 1974). Some instances of seemingly senseless aggression may serve this self-presentational function. A second function of aggression is to preserve one's image in the face of physical or verbal attacks. Retaliatory aggression does this by showing others than one is not to be trifled with (Brown, 1968). One study of gang violence showed that the most common precipitating factor was a perceived insult to the honor of the gang or one of its members (Horowitz & Schwartz, 1974). The purpose of the violence was to restore the offended gang's social image in the eyes of other gangs. Self-presentations of aggressiveness are also directly reinforced by certain societal subgroups, such as gangs. The members who give the impression of being the most dangerous are often the most admired (Bandura, 1973). We'll take a closer look at the role of self-presentation in aggression in Chapter 6.

Sport and Exercise

The sports and recreational activities people enjoy have self-presentational implications. People hold stereotypes about people who enjoy different sports: people have different impressions of those who enjoy tennis versus bowling versus motocross racing, for example (Sadalla, Linder, & Jenkins, 1988). Thus, we should not be surprised that people's choices of sport activities are sometimes affected by self-presentational concerns (Leary, 1992).

This is not to say that people choose sports just to make an impression (although I'm certain that happens on occasion). Rather, their awareness of the impressions associated with certain sport activities is but one consideration. Why aren't most men willing to go to aerobics classes or to take ballet, for example? Because participating in such activities is not consistent with the image they want others to have of them. Likewise, some women won't lift weights because they're afraid they'll be perceived as unfeminine.

Furthermore, some people won't exercise because they are worried about the impressions they make while doing so. People who think they are overweight, scrawny, or badly disproportioned may be unwilling to be seen bouncing around an aerobics class, swimming at the local pool, or jogging in a public place (Leary, 1992).

Eating

Although we tend to think of eating as a necessary, biological process, what and how we eat is greatly affected by social factors. Do you eat as well when you eat alone at home—either in terms of the quality of the food or your table manners—as when you eat in public with other people? Have you ever passed up an extra dessert you really wanted because you didn't want others to think you were a pig? Have you ever struggled to control how much you ate because you thought losing weight would lead you to make a better impression on other people? Studies have shown that eating can be affected by self-presentational motives (Mori, Chaiken, & Pliner, 1987; Pliner & Chaiken, 1990). Later in the book, we'll take a deeper look at the role of self-presentation in eating, including its role in eating disorders.

Risk-Taking

Because being daring is valued in come circles, risk-taking behaviors are sometimes motivated by self-presentation. For example, some people, particularly young men, drive fast to make an impression on their friends. The old game of "chicken"—in which two drivers speed toward one another to see who swerves first—is essentially a self-presentational game. (I wonder how many automobile accidents are solely the result of risk-taking self-presentations.) Some people smoke, take drugs, or drink excessively because they think doing so makes a certain impression—that they're reckless or adventuresome, for example. Some people seem unwilling to take necessary precautions to protect their safety—such as wearing seat belts in cars, life vests in boats, and helmets on motorcycles—because they don't want to appear overly cautious to others.

People are also more likely to make risky investments when they think others will think highly of them for doing so (Brockner, Rubin, & Lang, 1981). Also, as we'll discuss in a later chapter, people sometimes take risks with their health, such as not practicing safe sex, because of concerns with what others will think of them (Leary, Tchividjian, & Kraxberger, 1994).

Teamwork

Most of the examples of self-presentational tactics I have given so far have involved a single individual managing his or her own impressions. However, people sometimes work together as impression-management **teams** (Goffman, 1959).

In some cases, people manage others' impressions primarily for the others' benefit. When I write letters of recommendation for students, for example, my primary goal is to present an image of the student that helps him or her get a job, gain admission to graduate school, or whatever. In most business settings, co-workers do not publicly criticize one another in front of clients or customers (although they may disagree violently in private). In medical settings, a code of etiquette specifies that one physician should never say anything to a patient that would call into question the competence of another doctor. In these cases, members of a "team" agree, explicitly or implicitly, to help to convey or maintain certain impressions of other members of the team.

In other cases, people manage the impressions others have of a team member as a way of indirectly conveying an image of themselves. One member of a romantic couple may describe his or her partner favorably to other people because the partner's characteristics reflect back on him or her. Parents often present certain images of their children for the same reason. These kinds of team self-presentations are examples of boosting and burnishing that we described earlier.

Third, sometimes people work together to convey an impression of the team itself. Most couples, for example, try to put on a positive face in public no matter how strained and unhappy their relationship really is. Members of a department in a company may work together to convey a particular impression of the department to administrators, and administrators may work together to present a particular image of the company to the public.

Summary

Virtually any observable behavior can serve self-presentational goals. A summary of the more common self-presentational tactics is shown in Table 2.1. Through a wide variety of behaviors, people try to convey certain impressions of themselves to others. I must stress that a self-presentational analysis of social behavior does not imply that all of these behaviors are "nothing but" self-presentation. People's behavior is affected by a plethora of factors, of which impression motivation is only one.

Yet, people's concerns with others' impressions of them clearly produce strong effects on their behavior. In some cases, an interest in conveying a certain impression is the primary or only factor that causes a person to behave in a particular way. When the teenager untruthfully tells her parents that she's opposed to premarital sex, the expression of this attitude is prompted by her desire for her parents to view her in a certain manner. In other cases, impression motivation is but one of many factors that determine a person's behavior. When the father disciplines his unruly toddler in the supermarket, his actions reflect many motives,

TABLE 2.1 Common Self-Presentational Tactics

Self-Descriptions	Describing oneself in ways that convey a desired impression to others
Attitude Expressions	Expressing attitudes to connote that one possesses certain attributes
Attributional Statements	Explaining one's behavior in ways that support a particular social image
Memory Contrivances	Real or feigned remembering and forgetting for self-presentational reasons
Nonverbal Behaviors	Facial expressions, gestures, body positions and movements
Social Associations	Publicly associating oneself and disassociating oneself from particular other people
Conformity and Compliance	Behaving in ways that are consistent with social norms and/or others' preferences
Sets, Props, and Lighting	Using aspects of the physical environment for self-presentational purposes

only one of which is self-presentational. He wants to stop the child's outburst as quickly as possible, to help the child learn to behave appropriately in public, and to successfully complete the shopping trip. Yet, he will likely try to do so in ways that don't make him look foolish, ineffectual, or like a bad parent to onlookers.

If you watch your own and others' behavior carefully, you will begin to see its self-presentational elements everywhere. When in social settings, we are rarely completely freed of our concerns with how we are being perceived and evaluated by others.

CHAPTER

3

The Self-Presentational Motive

CHAPTER OUTLINE

The study of self-presentation assumes that people are often concerned about what others think of them and that, at least occasionally, they behave in ways that help them make certain impressions on other people. In this chapter, we explore the rather complex question of *why* people engage in impression management.

To answer this question, we really must address two separate issues. The first involves why people should be concerned with others' impressions of them in the first place. Why do people go out of their way to control others' impressions of them, sometimes to the point of doing things that are self-destructive or purposefully conveying images of themselves they know are not accurate? Given the pervasiveness and strength of the self-presentational motive and people's proclivity to impression-manage, it almost seems as if people are inherently predisposed to worry about how other people view them.

The second question involves why people are more motivated to manage their impressions in some situations than in others. People don't engage in self-presentation all of the time. In some settings, they don't seem to care about what others think of them, whereas in other settings, their primary goal is to create an impression. Thus, we will address the question of why impression motivation fluctuates across situations, along with the related question of why some people are characteristically more concerned about their impressions than others.

As I mentioned earlier, in some people's minds, the whole idea of impression management runs counter to the widely accepted dictum that people should be "true to themselves." In American society, the belief that people should be themselves and act according to their personal beliefs and standards is widely endorsed. Conscious attention to one's public image is often viewed as vain, shallow, insecure, deceitful, or narcissistic. Yet, everywhere we see evidence that we are living a lie—that most people *are* concerned with what other people think of them, at least occasionally.

One of the conclusions I hope you will reach by the end of this chapter is that, contrary to the idea that impression management is bad, there are very good reasons for being concerned with what other people think. Certainly, people can be too concerned with others' impressions or concerned in situations in which such concerns are inappropriate. And, people sometimes do things that are maladaptive simply to make impressions on others. But these self-presentational excesses should not blind us to the fact that a certain amount of self-presentational motivation is a good thing both for individuals and for society.

Personal Functions of Self-Presentation

Self-presentation has at least three primary functions for the individual. It can serve as a means of interpersonal influence, enhance the construction of personal identity and the maintenance of self-esteem, and promote positive emotions.

Interpersonal Influence

In most instances in which people engage in impression management, they do so because they believe, rightly or wrongly, that important outcomes are riding on the impressions they make on others. Put differently, they think that they can increase their rewards and/or decrease their costs in life by leading others to form certain impressions of them (Schlenker, 1980).

As it turns out, they are often right. The impressions that people make on others are a primary determinant of their outcomes in life. In fact, social interactions are mediated, in part, by the impressions that the interactants form of one another. When people respond to us, they are really responding to their impressions of the kind of people we are—our abilities, our personalities, our attitudes, our intentions, and so on. Thus, how they respond is very much determined by the impression they've formed.

Think for a moment about how differently you act toward people of whom you hold a "good" impression as opposed to people of whom you hold a "bad" impression. Do you treat them differently? Do you talk about them differently to other people? Would you be more likely to offer help to one as opposed to the other? Would you give them the same kind of feedback if you were their boss? Would you be equally willing to be their friend or to date them? My guess is that you respond much differently to people who make a good impression on you than to those who make a bad impression. As a result, making a "good impression" increases the quality of one's daily interactions. People are simply more pleasant, accepting, and affirming when they interact with someone of whom they hold a positive impression.

But impressions do much more than that. They affect the overall quality of the person's life in the long run. People who make bad impressions don't have as many friends. Others don't tend to invite them to social events or respond positively to their invitations. They have trouble getting others to like them, much less to fall in love with them. They may have more trouble landing the job they want or getting raises and promotions once they get the job. Self-presentational failures, then, can spread beyond social outcomes to financial and material consequences. Given the social and material stakes, is it any wonder that people are concerned with others' impressions of them?

More broadly, much self-presentation can be regarded as a mode of social influence, specifically as a way of affecting how other people respond to oneself. Jones and Pittman (1982) suggested that self-presentation serves to maintain or augment one's power in relationships with other people. When social psychologists use the word *power*, they are simply referring to the ability to intentionally produce desired changes in other people. One person has power over another to the extent that his or her actions can get the other person to behave in certain desired ways (Jones, 1990).

People can often influence others to respond to them in desired ways—that is, they can exercise power over others—by presenting certain impressions of themselves. For example, I may be able to get you to respond positively to me by showing you what a nice, cooperative, friendly fellow I am, or I can scare you into submission by appearing gruff, intolerant, and intimidating.

Constructing and Maintaining the Self

It is easy to understand why people impression-manage when they want to influence people to provide desired outcomes such as friendships, jobs, pay raises, and so on. But, people sometimes impression-manage even in situations in which there seems to be absolutely no reason to influence other people's behavior, and there are no direct implications of making a particular impression. People sometimes worry about looking foolish in front of others even when they consciously know it really doesn't make any difference. Thus, there must be another reason that people worry about their impressions other than because they want to influence others.

A friend of mine agonized for days after he vomited in front of two women who were coming out of a bar. He didn't know the women; he never expected to see them again, and what they thought of him really made no difference in the quality of his life. Yet, he worried about having looked like a disgusting slob. Similarly, I've watched people walking on the beach suck in their stomachs each time they passed a group of people. They didn't know the other people and had no intention of getting to know them. They were just passing by. Even so, they clearly were concerned with the impressions others formed. I suspect that, at one time or another, we've all felt like idiots in front of perfect strangers who had no social, financial, or material outcomes we wanted. Why? There are at least three explanations of self-presentation (and distress at self-presentational failures) in situations in which others' impressions really have no consequences for the person.

First, self-presentational failures often lower one's self-esteem and cause negative emotional reactions, whereas self-presentational successes typically raise self-esteem and cause people to feel good. Making a fool of oneself in front of one's ninth grade girlfriend or boyfriend not only damages his or her perceptions of you, but your perceptions of yourself. On the other hand, receiving an award not only indicates that others think highly of you, but it bolster's your own self-evaluation and mood. Over time, then, people become conditioned to experience negative emotions when they think they've made undesired impressions and positive emotions when they think they've made desired impressions.

Often in our past, making undesired impressions resulted in negative experiences—derision, punishment, loss of desired outcomes, and so on. So we come to associate self-presentational failures with aversive emotions.

Because behaviors that make good or bad impressions are often associated with changes in self-esteem and emotional state, our self-esteem and emotions can be affected by simply *imagining* what others think of us. Knowing that the two women outside the bar viewed him as a drunken, disgusting slob, my friend's self-esteem was affected; for all practical purposes, he was at that moment, a drunken disgusting slob. Even though you don't plan to interact with others on the beach, it hurts to imagine that others might be groaning, laughing, or wretching at your physique as you pass. Because the impressions we make (or, more accurately, think we make) affect our self-esteem and emotions, we are often motivated to impression-manage even when no direct implications of those impressions exist.

A second reason that people impression-manage even when they have no reason to influence others' behavior is that engaging in self-presentation helps to construct and maintain people's private identities (Baumeister, 1982a; Wicklund & Gollwitzer, 1982). Acquiring a particular identity requires people to behave in ways that are relevant to that identity (Gollwitzer, 1986). Before one can really see himself or herself as a certain kind of person, one must enact behaviors that are consistent with being that kind of person.

For a new college professor, for example, presenting images that are consistent with being a professor will help to solidify his or her new identity. Because conveying new images of oneself will lead to corresponding changes in one's self-concept (Rhodewalt, 1986; Tice, 1992), people's self-presentations help them internalize new roles (Goffman, 1959). Furthermore, if other people signify that they perceive him or her as possessing the characteristics of a professor—a process called **signification** (Jones, 1964)—it will help him or her to believe that he or she really possesses those traits. In Chapter 8, we'll look in greater detail at how people's self-presentations can change their views of themselves. For now, simply realize that people's self-presentations can affect their own identities and self-concepts.

The third explanation of why people impression-manage when it seems to make no difference is that self-presentation is such a well-ingrained habit that we find it difficult to be unconcerned with what others think even when we know it doesn't matter. From an early age, we learn that the impressions that parents, teachers, peers, and others have of us do have implications for our well-being. We learn early to be concerned with what others think and that there are few instances in which it is perfectly okay for us to behave in ways that others view as incompetent, immoral, inappropriate, or undesirable. Because self-presentation so often does matter, we find it hard to escape the pressure to manage our impressions even when it doesn't.

Emotion Regulation

Self-presentation can also reduce negative emotions and promote positive emotions. Because being approved of and accepted by others makes most people feel good, they can bolster their moods by behaving in ways that promote approval and acceptance. And, given that self-presentation is one way to obtain approval, people may impression-manage to improve how they feel (Baumgardner, Kaufman, & Levy, 1989). For example, the **negative state relief model** proposes that people often behave in ways that will relieve negative emotions and facilitate positive ones. By presenting images of themselves that they personally value or that will result in favorable reactions from others, people can make themselves feel better.

A second way in which self-presentation can regulate emotion involves the fact that, under certain circumstances, merely telling other people things about oneself can reduce negative feelings. Negative emotions motivate people to talk about themselves to others. When they are hurt, anxious, depressed, tense, or angry, people often feel the need to talk to somebody. Stiles (1987) compared the relationship between self-disclosure and psychological distress to the relationship of fever to physical infection. Just as fever can indicate the presence of an infection, high self-disclosure may indicate the presence of psychological distress. In addition, just as a fever helps to fight the infection and restore physical health, self-disclosure helps to reduce the person's inner distress.

When people experience dysphoric emotions, they tend to focus their attention inward. As a result, they think more about their thoughts, feelings, values, desires, and intentions, and less about the external world. Because people talk about whatever happens to be on their minds, distressed people end up talking more about themselves. When researchers asked students who differed in general trait anxiety to talk about anxiety-arousing versus happy topics, they found that highly anxious students disclosed more private information when speaking about anxiety-ridden topics than happy topics (Stiles, Shuster, & Harrigan, 1992).

Several studies support the idea that talking about oneself actually reduces internal distress. Pennebaker and his colleagues showed that simply expressing one's feelings improves affect, reduces stress, enhances physical health, and even increases the functioning of the person's immune system (Pennebaker, 1990).

The Evolutionary Basis of Self-Presentation

So far we have discussed the three primary personal functions of self-presentation—social influence, self-construction, and emotional regulation. Recently, researchers have begun to consider the possibility that the tendency to be concerned with others' impressions may have evolved because it promoted survival and reproduction.

To the extent that being included in supportive social groups increases one's chances for survival, human beings may have evolved a motive to seek social inclusion and to foster and maintain supportive relationships with other people (Ainsworth, 1989; Barash, 1977; Baumeister & Leary, 1994; Baumeister & Tice, 1990; Bowlby, 1969; Leary, 1990a). From the standpoint of contemporary industrialized society, it is easy to forget that most cultural features that you and I take for granted (such as agriculture, government, medical care, education, and the control of indoor climates) are creations of the past few thousand years. For the two million years before that, early humans lived as hunter-gatherers, and for several hundred million years before that, prehumans survived as foragers. The biological and psychological adaptations that human beings developed in the service of survival and, thus, reproductive fitness evolved during this immense expanse of time before recorded history (Cosmides, Tooby, & Barkow, 1992). Although people today may successfully survive and reproduce without being integrated into a supportive social network, such was not the case with our primitive ancestors (and, indeed, with certain aboriginal peoples today).

Early prehumans and humans who sought out the company of others, who stayed with the clan, and who were integrated into the social group were more likely to survive, reproduce, and pass on their genes than those who tried to strike out on their own. Because we are the descendents of the most gregarious people who ever lived, we may possess a motivational system that prompts us to establish supportive relationships with others and that causes distress when those relationships are damaged.

From the standpoint of self-presentation, one of the primary reasons that people are rejected or excluded is that others have formed undesirable impressions of them. People are typically rejected by others when they appear to possess characteristics that others find objectionable. For example, being perceived as immoral, incompetent, or otherwise socially undesirable is likely to weaken one's connections to other people (Baumeister & Tice, 1990). Conversely, being judged positively by the group's standards—as moral, competent, and socially desirable, for example—increases the chances that the person will be accepted, integrated into the social network, and helped when needed.

One way to avoid rejection, then, is to convey images of oneself that promote social inclusion and to avoid conveying images that lead to exclusion. This is not to say that we have inherited a gene for strategic self-presentation. But it is not unreasonable to conjecture that some self-presentational behavior is motivated by this innate tendency to be accepted and included.

A sociobiological or evolutionary analysis of the personal benefits of self-presentation helps to explain why self-presentational motives are so pervasive. In many instances, real tangible outcomes—both social and material—are riding on the impressions we make. But, even when no such outcomes exist, we continue to monitor how others see us because nature and nurture have combined to create self-presentational habits and because we stand to experience psychological distress in the form of negative emotions and lowered self-esteem if we don't.

Societal Benefits of Self-Presentation

Because they deal primarily with individual behavior, psychologists interested in self-presentation have focused on the personal, individualistic functions of self-presentation. But one person's self-presentational motives have benefits not only for that individual but for other people as well as for social groups. To see this, think again about what the world would be like if nobody ever cared what other people thought of them. The image is staggering. Many of the little things we do to make ourselves minimally tolerable to other people, we do so we don't make a "bad" impression, and I'm not sure that is a bad thing.

As a sociologist, Goffman (1959) dealt extensively with the benefits of self-presentation to the social group. Goffman suggested that social interaction could not effectively occur if people didn't construct public identities. Without having information about other people—about their personalities, competencies, attitudes, motives, and so on—we would have great difficulty interacting meaningfully with them. Think for a moment about how awkwardly we interact with strangers until we find out something about them.

We glean cues about what others are like from their behavior and appearance, as well as from our stereotypes about what certain kinds of people are like. But, as Goffman (1959) noted, "during the period in which the individual is in the immediate presence of the others, few events may occur which directly provide the others with the conclusive information they will need if they are to direct wisely their own activity" (p. 1). As a result, people *must* engage in self-presentation if others are to have enough information to interact smoothly, effectively, and pleasantly with them. Put differently, a certain amount of self-presentation is essential for meaningful interaction to occur and, indeed, according to Goffman, for the smooth working of society. From a sociological perspective, then, self-presentation functions to grease the wheels of interaction.

As we have seen, there are many good reasons—both personal and societal—for people to pay attention to the impressions they are making on others, but this should not lead us to conclude that people are always monitoring and controlling the impressions others form of them. On the contrary, people go about much of their everyday lives with little thought of how others are perceiving them. Not all behavior is self-presentational. Only in certain circumstances are people motivated to control others' impressions of them, and only in some of those situations do they actually try to do so.

In the remainder of this chapter, we examine factors that affect *impression motivation*—the degree to which people desire to create certain impressions in others' minds in a particular situation. What leads people to want others to perceive them in certain ways and to behave in ways to create those perceptions? The first step in self-presentation is for the individual to be aware of others' impressions (or aware of the potential for others to form impressions), so we will begin with a look at how people monitor their impressions.

Impression Monitoring

For people to engage in self-presentation, they must monitor, at one level or another, how they are being perceived and evaluated by others. To use a term we introduced earlier, they must be "dramaturgically aware." A person who is not dramaturgically aware is not attuned to what others might be thinking and will not be motivated to make certain impressions.

Levels of Impression Monitoring

A disagreement has existed between two factions of social psychologists regarding the pervasiveness of impression management. Some researchers see self-presentation lurking around every corner. They propose that self-presentational motives are pervasive and that a great deal of behavior is influenced, at least indirectly, by people's concerns about others' impressions of them. In contrast, other researchers argue that self-presentation is only a minor influence on behavior. They accurately note that, except in unusual circumstances (such as job interviews, legal trials, and blind dates), people do not often think consciously about how others regard them. If people think consciously about others' impressions of them only occasionally, how can self-presentational motives be as pervasive or as potent as some have suggested?

These two views can be reconciled once we recognize that people can monitor others' impressions at more than one level. Although in reality, impression monitoring is a continuum, for heuristic purposes, I'll act as if people monitor their impressions at one of four levels (which are shown in Table 3.1).

Impression Oblivion

At one extreme are situations in which people are oblivious to others' reactions to them. They are absolutely unaware at any level of how others are seeing them or even of the possibility that others are forming impressions. They are dramaturgically *unaware*. Two general processes can make people oblivious of others' reactions.

First, some situations are so compelling that they dominate the person's attention to the exclusion of other thoughts. Events can be so interesting, threatening, or stimulating that people devote all of their attention to the external world and literally have no attentional resources left to ponder what others might be thinking. Watching a spellbinding movie, witnessing a large fire, or finding oneself in the middle of a riot focuses one's attention on the outside world and away from an analysis of how one is being perceived and evaluated. The person's psychological state in such situations is one of **subjective self-awareness** (Duval & Wicklund, 1972).

Second, the person's own psychological state can interfere with impression monitoring. A person who is drunk or in a drug-induced haze may give little thought to others' impressions (Hull, 1981). The same is true of a person who is experiencing an intense emotion, such as rage or ecstasy. When in such powerful states, people often say and do things that they later regret, partly because they didn't consider others' likely reactions.

People who have temporarily lost their ability to think about themselves, whether because of compelling external stimuli or because of internal impediments to self-reflection, are in a state of **deindividuation.** Among other things, when people are deindividuated, they have difficulty monitoring and regulating their own behavior and are less concerned with others' evaluations of them (Diener, 1980). A fully deindividuated person is not impression-monitoring and, thus, has no impression-motivation. In fact, the necessary and sufficient cause of deindividuation may involve conditions that lower the degree to which a person is individually identifiable, thereby decreasing his or her concern with others' impressions and evaluations (Lindskold & Propst, 1981).

TABLE 3.1 Levels of Impression-Monitoring

Impression Oblivion	The person is unaware at any level of how he or she is being perceived by other people or even of the possibility that others are forming impressions of him or her.
Preattentive Impression Scanning	The person monitors others' impressions at a nonconscious or preattentive level while devoting his or her conscious attention to other things.
Impression Awareness	The person is consciously aware that others may be forming impressions of him or her and may think about the impressions others are forming.
Impression Focus	All of the person's thoughts involve others' impressions of him or her and the possible consequences of the impression he or she is making.

Preattentive Scanning

My sense is that true deindividuation in which the person *can't* monitor his or her impressions is relatively rare. More commonly, people monitor others' reactions at a **preattentive** or **nonconscious level.** People process a great deal of information about their environments without consciously thinking about it. In fact, they are able to do so even while they are consciously engaged in some other task.

This effect can be seen easily in the **cocktail party effect.** People at a party who are consciously and intently engaged in a conversation (and who appear to be generally oblivious to what is happening around them) will suddenly become attuned if they hear their name mentioned in the hubbub of the party. This effect demonstrates that the brain can monitor the environment at a nonconscious level even while conscious processing is devoted to other tasks. Most information is ignored, but if a personally-relevant stimulus, such as one's name, is detected, conscious attention may shift to that stimulus (Cherry, 1953; Schneider & Shiffrin, 1977).

People seem to monitor the impressions they are making in much the same way. People do not wander through life always thinking consciously about others' impressions of them. However, even when they are not consciously considering how others are perceiving them, people nonetheless scan the social environment nonconsciously for information about how others regard them. When no such information is detected (or sometimes if the information indicates that all is well with the person's public image), scanning continues at a nonconscious level. However, if impression-relevant cues are detected, the person may shift conscious attention to them. For example, a woman may be mindlessly conversing with her boss when she nonconsciously detects some cue that conveys disapproval—perhaps a frown or a lack of interest. Then she may begin to wonder consciously what her boss is thinking about her.

Viewing impression-monitoring as preattentive helps to explain why people are seldom consciously aware of thinking about others' impressions, yet can become so quickly attuned to particularly good or bad appraisals from others. Given that others' impressions of us are critical in so many ways, we should not be surprised that we regularly scan the social environment for information regarding others' reactions to us.

Furthermore, it explains why many people deny that they worry about others' impressions of them, yet use self-presentational tactics so readily. People don't typically think *consciously* about others' impression of them, which may give them the sense that they are unconcerned with others' impressions. Yet, the ease with which they detect evaluative cues even while devoting their conscious attention to other things suggests that impression-monitoring is occurring, albeit at a nonconscious or preattentive level.

Impression Awareness

As I just noted, people sometimes do become aware that others are forming impressions of them and/or think about the nature of others' impressions. The simple thought, "Geez, I just looked stupid," indicates a conscious awareness of others' impressions. When impression-monitoring occurs at a conscious level, people are in a cognitive state that Wegner and Giuliano (1982) called *tacit-other/focal-self awareness.* When in tacit-other/focal-self awareness, people view themselves from the perspective of others. This is probably the state people are in when most deliberate self-presentation occurs.

Impression Focus

Finally, we occasionally find ourselves in situations in which impression-monitoring completely dominates our thoughts. Every thought we have is focused on others' impressions of us. This is most likely in situations in which we are highly motivated to make a particular impression and either are unsure of the impression we're making (What is the audience thinking? How am I coming across?) or are convinced that we're making an undesired impression (Geez, I look like an idiot! What must they think of me? What should I do?).

Being mentally consumed with others' impressions can have undesirable effects. When people are focused on the impressions others are forming, they have no attentional capacity for other kinds of thoughts. For example, a person in a conversation who is focused exclusively on others' impressions will have difficulty interacting smoothly, devoting enough attention to other people, or being empathic. In many cases of stage fright and test anxiety, people's ruminations over their poor performance and what others will think of them interferes with other, task-oriented thoughts, resulting in impaired performance (Wine, 1971). In fact, people in such situations sometimes report that their "minds went blank." In reality, their minds didn't actually go blank; in fact, they were probably thinking quite actively about how poorly they were doing and about the horrible implications of it. However, such cognitions pushed out the thoughts they wanted to have—those that were relevant to the task at hand.

In addition, being in a state of impression focus may lead to behavior that is single-mindedly self-presentational and that fails to consider the effects of one's behavior on oneself or others. If all a person thinks about are the impressions he or she is making, those thoughts will dominate his or her behavior, sometimes to the exclusion of other factors (such as one's own or others' safety). Ironically, then, people may be so consumed by thoughts of the impressions they are making that they end up making undesired impressions. We'll return to this point in Chapter 9.

Public Self-Consciousness

The immediate situation determines, in part, the degree to which people monitor their social impressions. Even so, some people monitor others' impressions of them more frequently or more carefully than other people. Specifically, people who are high in **public self-consciousness** tend to think more about those parts of themselves that are public—that is, those parts that are easily observed by other people—than people who are low in public self-consciousness. Compared to people who are low on this characteristic, people who are high in public self-consciousness tend to spend more time thinking about things such as their physical appearances, their reputations, their way of doing things, and others' impressions of them (Buss, 1980; Carver & Scheier, 1985).

Public self-consciousness is measured by the Public Self-Consciousness Subscale of a longer personality inventory called the Self-Consciousness Scale (Fenigstein, Scheier, & Buss, 1975). People high in public self-consciousness tend to indicate that statements such as those below are more true of them than do people low in public self-consciousness:

- I'm concerned about what other people think of me.
- I'm usually aware of my appearance.
- One of the last things I do before I leave my house is look in the mirror.

Because they think more about the public aspects of themselves, people who score high in public self-consciousness are more attuned to others' evaluations of them and, thus, more concerned with managing their impressions than people who score low on the scale (Buss, 1980; Carver & Scheier, 1985; Doherty & Schlenker, 1991; Fenigstein, 1979). Publicly self-conscious people seem more sensitive to rejection from others (Fenigstein, 1979) and place a greater emphasis on makeup and clothing to improve the impressions they make (Miller & Cox, 1982; Solomon & Schopler, 1982). They are also more likely to conform in group situations (Froming & Carver, 1981) and are more accurate in assessing the impressions other people have of them (Tobey & Tunnell, 1981). Not surprisingly, they are also more worried about other people evaluating them negatively and, as a result, tend to be more anxious in social encounters (Buss, 1980; Fenigstein et al., 1975; Leary & Kowalski, 1993).

Master Status

Another factor that can lead people to impression-monitor is the possession of a master status condition. A **master status condition** is a personal characteristic that is culturally defined as central to the understanding of a person's character (Frable, Blackstone, & Scherbaum, 1990). Some master status conditions are negatively valued by the culture (such as being obese, deformed, or paralyzed), whereas others are positively valued (such as being academically gifted, exceptionally attractive, or very wealthy). Either way, master status typically involves characteristics that are statistically infrequent.

A master status condition tends to dominate others' impressions of the person, pervade his or her interactions with others, and play a central role in how they react to him or her. A paraplegic can never be regarded just as a student, computer programmer, or lawyer, but as the *paralyzed* student, computer programmer, or lawyer. In light of this, people who possess such a characteristic are likely to think a great deal about how others perceive and evaluate them. Over time, people who possess a master status condition may think less and less about others' reactions to their socially defining attributes, but they can rarely ignore their social implications entirely.

Frable et al. (1990) analyzed the spontaneous interactions of pairs of subjects who had reported for an experiment. One member of each pair had a master status condition, whereas the other member did not. Their data showed that master status subjects were more "mindful" during the interaction. They thought more about what the other person was thinking and paid closer attention to the other person and the immediate environment, and this occurred whether the condition was positively valued (such as being beautiful or gifted) or negatively valued (such as being an incest or rape victim).

Interestingly, the effects of master status conditions on social behavior occur partly because the person who possesses the characteristic *thinks* others will react to it. In an investigation of this effect, Kleck and Strenta (1980) found that subjects who thought that another person believed they possessed a negatively valued characteristic felt and behaved differently during an interaction with the other person *even though the other person did not, in fact, think that the subject possessed such a characteristic*. Because subjects anticipated that others might respond negatively, they perceived that the other person was affected by their undesirable characteristic, felt tense during the interaction, and behaved differently.

Impression Motivation

The fact that a person monitors others' impressions does not imply that the person will necessarily impression-manage. Indeed, most of the time, people impression-monitor simply to be sure their public images remain intact, yet they do not become motivated to engage in particular self-presentational behaviors. In some situations, however, people become motivated to control how others perceive them. In this section, we will explore the factors that determine **impression-motivation.**

At the most general level, the motive to impression manage springs from the same motivational source as all behavior. People impression manage to maximize rewards and minimize punishments (Schlenker, 1980). However, three factors are particularly likely to motivate people to try to control others' impressions of them: the goal-relevance of impressions, the value of desired goals, and discrepancies between one's desired and current image (Leary & Kowalski, 1990). We'll discuss each of these in turn.

PRINCIPLE:

People are more motivated to regulate how they are perceived by others to the extent that: (a) they believe that the impressions others form of them are relevant to attainment of their goals, (b) these goals are particularly valuable or important to them, and (c) a discrepancy exists between the impression they desire others to have of them and the image they think others actually hold.

Goal-Relevance of Impressions

Some of our outcomes in life are clearly affected by the impressions others form of us, whereas other outcomes are independent of the kinds of impressions we make on others. Whether one lands a particular job, for example, is likely to be affected by others' impressions of a job applicant, whereas whether one successfully repairs a broken lamp is not likely to depend on self-presentation.

People are motivated to impression-manage to the extent that they think that conveying certain impressions will increase their chances of obtaining outcomes they desire. In situations in which the impressions people make have few, if any, implications for their outcomes, the motivation to impression-manage will be low, if not zero. As the degree to which impressions are relevant to their goals increases, however, people become increasingly motivated to impression-manage. Several factors determine the degree to which people think others' impressions of them are "goal-relevant."

Publicity

Perhaps the most important determinant of goal-relevance is the **publicity** of one's behavior—the degree to which others might observe it firsthand or learn about it from secondhand sources. The more public one's behavior, the more relevant it is to the person's public image, and the more motivated the person will be to impression-manage (Arkin, Appleman, & Berger, 1980; Baumgardner & Levy, 1987; Bradley, 1978; House, 1980; Reis & Gruzen, 1976; Schlenker & Weigold, 1992).

Publicity affects impression-motivation because public behaviors are more likely to be relevant to the accomplishment of one's goals than behaviors that one performs in private. All of the functions of self-presentation described earlier in this chapter are more likely to be fulfilled when one's behavior is potentially public.

Even so, behaviors that a person performs while entirely alone can be affected by self-presentational motives. For example, people may prepare privately for self-presentations they will later execute publicly. An obvious example of this is personal grooming. Although we may shower, comb our hair, and dress in private, we do so partly because of the public impressions we will make later. Similarly, people sometimes privately rehearse what they will say to someone else to make the "right" impression or work behind the scenes to be sure that certain information about them does or does not come to others' attention. In addition, some public behaviors that were initially performed primarily for self-presentational reasons may become so habitual that we continue to perform them even when we don't expect others to see them.

Motivating Self-Presentation in the Laboratory

Much research on the topic of self-presentation has been designed to show that certain behaviors occur because of people's desire to be perceived in certain ways. The most common strategy researchers have used to demonstrate that a particular behavior results from self-presentational motives is to compare people's behavior when they believe it is public and observed by others to their behavior when they believe it is private and known only to them. The assumption has been that behaviors performed in public should be affected by self-presentational motives, whereas those performed in private should not.

For example, in studies designed to determine the extent to which people make self-serving attributions to bolster their images in others' eyes, subjects who have succeeded or failed on a task have been asked to answer questions about their performances, believing that their responses would be seen immediately by other people or that their responses would be anonymous and private. Similarly, studies designed to see whether people appear to change their attitudes so as to present positive images to others have told subjects that their identities would or would not be revealed on the attitude questionnaires.

In an influential article, Tetlock and Manstead (1985) argued that these sorts of public-private experimental manipulations do not provide an adequate test of self-presentational theories for two reasons. First, although it is true that people are generally more motivated to impression-manage when others will observe their behavior than when their behavior is private, publicity has effects on behavior other than simply increasing impression motivation.

Continued

For example, the presence of other people can increase physiological arousal, induce self-awareness, and change how people process information. As a result, simply demonstrating that people behave differently in public than in private does not necessarily mean that the difference is due to increased self-presentational motivation under public conditions.

Second, even private behaviors are sometimes affected by self-presentational motives. Although I shower, shave, and comb my hair in the privacy of my own bathroom, I do so because I want to be perceived in desired ways by other people. Even when they are completely alone, people often worry about how others will perceive them, prepare for upcoming self-presentations, and even practice how they will come across.

In laboratory studies of self-presentation, this problem is compounded by the fact that it is difficult to convince subjects that their responses are truly private or anonymous. Research subjects are often skeptical of researchers' truthfulness (with good reason) and sometimes suspect that their responses will be identifiable even when the researcher assures them that their responses will be private and anonymous. Thus, subjects may respond *as if* other people might observe their responses regardless of what the researcher has told them.

Tetlock and Manstead (1985) concluded that these problems make it virtually impossible to test self-presentational explanations of behavior. Although I share their concerns about certain research designs used in studies of self-presentation, I personally am more optimistic about the viability of self-presentational research (Leary, 1993).

Dependency

A second factor that determines the degree to which one's impressions are goal-relevant (and, thus, leads impression-motivation to be high) involves one's dependency on others. In this context, **dependency** refers to the degree to which a person's outcomes are contingent on the behavior of another person. When a person is dependent on others for valued outcomes, the impressions he or she makes are more important, and the person will be more motivated to impression-manage. As a result, people are more likely to try to control how they are perceived by their bosses and teachers than by their friends (Bohra & Pandy, 1984; Hendricks & Brickman, 1974). In the same way, subordinates ingratiate themselves with their superiors more than superiors ingratiate themselves with their subordinates (Pandey, 1981, 1986). Furthermore, people are more likely to impression manage to authority figures when these authorities have greater power to dispense or withhold valuable outcomes (Jones et al., 1965; Stires & Jones, 1969). If others do not control any social or material outcomes they desire, people have less reason to be concerned with how they are viewed.

In an experiment that I conducted with Robin Kowalski (Kowalski & Leary, 1990), subjects played the role of a worker in a company who was going to perform either an onerous task (singing "The Star-Spangled Banner" *a capella*) or a nonthreatening task (listening to a recording of "The Star-Spangled Banner"). (I know this sounds like a wierd thing to ask subjects to do, but subjects thought the company they pretended to work for specialized in political campaign ads.) Half of the subjects were told that another subject who was playing the role of their supervisor would decide which tasks they would perform, whereas the other subjects were told that the tasks would be assigned randomly. Thus, in the first condition, dependency on the supervisor was high—he or she had the power to assign the subject to the pleasant or unpleasant task—whereas in the second condition, the subject was not dependent on the supervisor for valued outcomes. Before the supervisor was to make the task assignments, subjects described themselves to the supervisor. The results showed that subjects' self-presentations were affected only when the supervisor had the power to make task assignments—that is, when subjects' dependency on the supervisor was high.

Future Interaction

Other things being equal, people's impressions are more relevant to their attainment of valued goals the more they expect to interact with another person in the future. Although there are instances in which important outcomes rest on making certain impressions during a single interaction (such as when a speeding motorist is pulled over by the police), the stakes in one-shot interactions are often quite low. In one-shot interactions with strangers (while waiting in line, for example), the impressions one makes are rarely relevant to important goals. But when we expect that we will interact with a person repeatedly in the future, we realize that the impressions we make may have implications for how we get along with that person for a long time to come (Gergen & Wishnov, 1965; Schneider, 1969). As a result, people tend to be more concerned with how others view them when they anticipate future interaction with them.

However, impression-motivation may begin to decrease after people get to know one another well and interact again and again. Not only are others' impressions less likely to be influenced by a particular self-presentational behavior as times goes by, but after a person knows someone pretty well, that person has less reason to try to create an impression. Some of my research showed, for example, that university students were less motivated to impression-manage in interactions with their same-sex best friends than with people of their sex they knew less well (Leary, Nezlek, Downs, Radford-Davenport, Martin, & McMullen, 1994).

Value of Desired Goals

Most theories of motivation assert that motivation increases as a function of the value or importance of desired goals (Beck, 1983). I'm sure it doesn't surprise you that people are more motivated to try to attain things that they view as valuable in one sense or another. This is also true of impression-motivation. Given that people think their impressions are relevant to the attainment of certain goals, they will be more motivated to impression-manage the more valuable or important the goal they wish to attain. Several factors affect the value of people's goals.

Availability of Resources

In economic systems, the value of something typically increases as it becomes more scarce, and a similar principle operates in social life. As a result, impression motivation is higher when resources are scarce. You can see this easily if you imagine being interviewed for a job; in which case would you be most concerned about the impressions you make—a job for which only one other applicant was being interviewed or one for which the company was interviewing 15 people? A study by Pandey and Rastagi (1979) showed that people were more likely to ingratiate a job interviewer as competition for the job became more fierce. Similarly, I suspect that impression management to potential romantic partners increases as the pool of potential partners gets smaller.

Characteristics of the Target

If you're like most people, you are probably more likely to impression manage when dealing with people who possess desirable characteristics, and this seems to be true of virtually any characteristic you might imagine. Who are you most likely to want to impress: An attractive person or an unattractive one? A person who is intelligent and competent, or one who is not very bright? A socially skilled person or a socially inept one? Someone who is likable or unlikable? Those of high status or those of low status? An individual with a pleasing personality or an individual with the personality of a planaria? Studies show that people are more likely to manage their impressions when interacting with those who are physically attractive or otherwise socially desirable (Forsyth, Riess, & Schlenker, 1977; Mori et al., 1987; Shaw & Wagner, 1975; Zanna & Pack, 1975).

This may be because we value the reactions of people with desirable characteristics more highly than those of less desirable people; put simply, their reactions are more valuable. For one thing, we often assume that attractive, powerful, competent, and high status people are harder to impress. Thus, when we do make a desired impression and receive affirming feedback, we feel better about it.

In addition, people with socially desirable attributes are often in the position to mediate important outcomes that we desire. Overall, bright, attractive, skilled, and personable people are more likely to be in positions of power and authority than stupid, unattractive, unskilled, and unpersonable ones.

The Value of Approval

Given that people often impression-manage to enhance others' evaluations of them and to get social approval, we would expect people who particularly need approval or fear disapproval from others to be more motivated to manage their impressions. Because people who have recently suffered a blow to either their self-esteem or to their esteem in others' eyes value approval more highly, failure, rejection, and embarrassment increase people's desire for social approval and, thus, their motive to impression manage (Miller & Leary, 1992). In some cases, a person who has been publicly embarrassed in front of one person may be motivated to convey a particularly positive impression in front of someone else (Apsler, 1975).

Although our need for approval varies across situations, some people are characteristically more concerned about receiving approval and avoiding disapproval. People who score high in **fear of negative evaluation** worry more about others' evaluations of them, score higher on measures of approval-seeking, and are more concerned about making good impressions on others (Gregorich, Kemple, & Leary, 1986; Leary, 1980, 1983a; Leary, Barnes, & Griebel, 1986; Watson & Friend, 1969). Similarly, people who score high in **need for approval** (Crowne & Marlowe, 1964; Paulhus, 1984, 1991) are generally more motivated to control how others see them than people who are low on this trait (Dies, 1970; Jones & Tager, 1972; Leary, 1983c; Millham & Kellogg, 1980; Schneider & Turkat, 1975).

People who are high in fear of negative evaluation and need for approval tend to have higher impression motivation because they value approval more highly than people who are low on these dimensions. Because they value it more highly, they are more motivated to behave in ways that will gain approval and avoid disapproval, including self-presentation. People high in fear of negative evaluation, for example, work harder on tasks when they believe that hard work will gain them explicit approval (Watson & Friend, 1969). They also are more likely than lows to offer excuses when the possibility of negative evaluation exists (Leary et al., 1986).

Discrepancy between Desired and Current Image

The third factor that motivates self-presentation involves the degree of discrepancy that exists between the image one would like others to have of oneself (the **desired image**) and the image that others appear to hold (the **current image**). As long as people think they are making the kind of impression they want to make, impression-motivation should be minimal. However, to the degree that people become aware that others are not forming the impressions of them they would like, they will be motivated to manage their impressions to convey the desired images.

As a result, people who have made undesired impressions are particularly motivated to impression-manage. In some experiments, subjects have been led to think they failed on an important task or have been embarrassed in front of others. Both failure and embarrassment increase impression-motivation as people try to repair the damage they sustained to their social images (Apsler, 1975; Baumeister & Jones, 1978; Baumgardner, Lake, & Arkin, 1985; Brown, 1968, 1970; Brown & Garland, 1971; Leary & Schlenker, 1980; Modigliani, 1971; Schlenker, 1975; Schneider, 1969).

People who perceive a discrepancy between their desired and current images use a variety of self-presentational tactics in their attempts to reduce the discrepancy. For example, they may stress other positive attributes (Baumeister & Jones, 1978; Schneider, 1969) or make self-serving attributions for the events that damaged their images to begin with (Baumgardner et al., 1985; Frey, 1978; Weary & Arkin, 1981). They are also more likely to do favors for others to show what nice people they are (Apsler, 1975) and to associate themselves with other successful people (Cialdini & Richardson, 1980), hoping to "bask in reflected glory."

Nonconscious Self-Presentation

People are not always aware of their motives for doing things. Although we can usually give *reasons* why we did this or that, the reasons we give may or may not reflect the true causes of our behavior (Nisbett & Wilson, 1977). As a result, people's behaviors are sometimes affected by self-presentational motives even though they are not consciously thinking about others' impressions at the time and even though they may deny that self-presentation entered into their behavior at all.

First, some self-presentational behaviors are performed so regularly that they become mindless habits. Although the behavior may have begun because the person consciously wanted to create a certain impression, the person now performs the behavior without consciously thinking about its self-presentational roots. For example, why do you comb your hair? Obviously, there is little reason rather than to make a better impression on other people. Yet, I doubt that you *consciously* think, "I'd better comb my hair so I'll look okay today." Similarly, we are so used to conveying positive, socially desirable impressions of ourselves that we often do so mindlessly, without consciously thinking about our self-presentational goals in doing so.

A second reason that people sometimes engage in self-presentational behaviors nonconsciously is that they are simply not consciously aware of the stimuli that are causing their behaviors. One experiment showed that how a subject presented himself or herself to a conversation partner clearly depended on how the conversation partner presented him- or herself: subjects who interacted with self-enhancing partners presented themselves more positively than subjects who interacted with modest partners. Yet, subjects seemed completely unaware that their own self-presentations had been influenced by those of their partners. In fact, subjects insisted that they would have presented themselves the same way in other situations as they did during the study. They seemed unaware of deliberately or strategically changing their self-presentations (Baumeister, Tice, & Hutton, 1989). Thus, people sometimes engage in self-presentational behaviors without being aware of doing so.

Self-Monitoring

People differ in the degree to which they typically manage their impressions. Some people carefully monitor how they're coming across and adjust their behavior to convey the "right" impressions, whatever they might be in a particular situation. In contrast, other people give relatively little thought to their public impressions and, even when they do, rarely try to make particular impressions on others. Several different personality characteristics may underlie these individual differences in self-presentation. As we've already discussed, people who are publicly self-conscious tend to think more about others' impressions of them (Buss, 1980), and people who are high in fear of negative evaluation impression-manage so that others will evaluate them favorably (Leary, 1983a).

The personality characteristic that has been studied most closely in relation to self-presentation is **self-monitoring.** According to Mark Snyder, who first identified this construct and developed the "Self-Monitoring Scale," a **high self-monitor** is a person who, "out of a concern for social appropriateness, is particularly sensitive to the expression and self-presentation of others in social situations and uses these cues as guidelines for monitoring (observing and controlling)" his or her own self-presentations (Snyder, 1974, p. 528). High self-monitors are sensitive to cues regarding appropriate demeanor, have the ability to adjust their behavior to the contingencies of particular encounters, and use this ability to control how they come across to others. As they enter social situations, they seem to ask themselves "Who does this situation want me to be and how can I be that person?" (Snyder, 1987, p. 46).

Low self-monitors, in contrast, are not as sensitive to social cues regarding appropriate behavior and self-presentation, are not as capable of controlling the impressions others form of them, and attempt to manage their impressions less often than high self-monitors. Low self-monitors may be as expressive and self-revealing as highs, but their expressiveness derives less from strategic attempts to control how they are perceived in social settings. Snyder (1974) originally argued that low self-monitors are more strongly controlled by their inner dispositions and attitudes than highs. However, research suggests that although low self-monitors are less responsive to social cues than highs, they are not necessarily more inner-directed (Briggs & Cheek, 1988; Lamphere & Leary, 1990).

Snyder (1974) developed the Self-Monitoring Scale to measure people's proclivity for self-monitoring. High self-monitors are more likely than lows to say that statements such as those below are true of them:

- In different situations and with different people, I often act like very different persons.
- I may deceive people by being friendly when I really dislike them.
- I'm not always the person I appear to be.

Low self-monitors, in contrast, tend to endorse statements such as:

- I can only argue for ideas which I already believe.
- I have trouble changing my behavior to suit different people and different situations.
- I find it hard to imitate the behavior of other people.

Successful impression management requires that people successfully "read" the social situation for cues about how to respond, then adjust their behavior accordingly. High self-monitors are better on both of these dimensions than lows. For example, high self-monitors are more likely to seek information about other people (Snyder, 1974, 1987). They pay more attention to information they learn about those they meet and are better at remembering such information. Presumably, such information helps them tailor their self-presentations to specific targets (Berscheid, Graziano, Monson, & Dermer, 1976). High self-monitors are also better at reading other people's emotions from their expressions; for example, highs were more accurate than lows at identifying truthful from lying contestants on videotapes of the television show "To Tell the Truth" (Geizer, Rarick, & Soldow, 1977). Highs are also better than lows at detecting when other people are being manipulative and ingratiating (Jones & Baumeister, 1976).

As you would expect, high self-monitors are more likely to use tactical self-presentation than lows. High self-monitors are better at tailoring their behavior and self-presentations to the contingencies of the particular situation in which they find themselves (see Snyder, 1987). For example, high self-monitors are more likely to match their level of self-disclosures to the self-disclosures of the people with whom they interact; in one study, high self-monitors tended to disclose more about themselves to others who were highly disclosing, whereas lows were relatively unaffected by others' disclosures (Shaffer, Smith, & Tomarelli, 1982). High self-monitoring men have more different styles of clothing in their wardrobes than low self-monitors. Presumably, high self-monitors use clothing to make different impressions, depending on the social context. (It is not clear why this difference occurs for men, but not for women; Zaidman & Snyder, 1983, cited in Snyder, 1987).

Other people can pick up on these differences in how low and high self-monitors approach interpersonal encounters. Other people rate high self-monitors as more skillful than lows in controlling their social behavior and emotional expressions (Snyder, 1974).

Not surprisingly, high self-monitors tend to be more successful in situations that require them to tailor their behaviors to specific features of the social context. For example, in business organizations, high self-monitors are more effective than lows in jobs that involve "boundary spanning." Boundary spanning positions are those that require employees to interact with highly disparate groups, such as management and labor in contract disputes. Because these organizational "go-betweens" must vary their approach as they work with different groups and must possess good interpersonal skills, high self-monitors tend to fulfill such roles better than lows (Caldwell & O'Reilly, 1982). High self-monitors also tend to emerge as leaders in groups and organizations more often than lows (Snyder & Copeland, 1989), possibly because they are more flexible across different situations.

Despite research findings showing expected differences between low and high self-monitors, the Self-Monitoring Scale has generated a great deal of controversy. Several studies showed that the scale taps at least three distinct attributes that do not perfectly match Snyder's original conceptualization of self-monitoring (Briggs, Cheek, & Buss, 1980; Gabrenya & Arkin, 1980). This led some researchers to advocate a reconceptualization of the trait and the development of new measures (Lennox & Wolfe, 1982), which spurred spirited debates between Snyder and critics of the scale. In an attempt to address some of the concerns about the scale, Snyder and Gangestad (1986) offered a shortened 18-item version of the Self-Monitoring Scale (the original scale consisted of 25 items). In any case, despite lingering questions about the Self-Monitoring Scale, most research supports Snyder's hypotheses regarding the relationship of self-monitoring to self-presentation.

Summary

People manage others' impressions of them for three general reasons—to influence others to respond in desired ways, to construct and maintain their private self-identities and self-esteem, and to regulate their emotional experiences. In addition, some instances of impression management may be traced to people's inherent need to be accepted and included by other people. Whatever benefits self-presentation has for the individual, it is also beneficial for social interaction and, more generally, for society.

Although people sometimes think consciously about how other people are perceiving them, more often they monitor the impressions they are making at a nonconscious or preattentive level. In some cases, however, people are in a state of impression oblivion in which they are not at all attuned to others' impressions of them or even aware of the fact that other people are forming impressions. People who are high in the trait of public self-consciousness are particularly likely to monitor how they are being viewed by others.

People are motivated to manage their impressions to the degree that (a) they believe that the impressions they make are relevant to their attainment of desired goals, (b) those goals are important, valuable, or otherwise desirable, and (c) a discrepancy exists between the impressions they would like others to have of them and the impressions they think others have formed. Although a great deal of behavior is affected by concerns with others' impressions, people are not always aware of this. In some cases, self-presentational behaviors are performed "mindlessly," whereas in others, people may not be cognizant of why they are behaving as they are. People who are high in self-monitoring are particularly likely to manage their public impressions.

CHAPTER

4

The Social Context: Norms and Roles

CHAPTER OUTLINE

Once people become motivated to manage their impressions in a particular encounter, they face the task of deciding precisely the kinds of impressions they would like others to form. Sometimes, only one impression will achieve their goals in the interaction, and the choice is clear. For a boy trying out for the baseball team, for example, only one impression is salient—appearing to be a good baseball player. Being perceived as good in math, as empathic, or as humorous will do him little good.

In other instances, the self-presentational choice is quite large. We each could honestly convey a variety of images of ourselves, any one of which could facilitate our attainment of social goals. For example, we could conceivably make good first impressions on our dates by appearing humorous, interesting, empathic, courteous, intelligent, or attractive. But we can't convey all of these images at once and must choose which aspects of ourselves to emphasize in a given social encounter. What determines the kinds of impressions people will try to convey of themselves? In the next five chapters, we examine the primary factors that affect the kinds of impressions people try to make. We begin in this chapter with the effects of the social context on self-presentation.

Norms and Roles: The Unwritten Rules

Imagine yourself on a crowded city bus or subway. Like many of the passengers, you stand, clinging to a metal pole. Now imagine yourself turning to a frail, elderly woman seated by the window and saying, without elaboration or explanation, "Excuse me, could I have your seat?" The woman regards you suspiciously but shrugs and relinquishes her seat. Other nearby persons watch the exchange and stare at you as you sit down. How would you feel? When Stanley Milgram asked subjects to perform these kinds of unusual actions, most of them had great difficulty doing so. And those who managed to perform the behaviors experienced intense feelings of social discomfort afterward. But why?

Our focus in this chapter concerns the effects of norms and roles on people's self-presentations. In the example above, you felt distressed not only because you violated a social norm that says that an able-bodied person shouldn't take an old woman's seat without a good explanation but because this norm violation had *self-presentational* implications for you. Put simply, you looked like an inconsiderate louse.

In the course of everyday life, we are rarely aware of the profound influence that norms and roles have on our behaviors. After all, neither norms nor roles have any physical existence; they aren't written down in books or posted on signs (as laws are), and, typically, no one explicitly forces us to follow their dictates. Yet, much of our behavior is a direct consequence of the fact that we typically behave in line with social norms and the roles we play.

Behavioral researchers who study norms and roles have emphasized the fact that these social guidelines dictate what people should and should not do as a function of the situations they are in and the positions they occupy. For our purposes, it is important to recognize that many norms and roles also have self-presentational requirements that dictate how people in certain situations or positions *should appear to be* to others. When such self-presentational norms and roles are in effect, people often tailor their self-presentations to comply with those norms and roles.

PRINCIPLE:

Unless explicitly motivated to do otherwise, people try to project images of themselves that are consistent with the norms in a particular social setting and with the roles they occupy.

Self-Presentational Norms

A **norm** is a rule or standard for action. Norms are usually implicit and unwritten (as opposed to regulations and laws, which are more explicit). Norms not only specify how people should act but also the nature of the public images they should and should not convey in particular situations. I will call norms that are relevant to the impressions people should convey of themselves **self-presentational norms.**

Some self-presentational norms are *prescriptive*—they prescribe or dictate particular impressions that should be conveyed. At a funeral, self-presentational norms prescribe that those in attendance maintain expressions of solemnity regardless of how they actually felt about the deceased. A funeral-goer who smiled broadly throughout the service would be viewed as quite deviant even if everyone knew that he or she had just won the state lottery or was the deceased's worst enemy.

Other self-presentational norms are *restrictive*—they restrict or constrain the images people present without indicating the precise impression that a person should foster. In many situations, norms do not dictate precisely the kinds of impressions people should convey. Instead, they constrain or limit the possible images that should be conveyed in that setting. As long as people stay within those limits, their behavior will be seen as appropriate, but projecting images outside of those limits may result in negative responses from others. For example, the self-presentational norms relevant to behavior on a city street permit a great deal of latitude in the images people may convey. No one cares much whether we look happy or sad, rich or poor, confident or insecure, athletic or nonathletic, or whatever. Even so, the norms prohibit certain self-presentations. A man who stands on the corner and claims to be Jesus is not staying within the normative limits on who or what he may claim to be.

Some self-presentational norms apply to a broad range of social settings. These are norms that socialized and well-intentioned people are expected to follow in most, though not necessarily all, social contexts. The failure to maintain general, omnibus impressions such as these usually leads others to conclude that the person is unsocialized, rude, disturbed, or purposefully trying to appear deviant. There are many general self-presentational norms that apply in most situations, but I'll discuss only five of the more common ones—decorum, modesty, matching, consistency, and civil attention.

Decorum

Decorum refers to behavior that conforms to established standards for proper behavior. Many of the most basic norms specify minimum criteria for socially acceptable behavior. One aspect of decorum involves people's public images.

Many of the polite and socially appropriate things that we do in public (and perhaps more importantly, many of the things that we don't do) we do and don't do, not because they're harmful to anyone but because of self-presentational norms. Think for a moment of all of the things you do and don't do simply because other people would form unfavorable impressions of you—impressions of being rude, inappropriate, uncouth, or otherwise undesirable.

Why don't you pick your nose in public? Or belch loudly? Or interrupt other people while they're talking? Why do you not lie down on the classroom floor during the professor's lecture or gulp down your food at the restaurant? Why do you say, "Excuse me," when you've accidentally bumped into someone, and "thank you" when you've received a gift? The primary reason is that violating norms such as these will lead others to regard you as a person who cares little for social rules or for others' feelings. Norm-violators are not only negatively evaluated, but they are sometimes outright rejected (Baumeister & Tice, 1990; Schachter, 1951).

Many self-presentational norms involving decorum are so strong that people try to abide by them even under extreme stress. For example, no matter how emotionally distraught they may feel, most people try not to break down in public. In their eyes, it's not something a person is supposed to do because others would think badly of them for it. Even prisoners who are being executed seem intent to die with grace even though no one could blame them for crying, shouting, cursing, or pleading as they were brought to the execution chamber.

Modesty

The **modesty norm** puts impression managers in a bit of a dilemma. On one hand, we usually want other people to perceive us as positively as possible but, on the other hand, self-presentational norms require that we not be *too* self-aggrandizing. People who violate this norm are regarded

Figure 4.1
Modesty is not always an effective self-presentational tactic.

as braggarts, boasters, show-offs, or megalomaniacs. In fact, if we are actually quite superior on some dimension, others are likely to evaluate us more favorably if we downplay our achievements in a show of modesty (Rosen, Cochran, & Musser, 1990; Schlenker & Leary, 1982a). The difficulty is that modest self-presentations risk the possibility that others will accept our self-deprecation as accurate or, if others already regard us highly, as an indication of low self-esteem or lack of self-insight.

Interestingly, people seem to implicitly recognize these hazards and manage their impressions accordingly. When they think others are not aware of their positive attributes or successes, people tend to present themselves somewhat positively (but not so much as to be seen as braggardly). Perhaps they sense that it is better to be seen as possessing positive attributes even at the risk of seeming a bit self-aggrandizing. On the other hand, when they think others already regard them favorably or that others are aware of their accomplishments, people tend to downplay their virtues slightly (Baumeister & Jones, 1978; Jones & Wortman, 1973; Schlenker, 1980; Stires & Jones, 1969).

Modesty is not simply a matter of downplaying or denying one's accomplishments or positive characteristics. When people want to appear modest, they often do so by actually describing their behavior in different terms. Specifically, people who want to appear modest tend to describe their behavior at a relatively low level of meaning; whereas, those who want to self-aggrandize describe their behavior at a higher level of meaning (Vallacher, Wegner, & Frederick, 1987). For example, if someone asked me what I did today, I could honestly describe precisely the same activity—I worked on this chapter—in a number of ways, some of which convey more positive impressions than others. If I didn't want to seem boastful, I might reply, "I typed on the computer all day." If I wanted to convey a more positive impression, I might say, "I worked on the self-presentation book I'm writing."

Before you go out and try to show everyone how modest you are, four words of caution are in order (Schlenker & Leary, 1982a). First, modesty is more effective after the fact than before. People who underestimate their performance beforehand are not regarded as favorably as those who understate their performance afterward. Second, slight modesty is apparently more effective than extreme modesty. For example, claiming to have done "all right" after doing well makes a better impression than claiming to have done poorly. Third, people do not react favorably to those who accurately state that they did well, but downplay the importance of the performance (e.g., "I did well, but it's no big deal"). In fact, such statements may be seen as boastful rather than modest. Finally, downplaying one's accomplishments is an effective self-presentational tactic only if others know the person did well. When others don't know anything about the person's performance, they seem to accept his or her modest claims at face value so that self-derogation results in less favorable impressions.

Incidentally, if people don't know how well they will perform on an upcoming task, their safest bet is to claim that they expect to perform about average. If they subsequently do well, people who expect to do just average are evaluated as favorably as those who expected to do well. If they subsequently do poorly, they are evaluated as favorably as those who made unfavorable predictions. No other self-presentational strategy provides as much flexibility without the risks of being blatantly incorrect (Schlenker & Leary, 1982a).

Self-Presentational Matching

Two different norms specify that people should present themselves similarly to how other people in an interaction are presenting themselves. The **self-presentation positivity norm** specifies that people should present themselves just about as positively as others in the interaction. This norm was first demonstrated in a study by Gergen and Wishnov (1965) in which subjects received another person's self-ratings, then described themselves to this person. Subjects who received egotistical self-ratings from the other person subsequently described themselves more positively, whereas subjects who received humble self-ratings described themselves more negatively. (See, also, Schneider & Eustis, 1972).

Baumeister, Hutton, and Tice (1989) showed that people are not always aware that they conform to this norm. In their study, subjects were induced to present themselves either favorably or modestly to an interaction partner. In accordance with the positivity norm, the images that the interaction partners subsequently conveyed of themselves were influenced by the positivity of the subjects' earlier self-presentations: partners presented themselves more positively if the subject had previously presented a favorable impression than if the subject had presented a modest impression. However, the interaction partners seemed unaware that their self-presentations had been affected by the impressions the subjects had conveyed earlier.

A second self-presentational matching norm is the **depth of disclosure norm.** This norm specifies that people should match the depth or intimacy of other people's self-disclosures (Derlega et al., 1993). People tend to reveal more about themselves to those who reveal more about themselves than to those whose self-disclosures are relatively unrevealing.

Among strangers, this effect occurs within single interactions; if I tell you something personal about myself, you will feel a certain amount of pressure to reciprocate immediately. Among people who know each other well, this norm operates over a longer time span. If you are a close friend, you may not necessarily reciprocate my disclosing statement right now, but you are likely to do so some time in the future (Derlega, Wilson, & Chaikin, 1976). If people in long-term friendships and romantic relationships violate this norm over the long run, relationship stress may occur because of inequity in the degree to which the two people confide in one another (Rosenfeld & Bowen, 1991).

Consistency

A fourth general self-presentational norm involves **self-presentational consistency.** This norm dictates that people should behave consistently with their beliefs and attitudes, as well as show a reasonable degree of consistency in how they behave across different situations (Gergen, 1968; Goffman, 1959). People who do not appear consistent are often viewed as weak, unreliable, hypocritical, deluded, or even mentally unstable. No one wants to be so rigidly consistent that they're utterly predictable and boring, but a high degree of consistency is valued nonetheless.

Of course, everyone occasionally behaves in ways that are inconsistent with their true beliefs. We feign our enjoyment of our host's truly tasteless meal, laugh at jokes that aren't funny, agree publicly with opinions we privately reject, and so on. One of the more interesting social psychological findings of the past 40 years is that, under certain circumstances, engaging in these kinds of inconsistent or attitude-discrepant behaviors leads people's attitudes to change in the direction of their behavior. Under certain circumstances, complimenting our host's meal may lead us to adopt a more positive attitude toward it.

During the 1960s, the most widely accepted explanation of this phenomenon was based on Festinger's (1957) cognitive dissonance theory. According to cognitive dissonance theory, people have an inherent drive to maintain consistency among their various thoughts and experience an unpleasant state of tension (dissonance) whenever they have thoughts that are in conflict. As a result, people are motivated to avoid cognitive inconsistency and to reduce inconsistency whenever it occurs.

According to dissonance theory, people who engage in an action that is contrary to their attitudes are likely to experience dissonance because they recognize that their attitudes and behavior are inconsistent. To resolve this inconsistency and the accompanying dissonance, the individual's attitude changes so that the discrepancy between behavior and attitude is reduced. Put simply, if the person comes to believe in what he or she did, dissonance will disappear. One essential condition for dissonance is that the person feel responsible for engaging in the attitude-discrepant behavior. If the person were coerced or induced by strong incentives to perform the behavior, little or no dissonance and, thus, little or no attitude change should occur.

This effect was first demonstrated in a now classic study by Festinger and Carlsmith (1959). In this study, subjects were induced to lie to another person (telling him or her that a boring task was interesting). Consistent with the predictions of cognitive dissonance theory, subjects who were paid a pittance for lying changed their attitudes more than subjects who were paid handsomely. Cognitive dissonance theory explained this finding by arguing that subjects who were paid a small amount to say something against their real attitudes subsequently experienced a great deal of dissonance. To reduce their unpleasant feelings, these subjects' attitudes changed in the direction of the lie to reduce the inconsistency. In contrast, subjects who were paid a larger sum had a strong external justification for saying that the boring task was interesting.

As a result, they experienced less dissonance and had no reason to change their attitudes. This explanation of attitude change following counterattitudinal behavior was widely (though not universally) accepted for many years. However, in the late 1960s, James Tedeschi and two of his students, Barry Schlenker and Thomas Bonoma, began to have doubts about the dissonance explanation of this variety of attitude change.

Tedeschi came to social psychology via an indirect route, initially being interested in learning and motivation. But his involvement in the political unrest of the 1960s evoked both a personal and professional interest in power. Leaving his work in animal learning behind, Tedeschi began a program of research on the role of threats and promises in conflict situations. In the context of this research, he became intrigued by the fact that both nations and individuals often try to create the impression that they have power even when they had none, thereby stimulating his interest in impression management (Tedeschi, 1992).

Tedeschi, Schlenker, and Bonoma's insight was that many behavioral effects that psychologists had explained in terms of cognitive dissonance were, in fact, affected by self-presentational concerns. In a review of the research literature, they concluded that there was little evidence that the attitude change obtained in these studies was, in fact, due to cognitive inconsistency or to the subjective experience of dissonance. Rather, they claimed that attitude change after attitude-discrepant behavior occurs because subjects are concerned with *appearing* consistent to others (Tedeschi, Schlenker, & Bonoma, 1971).

Norms insist on consistency between what people say and what they do. Indeed, such norms are essential for organized, predictable, and mutually beneficial interactions. We would find it difficult to negotiate social life if people didn't generally keep their promises, behave consistently with what they said, and, in general, live up to who and what they claimed to be (Dollard, 1949; Gergen, 1968; Goffman, 1959). As a result, we are under considerable social pressure to behave consistently and are likely to be regarded unfavorably for unjustified inconsistency. Given these social pressures, people are understandably motivated to manage their impressions to appear reasonably (although not necessarily rigidly) consistent.

As a result, when a person freely behaves in a manner discrepant from his or her attitudes, then is asked what his or her attitudes are, the individual is in a self-presentational dilemma. To admit that he or she behaved in a manner that violated his or her true attitudes or beliefs would lead others to form negative impressions (such as that the person was unstable, hypocritical, or noncredible). As a result, the person who has acted contrary to his or her attitudes may subsequently report an attitude that is more consistent with his or her behavior than is really the case. Having told someone that the boring task was interesting, a subject may suffer less self-presentational damage by later claiming it *was* interesting than admitting that he or she lied. The person's attitude did not really change (the task was, after all, pretty boring); it only appeared to change.

Several studies have shown that impression management theory parsimoniously explains the effects of counterattitudinal behavior on attitude change as well, if not better, than cognitive dissonance theory. In a pair of studies, Gaes, Kalle, and Tedeschi (1978) convinced some of their subjects that they were attached to a machine that accurately measured their attitudes physiologically (a technique known as the **bogus pipeline**). After subjects were led to perform a behavior that was inconsistent with their attitudes (writing essays arguing against toothbrushing), they were asked about their attitudes toward toothbrushing. Subjects who believed that the machine could measure their true attitudes admitted that they really thought toothbrushing was important; that is, they showed no evidence of attitude change. The bogus pipeline prevented them from feigning agreement with their behavior. In contrast, subjects who were not connected to the bogus pipeline expressed attitudes that were more consistent with their essays (see also Reiss, Kalle, & Tedeschi, 1981).

Other studies showed that subjects who have performed an attitude-discrepant behavior change their attitudes only if other people *know* they have done so (Tedeschi & Rosenfeld, 1981). This pattern is not consistent with cognitive dissonance theory; dissonance should occur even if the person performing the behavior was alone on a desert island. Also, subjects who perform an attitude-discrepant behavior in front of a group of people show evidence of attitude change only if they subsequently report their attitudes to *that* group of people. Subjects who report their attitudes to someone who didn't know they performed the behavior show no evidence of attitude change (Schlenker, Forsyth, Leary, & Miller, 1980). Again, this finding is consistent with impression management theory but not with cognitive dissonance theory.

In brief, the proponents of impression management theory claim that the attitude change that one shows after he or she has engaged in behavior that is inconsistent with his or her existing attitudes is a self-presentational strategy designed to show the individual to be consistent and/or moral. The theory seems to be able to explain many of the research findings regarding attitude change, including findings that can not be easily explained by dissonance theory (Schlenker, 1982). This does not necessarily mean that cognitive dissonance never occurs or that attitudes do not really change (see Croyle & Cooper, 1983; Rosenfeld, Giacalone, & Tedeschi, 1984). But it shows the power of the norm of self-presentational consistency.

Civil Attention and Inattention

In certain settings, self-presentational norms specify how much attention people should appear to be paying to what others are saying or doing. In some situations, norms require people to appear to be attentive to or interested in what others are saying or doing. What do you do when you're listening to someone talk—in a conversation or lecture, for example—and he or she is boring you to tears? Do you tell him or her you're not interested, or walk off, or look around disinterestly?

Sometimes. But, most commonly you will try to look as if you're interested in what they're saying. As Goffman (1967) noted, "when a conversation fails to capture the spontaneous involvement of an individual who is obliged to participate in it, he is likely to contrive an appearance of being really involved" (p. 126). The **norm of civil attention** dictates that people appear to be at least minimally involved in social encounters. Even when someone bores us with long-winded accounts of his or her personal problems, poor health, esoteric hobbies, and mindless opinions, it is usually considered impolite not to *appear* at least minimally interested. As a result, people often try to appear interested and involved even when they are not.

In other settings, norms dictate that people should *not* pay attention to what others are doing—that they should mind their own business. We aren't supposed to stare at people who are engaging in odd behaviors, comment on others' actions, or eavesdrop on their conversations. Of course, we all violate this norm when we find others' behavior interesting. What is the couple in the park fighting about? Look at that vagrant digging through the garbage. Did you hear those two guys at the bar sizing up the women sitting across from them?

However, even when we pay more attention to others' actions than perhaps we should, we typically abide by the self-presentational **norm of civil inattention.** This norm specifies that people don't pay undue attention to things that aren't any of their business (Goffman, 1963). Thus, we often glance at other people obliquely, listen to them while we engage in other behaviors, and we talk about what they are saying or doing in hushed tones.

Such a norm is commonly in force when strangers meet in a public restroom. They glance at one another, perhaps nod or grunt a greeting, then pretend that one another is not there (Cahill et al., 1985). We would be regarded quite negatively if we started a loud and antimated conversation with the person in the adjacent stall or if we watched too closely while someone used the urinal or washed his or her hands.

A self-presentational norm that is closely related to that of civil inattention is that of "nothing unusual is happening" (Emerson, 1970). In certain instances in which people behave in unusual ways, we are expected to *act as if* nothing unusual were happening. Imagine you are at a party when a couple you know becomes embroiled in an argument. In such a situation, observers are inclined to give the impression that they notice nothing out of the ordinary. Similarly, we often give the impression that "nothing unusual is happening" when we pass street people who are ranting loudly to themselves.

Conveying the impression that "nothing unusual is happening" serves several functions. First, it allows the person to adhere to norms of inattention and politeness. To convey that we notice others' indiscretions shows that we really weren't minding our own business after all. Second, acting as if nothing were happening allows people to avoid responding to situations that may be awkward or dangerous. If I don't act as if the ranting vagrant is normal, how *do* I act? Finally, this tactic helps people stall for time until they figure out how to respond. If we show others that we regard the situation as unusual, dangerous, or whatever, we may be obligated to react immediately.

Gender-Related Impressions

In every society, norms specify that men and women should engage in a somewhat different range of behaviors. In most societies around the world, men are expected to be the primary breadwinners, and women are expected to take primary responsibility for the children. In addition to the norms that govern gender-related behaviors such as these, self-presentational norms specify that men and women should *convey different impressions of themselves*. For example, people often think that men should appear dominant, ambitious, assertive, and tough, but those same people may view dominant, ambitious, assertive, tough women negatively. Conversely, a woman who is sensitive and emotional may make a good impression, whereas a sensitive and emotional man may not.

In light of this, many of the differences we observe in the behavior of men and women in our society may reflect differences in the self-presentational norms for men and women (Deaux & Major, 1987). From an early age, boys and girls are rewarded for creating different public images. Little boys are encouraged to act independent and are teased for looking like "sissies," and little girls are encouraged to be expressive and nurturant and to act "feminine." As a result, adult men present themselves as more assertive, powerful, and competent than women, whereas women's self-presentations emphasize their interpersonal and communal attributes (Deaux, 1977; Forsyth, Schlenker, Leary, & McCown, 1985; Schlenker, 1975).

Males and females are also raised to be differentially expressive; girls are typically encouraged to be more open and expressive than boys. As a result, men and women differ in the amount and intimacy of the information they disclose about themselves to others. Women are typically more self-revealing than men (Derlega et al., 1993; Wheeler, Reis, & Nezlek, 1983). In part, this seems to be due to the fact that norms regarding self-disclosure lead men to worry about the impressions they will make if they are too disclosing, expressive, or open (Petronio & Martin, 1986).

Self-presentational norms even affect differences in how men and women eat. Because "eating lightly" is associated with appearing feminine in American society, women are more likely than men to eat less when they want to make socially desirable impressions (Pliner & Chaiken, 1990). One study showed that university women were particularly likely to reduce how much they ate when eating with a man whom they thought perceived them as unfeminine (Mori et al., 1987). The fact that eating and weight are more central to images of "femininity" than "masculinity" may help to explain why women of all ages are more concerned than men about how much they eat and weigh (Pliner, Chaiken, & Flett, 1990).

Self-presentational norms even require that men and women groom differently. Most American women wear makeup when they go into public, but men who wear makeup are openly ridiculed. Why? What is it about a woman's facial skin that isn't good enough unless it's covered up and artifically colored? This norm is so strong that, in 1991, Continental Airlines fired a ticket agent because she refused to wear makeup and lipstick. When the woman threatened to sue for sexual harrassment (after all, male employees weren't required to wear makeup), Continental backed down (Goodman, 1991).

Such norm-based prescriptions place both men and women in a bind. To the extent that men are, in fact, nurturant, or that women are dominant, they may feel they must maintain a public image that is, in some respects, inconsistent with who they "really are."

Furthermore, concerns with others' impressions constrain the range of behaviors that men and women are willing to enact in public. One clear example involves people's choices of sport and recreational activities. Although some physical activities, such as tennis and running, are enjoyed by both men and women, some activities are viewed as more appropriate for one gender than the other (Jackson & Marsh, 1986). Because people who engage in activities associated with the other gender are often ridiculed, some people will not engage in them. For example, why do so few men become involved in aerobic dance or ballet, and why do relatively few women box or lift weights? In part, it is because involvement in these activities conveys impressions that are inconsistent with the images most men and women in our culture want to project (Leary, 1992).

Gender and Self-Presentation on the Road to the White House

Hillary Rodham Clinton faced some tough self-presentational choices, choices that most candidates' and Presidents' wives have not had to face. By all accounts, Hillary Clinton has long been a capable, strong, assertive, ambitious, outspoken person. She is a successful lawyer (she was ranked among the top 100 in the country), as well as a public advocate for children and education. Such attributes are widely admired in men, but many people continue to have reservations about independent, outspoken, successful women. During the 1992 Presidential campaign, the Republican party hoped to gain votes by attacking Ms. Clinton as a "feminist who preferred the boardroom to the kitchen" (Carlson, 1992).

To counter the criticism against her and to prevent a backlash that might thwart her husband's political aspirations, Hillary Clinton managed her impressions to present an image that was more palatable to many Americans. She changed her hairstyle, eyewear, and clothing to convey a softer, more feminine image. After public criticism for her quip that she "could have stayed home, baked cookies, and had teas," she was photographed baking cookies and attending daughter Chelsea's soccer games. Instead of introducing her husband to the crowds at his campaign appearances, she began to stand in the background, gazing adoringly at him as candidates' wives have always done (Carlson, 1992; Quinn, 1992).

Some of Ms. Clinton's behaviors were designed as much to manage her husband's impressions as her own. Campaign strategists were concerned that an overly assertive wife might make Mr. Clinton look like a wimp. One commentator noted that the perception that his wife is telling him what to do "will only make him look weak," reducing his power and effectiveness (Quinn, 1992, p. 28).

Continued

After the election, however, Ms. Clinton's self-presentations changed slightly. She moved into an office in the west wing of the White House, the President appointed her to chair his task force on health care reform, and she was openly involved in the appointment of cabinet positions. Although many people criticized the return of the old, pre-campaign Hillary, few addressed the larger issue of why an intelligent, capable, assertive woman should have had to model a more traditional image in order not to hurt her husband's chances for election.

Context-Specific Norms

In addition to general norms that apply across many situations, some self-presentational norms apply only to specific social contexts. The variety of context-specific self-presentational norms is virtually endless, so I'll mention just a few to give you a sense of the degree to which our public images are constrained by the self-presentational norms operating in particular situations.

Consider how the self-presentational norms for a funeral, for example, differ from those of a wedding. I can imagine instances in which guests at a wedding are, in fact, more unhappy about the event at hand than mourners at a particular funeral, yet the wedding guests *look* happy; whereas, the mourners do not.

In highly cohesive groups—groups in which there is a great deal of "we-feeling"—norms discourage behaviors that threaten the group's solidarity. People who "rock the boat" are ignored, devalued, or ostracized. As a result, group members feel pressure to appear to agree with other group members even when they privately disagree. The fact that people are more likely to express opinions that go along with the group when they express their opinions publicly rather than anonymously shows that conformity is heightened by self-presentational motives (Deutsch & Gerard, 1955). When group members fail to express dissenting opinions because of concerns with what other group members will think of them, bad group decisions may result (Janis, 1982).

Even restrooms are governed by self-presentational norms. As I noted, when in public restrooms, people are expected to engage in civil inattention. Furthermore, they are expected to wash their hands after going to the bathroom, but I have the strong suspicion that people are more likely to do so when others are present than when they are alone.

Culture

Confusion and misunderstanding can arise when people from one culture engage in self-presentations that do not conform to the norms of another culture. A person may behave in a certain way to communicate a certain impression, yet find that persons from another culture draw an entirely different impression from the one he or she intended.

One way to examine self-presentational norms across cultures is to consider the personal characteristics that different cultures value (Bond, 1991). For example, cultures differ in the degree to which they value achievement, power, hedonism, respect for tradition, and conformity (Schwartz & Bilsky, 1987). We would expect people's self-presentations in a culture that values conformity to differ from those in a culture that values independence and autonomy. In a culture that values conformity, people will pretend to agree more than they really do, use a large number of moderating adverbs to qualify their statements (such as slightly, perhaps), and avoid taking strong positions against the group. In contrast, in a culture that values self-direction, people will be freer to express their true opinions and emotions. They will be more likely to experiment with their lifestyles and more willing to march to the beat of their own drummer. People in a culture that values independence may go out of their way not to give the impression of being overly provincial, conservative, or traditional.

The powerful role of culture in self-presentation has been inadequately explored. However, as our global society expands, we have increasing reason to understand cultural differences in self-presentation (Bond, 1991).

Roles

A social **role** is a set of behaviors that is associated with a particular position within a social system (Harre' & Lamb, 1986). The existence of a role implies that a person who holds a particular position is expected to enact the behaviors that are associated with the role. You can think of roles as a special kind of norm, specifically a norm that is attached to a particular position or part (Turner, 1990).

Some roles, such as "parent" or "minister," are relatively permanent. In these ongoing positions, the roles transcend situations and time. In other cases, people enact a role only for a specified period of time or for a particular occasion (Biddle, 1979). For example, a person may enact the role of "host" for the duration of the party, after which the role ceases to exist.

Many roles prescribe not only how people in a certain position are to behave but that people who occupy the position should appear to be a certain kind of person or to possess certain personal characteristics. Being in a certain position often requires certain self-presentations.

An obvious example involves members of the clergy. A minister, priest, or rabbi must not only possess certain knowledge and perform certain duties but must maintain a certain public image in others' eyes. He or she must be seen as caring, more selfless than the average person, highly moral, even tempered, and so on. At the same time, the clergy usually try not to be seen as overly hedonistic, carefree, or earthy. Most members of the clergy go out of their way to avoid situations that could lead others (particularly parishioners) to doubt their convictions or morals.

Importantly, failure to maintain a public image that is consistent with a self-presentational role may lead to loss of one's influence or effectiveness in the role, or even the right to hold the position. History is rife with religious leaders, politicians, and businesspeople who lost their claims to power not because they were incompetent in their positions but because they failed to convey the "right" impressions of themselves.

Prototype Correspondence

Role-determined self-presentations seem to be governed by a process of **prototype correspondence.** People hold cognitive prototypes regarding categories of people (Cantor & Mischel, 1979). They use these prototypes to classify people into categories based on the degree to which the individual resembles the relevant prototype. For example, each of us has a prototype of a minister (rabbi, priest, etc.) that specifies the characteristics that the generic minister possesses. Similarly, we have prototypes of college professors, prostitutes, business executives, and accountants. The greater the match between the perceived characteristics of a given individual and the perceiver's prototype, the more likely the individual will be regarded as appropriate and effective in that position. Knowing this, an individual in a particular position may manage his or her impressions to correspond to others' prototypes.

Violations of role prototypes precipitate impression management problems. If the violation is relatively minor—such as when President Lyndon Johnson showed his surgical scar to photographers or Franklin Roosevelt cursed a stuck voting machine handle ("The goddamned thing won't work")—the consequence is typically no more serious than a public outcry. More serious violations, however, can undermine a person's right to play a particular role. For example, the disclosure of Gary Hart's relationship with a Miami model during the 1988 Presidential campaign doomed his bid for the Democratic nomination. Apparently, Hart's behavior did not mesh with voters' prototypes of a viable presidential candidate, although in reality it said little about his ability *as president*.

Self-Presentation and Leadership

A good example of how people sometimes manage their impressions to match the prototype of their roles involves leadership. Leaders throughout history have recognized that their effectiveness and power depends, in part, on their public images. Military officers, heads of state, corporate executives, officers of civic groups, and small group leaders alike have realized that they must convey to others that they possess certain attributes and skills both to attain and to maintain their positions.

The importance of impression management to leaders becomes more apparent when we realize that what we call "leadership" is actually an inference that we draw about certain individuals (Calder, 1977). Certain patterns of behavior lead others to perceive a person as a leader or as possessing characteristics that are relevant to leadership. Other patterns of behavior lead people to regard a person as unfit for leadership. Thus, others' impressions determine in part who is and is not likely to become and remain a leader. The ability to establish one's suitability for the leadership role is critical for a person who wants to become or remain an effective leader (Leary, 1989).

Typically, a person who wants to become or remain a leader will try to convey images that correspond to others' prototypes of a leader, whatever those may be in a particular setting. This involves both conveying that they possess characteristics that are part of the leader prototype (appearing decisive, concerned for the group's welfare, effective, and so on) and avoiding appearances that are inconsistent with the prototype (such as appearing incompetent, unconcerned for the group, self-serving, or weak). American Presidents, for example, despite variations in their personal styles, typically try to appear "presidential"—that is, they try to match the public's prototype of a president, however that is defined at a particular time in history (Hall, 1979).

Five particular impressions are central to leaders' images. This is not to say that every leader must convey all five impressions at all times, but each is sometimes necessary for maximal effectiveness. The perception of competence is central to nearly every leader's effectiveness. Followers' perceptions of a leader's ability weigh heavily in their assessment of whether someone is appropriate for the position. In addition, perceived competence is one source of a leader's influence, forming the basis of "expert power" (French & Raven, 1959).

Second, leaders sometimes manage their impressions to be liked, believing that they can increase their influence through "attraction power" (French & Raven, 1959). Many leaders want to be viewed as both competent and likable, but sometimes find it difficult to impress their subordinates with their competence and task orientation while still being seen as friendly and approachable. One solution to this dilemma was demonstrated in a study of ROTC cadets (Jones, Gergen, & Jones, 1963). High status cadets who were instructed to get a low status cadet to like them became more self-deprecating on attributes that were not relevant to their leadership position. In this way, they could appear more friendly, modest, and approachable without undermining impressions of competence and authority.

Third, some leaders are interested in being perceived as moral and exemplary. Such concerns are probably most prominent for religious leaders who are unlikely to be effective if their followers get the impression that they are self-serving, cheating liars. More interesting is the fact that followers often expect their leaders to maintain an image of morality even in areas that are unrelated to the exercise of leadership per se. This can be seen in the case of American presidents and their families who are expected to "provide leadership in morals and taste as well as politics" (Klapp, 1964, p. 131).

Fourth, leaders usually want to be seen as powerful, calm, decisive, and in control. Self-presentations of potency are particularly important when a leader's group is under stress. For example, during national crises, such as a war, being seen as calm and confident has implications not only for a President's own public standing but for the people's morale and confidence. During World War II, Franklin Roosevelt seemed to work on presenting a confident, if not cocky impression, and during the Cuban Missile crisis, John Kennedy tried to be seen as calm. During the Persian Gulf War of 1991, George Bush made a concerted effort to project an image of being controlled, unruffled, and unflappable. As one White House official commented, "George Bush believed it was important he be as strong and as steady as he could be. His emotions were not relevant here. In fact, it was important to him that they not show" (Strong and Steady, Jan. 28, 1991, p. 34).

Finally, some leaders use self-presentations of intimidation. By maintaining an appearance of impatience and hostility, leaders can threaten their subordinates or enemies into submission. By conveying that they have a low threshold for anger, for example, supervisors can exert "coercive power" (French & Raven, 1959), though often at the expense of group morale. At the end of the Persian Gulf War of 1991, General H. Norman Schwarzkopf used intimidating self-presentations in his negotiations between American and Iraqi commanders. The tent that served as the site of the meeting was ringed with armored vehicles that were draped with American and British flags. Schwarzkopf himself arrived with a squadron of Apache attack helicopters (the Iraqi commanders rode in jeeps). Once at the negotiating table, Schwarzkopf maintained a stonelike expression, refusing even a hint of a smile. In all, the desired effect was obtained; the Iraqis were awed by the allied weaponry and chagrined by their position ("Allies Dealing Sternly with Iraqis," 1991).

Effective leaders are presumably quite aware of the importance of others' impressions of them. They also seem to be aware that, although there are general prescriptions for leader's images, they must occasionally foster different impressions depending on the situation. For example, leaders may want to be perceived as warm and supportive when they want to foster loyalty, but as gruff and intolerant to increase followers' unquestioning compliance.

In laboratory studies of leaders' self-presentations, leaders of ad hoc groups showed themselves quite adept at conveying impressions that were consistent with the kind of leader they thought the group needed at the time. When a task-oriented leader was needed, leaders described themselves to their followers more strongly in terms of their power and effectiveness than when a relationship-oriented leader was needed (Leary, Robertson, Barnes, & Miller, 1986). If college students playing the role of leader in a psychology experiment are adept at managing their impressions depending on the group context, we can only imagine that experienced leaders are even more so.

Charismatic Leadership

Some leaders do more than just lead. They instill in their followers a sense of trust, admiration, and confidence, if not awe. Such leaders are often said to have **charisma.** John F. Kennedy, Ghandi, Jesse Jackson, Jesus, Franklin Roosevelt, and Martin Luther King, Jr. are often named as examples of charismatic leaders. Even leaders who inspire others to behave destructively, such as Adolf Hitler, Jim Jones, and David Koresh may be said to have charisma to the extent that they have profound effects on their followers.

Charisma has proven difficult for researchers to define and operationalize. My dictionary defines charisma as "the special

Continued

quality that gives an individual influence or authority over large numbers of people" (*The Random House Dictionary*, p. 226), but researchers have had difficulty identifying precisely what that quality involves.

Whatever charisma is, however, it clearly has something to do with the leader's *image* in followers' eyes. Charismatic leaders project an extraordinary public image that leaves a lasting impression on other people. In fact, one theory suggests that charismatic leadership involves "the use of articulation and impression management practices to inspire followers in pursuit of the vision" (Conger & Kanungo, 1987, p. 29).

Earlier, I listed five impressions that are central to the prototype of leadership—competence, likability, morality, potency, and intimidation. Few leaders are able to convey impressions of themselves on all five of these attributes: some leaders seem likable and moral, but not very effective; other leaders come across as powerful and intimidating, but nobody likes them very much; still others appear competent and strong, but as not very ethical.

My sense is that charismatic leaders are unusually effective at maintaining a public image that includes most, if not all of these impressions, more or less simultaneously. Put differently, a leader is unlikely to be perceived as charismatic unless he or she is seen as outstanding on at least four of these dimensions.

Charismatic leaders tend to be excellent self-promoters who ensure that nothing contradicts their image of competence and effectiveness. They also tend to be liked and admired by their followers, often because they seem excessively selfless and concerned with their followers' welfare. Charismatic leaders often work to assure that they are seen as having morality on their side. In fact, many charismatic leaders sound as if they are on religious crusades as much as on political ones. They also try to portray themselves as being moral in their personal lives (even though reality may not mesh with the projected appearance). Even those who inspire their followers to harm themselves or other people often base their power on moral teachings. Finally, charismatic leaders can be intimidating when they need to be. However, they must use threatening self-presentations only for the benefit of the group (such as to discipline deviants and to scare the group's adversaries) and not for their selfish purposes.

A self-presentational analysis of charisma does not suggest that people can become charismatic leaders by simply pretending.

Continued

Over time, a person will be able to sustain an image of competence, likability, morality, potency, and intimidation only if he or she really possesses these attributes. Even so, no matter what his or her personal characteristics, a person will be seen as charismatic only to the extent that such images can be conveyed to followers.

Role Distance and Conflict

Sometimes, people find themselves in a role that has the potential to cast undesirable aspersions on the images they want other people to have of them. In such instances, people use impression management to distance themselves from the role they are playing. In essence they want to show others that they are not taking the role seriously and, thus, the role should not be taken as a reflection on their real selves.

Role distancing self-presentations are commonly seen in older children and adolescents who do not want their peers to see their parents treating them "like a child." People who are performing duties that they think are beneath them also use role distancing. For example, when an employer asks an employee to perform some menial chore, he or she may do so with an obvious air of detachment, sullenness, or disgust.

Goffman (1961) provided the example of a merry-go-round ride to demonstrate role distancing behaviors. Whereas very young children clearly take merry-go-round rides quite seriously, older children and adults seem determined to show onlookers that they do not. They may ride with casual nonchalance, refusing to hold on to the pole or reins. Or, they may ride recklessly, sitting backwards or leaning far back in the saddle. Adults who are riding with their children often adopt an expression of tolerant boredom. In all cases, they are trying to show others that they do not take the ride seriously.

Understandably, people try to avoid violating the self-presentational requirements of norms and roles. However, sometimes such violations seem unavoidable. One of the more interesting instances of this involves cases of **self-presentational role conflict** in which the public images required of one role are in opposition of those required of another role, or when the self-presentational requirements of one's role conflict with self-presentational norms.

Sometimes, people find themselves in a position where they must simultaneously play two roles whose self-presentational demands are incompatible. I recently read a newspaper story of a police officer who, in the course of a drug bust, found that his daughter was among the people he was arresting. What impression-management strategy did he adopt, I wondered—that of a concerned (or angry) father, that of a police officer doing his job, or something in between?

A related conflict occurs when a role requires self-presentations that are inconsistent with self-presentational norms. This is the dilemma in which many female business executives and leaders find themselves. As we've seen, the prototype of a leader involves someone who is dominant, assertive, and task oriented. Yet, gender-related norms discourage women from being seen in these ways. Women who appear too dominant or assertive are often derogated, even when such behaviors would be acceptable if done by a man.

Backstage Behavior

Although norms and roles require people to maintain certain public images in the eyes of certain targets, these public rule-dictated images are often knowingly contradicted when the individual retreats to a **back region or backstage area.** In the back region, away from the target, normal norm and role demands often do not apply. The individual "can relax; he can drop his front, forego speaking his lines, and step out of character" (Goffman, 1959, p. 112). Thus, when people can retreat to backstage areas, they need not worry about their self-presentations in the ordinary sense.

You should not think of back regions as places as much as social contexts in which the self-presentational demands of a role do not apply. In some cases, back regions are physically separate from the front region where such norms are in place. For example, school teachers may escape to a teacher's lounge where they are out of sight of their students and need not worry about maintaining the impressions appropriate to being a teacher. In other cases, however, a single area may serve as a front or back region depending on the social context. Executives' offices may be front regions as they meet with clients or lawyers but back regions when they sequester themselves behind closed doors with their best friends.

Backstage areas also serve as "staging areas" where people, either alone or collectively, prepare themselves for performances in the front region (Goffman, 1959). People in backstage areas can arrange their appearances, practice mentally or aloud things they will say to others, and otherwise prepare themselves for social contacts. Sometimes, "teams" of individuals use backstage areas to discuss problems involved in the staging of a collective performance (Cahill et al., 1985). For example, a couple throwing a party may retreat to a backstage area to discuss how they will handle an unruly guest.

When impression-relevant norms are suspended in back regions, people's behavior often takes on a "regressive" character. People in back regions tend to be excessively informal, status demarcations disappear, and people behave more playfully. At minimum, people in backstage areas often engage in behaviors that would be socially unacceptable to targets in the front region. Physicians joke among themselves about patients; teachers discuss topics in language that would shock their students; and waiters in a fine restaurant display degrees of informality that diners would find objectionable.

Furthermore, in some back regions, general norms regarding decorum are suspended. For example, belching and flatulance may be regarded as funny rather than as the breach of decorum they would be regarded in a front region. Back region behavior also tends to involve substandard speech, including swearing, as well as open sexual remarks (Goffman, 1959; Turner & Edgley, 1976). In discussing the regressive nature of back region behavior, Goffman (1959) raised the interesting question of whether "a backstage gives individuals an opportunity to regress or whether regression, in the clinical sense, is backstage conduct invoked on inappropriate occasions for motives that are not socially approved" (p. 128).

Although most ordinary self-presentational norms are suspended in backstage areas, some back regions have self-presentational norms of their own. Such norms go beyond suspending the requirements of the front area to flagrantly *violating* them. For example, in some back regions, it seems that people are expected to be excessively crude, to openly ridicule the people in the front area (customers, patients, students, or whoever), and to otherwise behave in ways that are in stark contrast to norms that operate in the front region.

The importance of back regions is perhaps nowhere more obvious than in the everyday work world. In nearly every line of work, workers have back regions where they escape the scrutiny of the people who use their goods, products, and services. In these areas, they need not play their roles as salespeople, teachers, waiters, physicians, ministers, or whatever, and they do not need to concern themselves with the self-presentational demands of their roles.

In some cases, the separation is absolutely essential for the performance of their work. For example, in funeral homes, mourners must be kept away from the places where personnel prepare the body for display and burial (Turner & Edgley, 1976). As Goffmann (1959) observed, "if the bereaved are to be given the impression that the loved one is really in a deep and tranquil sleep, they will have to be kept away from the area where the corpse is drained, stuffed, and painted for its final performance"

(p. 106). In other cases, the back region is merely a convenience for employees, a place where they can forego the impressions they must maintain in the front regions. Teachers, for example, don't need lounges to do their jobs effectively, but being able to escape to such places during the school day is undoubtedly a relief.

Of course, people must be very careful that the normal targets of their self-presentations do not have access to their back regions. Often, backstage areas are formally restricted by locked doors or "employees only" signs. Fortunately, people typically respect the sanctity of others' back regions. No matter how curious we may be, we typically don't intrude uninvited into the kitchen area of a restaurant, the medical lab of a funeral home, the employees' lounge at a school or store, or the executive washroom.

Restrooms as Backstage Areas

You probably think of bathrooms simply as places where people relieve their bodily needs. However, they also serve a social function as backstage areas where people can be temporarily free of the norms and roles that they must abide by outside the restroom door. As Cahill et al. (1985) observed, "public bathrooms offer individuals at least some relief from the behavioral harness that the frontstage audience's eyes impose upon them" (p. 45). For example, people sometimes retreat to bathrooms to compose themselves when they can not maintain the kind of images they would like to maintain, such as when they are crying, embarrassed, or otherwise upset (Cahill et al., 1985).

As I noted, back regions are sometimes used as staging areas where people prepare for public performances, and restrooms are noteworthy in this regard. Restrooms are often used as self-presentational "repair shops" where people check their appearances, comb their hair, tuck in their shirts, put on makeup, check to be sure no food is lodged between their teeth, and perform other behaviors to improve their public impressions. Furthermore, "teams" use restrooms to discuss their staging of certain social interactions, as when two women in a bar retreat to the restroom to talk about how they will handle the overtures of the two men they just met.

The backstage use of restrooms helps to explain why bathrooms are sometimes segregated by rank (Cahill et al., 1985). Often, executives use different washrooms than the rank-and-file; faculty use different restrooms than students, and officers use different latrines than enlisted soldiers. Even the segregation of restrooms by gender may serve as much a self-presentational as a biological function.

Bloopers and Backstage Behavior

Goffman's (1959) idea that our social lives contain audiences, front regions, and backstages was metaphorical.

For people who appear on radio and television, though, front and back regions are quite real. Behaviors that are acceptable in the back region—that is, when the mike or camera is off—may not be acceptable if seen or overheard by the audience in the front region.

Many of the "bloopers" that have become the focus of popular records and TV shows are instances in which a performer thought he or she was "backstage"—off the air—when, in fact, he or she was being seen or heard by thousands of people. Perhaps the classic blooper of this type involved Uncle Don, the host of a children's show during the early days of radio. In a now classic broadcast blooper, Uncle Don signed off his show, then, thinking he was off-the-air, commented "I guess that'll hold the little bastards for the night" (Pardon My Blooper, 1972).

Summary

People try to project images of themselves that are consistent with social norms and roles. Self-presentational norms involving decorum, modesty, matching, consistency, and civil attention apply to a wide range of social situations. Furthermore, norms specify that men and women should maintain slightly different public images.

Roles dictate not only that people in a certain position behave in specified ways but that they convey certain impressions of themselves to others. As a result, people try to project images that are consistent with the prototype of people in a certain role. One clear-cut case of this involves leaders who often try to present images of themselves that will facilitate their effectiveness. However, when people find themselves in roles that convey undesired impressions of themselves, they engage in role-distancing behaviors to show that the role should not be taken as a reflection on their personal characteristics.

In backstage areas, norm and role constraints on self-presentation are relaxed. As a result, people often engage in behaviors that are inconsistent with the impressions they try to maintain in the front area.

CHAPTER

5

The Target's Values

CHAPTER OUTLINE

When I was a kid, one of my favorite television shows was *Leave it to Beaver*. If you have watched the show, you know that Eddie Haskell was Beaver's brother's best friend. I suspect we all knew guys like Eddie in high school—the wisecracking, troublemaking smart alec our parents would have preferred would move away. The thing that fascinated me about Eddie was his ability to quickly change his persona as the targets of his self-presentation changed. When with Beaver and Wally in the boys' room, he was sarcastic and impudent, making fun of Beaver, bragging, and showing off. But, when Beaver's parents walked in, Eddie was charming and considerate. "Hello, Mrs. Cleaver. My, don't you look nice today. I was just telling Wallace and Theodore how lucky they are to have such fine parents."

Part of Eddie's appeal as a character, I think, lies in the fact that each of us recognizes that we are sometimes part Eddie Haskell. Our self-presentational changeovers may be less extreme and less obvious than Eddie's (his ploys were often transparent to Mr. and Mrs. Cleaver) but, like Eddie, we put on different faces for different audiences. And the faces we put on are often determined by what we think the target will value. We often show quite different sides of ourselves to our best friends than to our parents than to our employers than to our ministers, and so on.

PRINCIPLE:

Self-presentations are tailored to the perceived values and preferences of the target.

The realization that people try to make impressions they think others will value leads some people to conclude that we are little more than social chameleons who change color as we move from situation to situation. As we noted earlier, however, the fact that people tailor their public images to others' values does not necessarily imply that their self-presentations are deceptive. Even when people try to create impressions they think others will like, they often do so by selectively conveying accurate images of themselves. In such situations, their behavior may be tactical, but it is not deceptive. Of course, people do sometimes try to present self-images they know are not accurate simply to impress someone else. But, in the course of everyday life, self-presentation is more often accurate than not.

To understand the kinds of impressions people try to make, we examine in this chapter some of the images that people assume targets value. Some characteristics—such as honesty, competence, and loyalty—are so widely valued that we usually assume others will respond more positively if we convey these kinds of images. Other characteristics, on the other hand, are valued only by certain targets. One person may respond favorably to my disclosure that I enjoy Stephen King novels, whereas another may regard this fact as evidence of mental instability.

Physical Attractiveness

I don't know anyone who prefers unattractive people over attractive ones. We may complain about the fact that people place too much emphasis on what others look like—after all, beauty is only skin deep—but, whether we like it or not, people's reactions to others *are* affected by their physical appearance. Researchers have repeatedly found not only that we prefer to interact with attractive than unattractive people, but that we form more positive impressions of them. When researchers compare people's ratings of attractive and unattractive strangers, they find that attractive people are consistently perceived as more sociable, dominant, warm, mentally stable, intelligent, socially skilled, and so forth (Feingold, 1992).

Most people recognize that others value physical attractiveness and consequently do what they can to enhance their appearance. This is not to say that we all try to be stunningly beautiful or strikingly handsome; we don't. But most of us try to do the best we can with what we have to meet the minimum appearance standards of our reference groups. From a self-presentational standpoint, anything that people do to make themselves more attractive to others reflects impression motivation. I'll mention just three ways that people try to make better impressions by enhancing their physical appearance—cosmetic enhancements, weight regulation, and suntanning.

Cosmetic Enhancements

The most common way in which people enhance their appearance is through daily grooming and the use of cosmetic enhancements. Most of us try to stay reasonably clean, keep our hair combed, and wear clothing we think makes us look good in the eyes of our reference group. Of course, among some subgroups, being scroungy is valued, and members of such groups purposefully wear tattered clothing and try to appear unkempt. (I'm reminded of how scruffy many of us looked during the "hippy" era of the late 1960s and early 1970s.) In either case, appearance is used to foster certain kinds of impressions in others' eyes.

Many women regularly use makeup to enhance their appearance. Unfortunately, frequent use of cosmetics can have negative self-presentational consequences. Roughly one third of adolescent girls who regularly use makeup develop facial blemishes caused solely by the cosmetics, a condition known as *acne cosmetica* (Freedman, 1984). This problem can become cyclical as the make-up that is applied to cover blemishes in fact exacerbates the skin problem. Then the girl uses more makeup to cover up her pimples, and the pimples get worse. And so on and so on. The ironic thing about this is that *acne cosmetica* is caused solely by the desire to look better!

Of course, some people are not satisfied with how they look no matter what care they take to groom themselves regularly. Over 1.5 million people undergo cosmetic surgery each year in the United States (Findlay, 1988), representing a substantial increase during the past decade. For example, between 1981 and 1989, face lifts increased from 39,000 to 75,000, rhinoplasty ("nose jobs") from 54,500 to 95,000, and breast augmentation (usually breast enlargement) from 72,000 to 100,000.

Although some cosmetic surgery is conducted to repair serious disfigurements resulting from birth, accident, or disease, the vast majority involve elective surgery intended simply to enhance the individual's appearance. For example, the primary reason women give for seeking breast augmentation is purely self-presentational. They want to look better to others and to reduce their self-consciousness over the size of their breasts (Birtchnell, Whitfield, & Lacey, 1990). Similarly, 80 percent of people who seek orthodontic treatment do so for cosmetic reasons, not because they have difficulty chewing or talking (Giddon, 1983). We typically think of people seeking medical treatment because of illness or injury but, in the case of cosmetic surgery, medical "treatment" is sought for self-presentational rather than medical reasons.

Weight

In contemporary America, physical attractiveness involves not only facial appearance, but having an appropriate body weight and, often, being in good physical shape (Hayes & Ross, 1987). Many people regard being overweight as aesthetically displeasing and tend to draw negative inferences about overweight people—that they are lazy and self-indulgent, for example (Brownell, 1991b; Crandall & Biernat, 1990). Being overweight is a stigma in our society (Crocker, Cornwell, & Major, 1993).

Despite the fact that antifat attitudes create considerable distress for those who are overweight, they also have beneficial effects. Most people try to control their weight not because they want to be healthy per se but because they want others to regard them as attractive (or, at least, not as unattractive) (Hayes & Ross, 1987). (If you have ever been on a diet, ask yourself whether you did so primarily to be healthier or to look better.) I suspect that if our self-presentational concerns about weight and appearance suddenly vanished, most of us would soon become fatter and, thus, unhealthier. Thus, self-presentational motives regarding appearance and weight may benefit many people.

Unfortunately, excessive concerns with how others judge one's weight and appearance can also lead to unhealthy behaviors. Many people watch their weight who really don't need to diet; over twice as many people are on diets at any given time as need to diet for health reasons (Brownell, 1991a). Effects of unnecessary dieting include malnutrition, lack of energy, and increased susceptibility to disease. More seriously, excessive concerns with one's impressions lead certain people, particularly women, to develop eating disorders in an attempt to be thin (Hayes & Ross, 1987; Leary, Tchividjian, & Kraxberger, 1994). Consistent with a self-presentational analysis of eating disorders, women with eating disorders tend to have a high need for approval and an intense fear of rejection, particularly rejection by men (Dunn & Ondercin, 1981; Katzman & Wolchik, 1984; Weinstein & Richman, 1984).

Some have suggested that the increase in anorexia nervosa and bulimia that we've seen in this country in the last 25 years resulted from the idealization of thinness in American culture (Nasser, 1988). Eating disorders of the sort that are common in the United States are virtually nonexistent in cultures that prize "plumpness" (Nasser, 1988). As other cultures adopt American values about weight and dieting, we may expect to see an increase in eating disorders worldwide (Stein, 1991).

The fact that serious eating disorders are far more common among women than men may reflect the fact that eating behaviors and body weight are more important determinants of others' impressions of women than of men. Two studies found that subjects' perceptions of women were affected by how much they ate (women who ate less were viewed as more feminine and less masculine), whereas perceptions of men were not affected by their eating (Chaiken & Pliner, 1987; Pliner & Chaiken, 1990). We also know that the standards for men's weight are more lenient than the standards for women; men have greater freedom to be a few pounds overweight than women. Not surprisingly, at all ages, women are more worried about their weight than men (Pliner et al., 1990).

Sunbathing

The incidence of skin cancer has increased markedly during the past 30 years. In fact, the incidence of malignant melanoma (the form of skin cancer most likely to be fatal) has quadrupled since 1960 (Fears & Scotto, 1982). This recent increase is due to a number of factors, including increased time spent sunbathing, increased vacationing in southern latitudes, larger numbers of people living in the "sun belt," changes in clothing styles, the growth of popularity of tanning salons, and, possibly, the depletion of the ozone layer (Elwood, Whitehead, & Gallagher, 1989). Whatever the reason for this increase, the primary cause of skin cancer is excessive exposure to ultraviolet radiation from the sun or sunlamps.

In some cases, excessive exposure to the sun is incidental. People who work outside, such as farmers and construction workers, often receive too much sun as they go about their normal working days. For many people, though, excessive exposure to the sun is intentional and voluntary. They expose themselves to the sun's rays because they think that being tanned will improve their appearance and lead them to make better impressions on others. In fact, they may be right; tanned individuals are judged more positively than untanned ones (Broadstock, Borland, & Gason, 1992; Miller, Ashton, McHoskey, & Gimbel, 1990).

The role of self-presentation in skin cancer first dawned on me when I was at a professional conference in a seaside community. Because my dermatologist had warned me that I was at risk for skin cancer, I had stayed behind one sunny afternoon when many of the conferees headed to the beach. When they returned, one woman, who was beginning to turn bright red from her afternoon in the sun, asked why I hadn't gone to the beach. When I explained my reason, she said, "Oh, I've had skin cancer," and showed me a large scar where cancerous skin tissue had been removed. In response to my flabbergasted reaction, she replied, "Oh, I know it's dangerous. My dermatologist and husband both tell me to stay out of the sun. But I can't stand not to have a tan in the summer." At that moment, a lightbulb went on in my brain: this woman's self-presentational motives were putting her health at risk. How many other people, I wondered, are doing the same thing? Could it be that self-presentational motives are a risk factor for skin cancer?

The next year, I conducted a study with Jody Jones to answer this question (Leary & Jones, 1993). We administered an extensive questionnaire to a large sample of university students, asking about the degree to which they engaged in behaviors that put them at risk for skin cancer, such as staying in the sun for long periods, not using sunscreen, and not wearing a hat when in the sun for a long time. We also measured a number of cognitive, attitudinal, and motivational variables that we thought might be associated with excessive sun exposure.

Our results showed that the best predictors of behaviors that increase the risk of skin cancer involved concerns with others' impressions generally and with one's appearance specifically. The variable that best predicted tanning behaviors was the belief that being tan improves one's appearance. In addition, respondents who were most concerned with others' impressions of them reported that they engaged in more risk behaviors, as did people who were more concerned about others' appraisals of their bodies.

Once we realized that people's self-presentational motives were putting them at risk for skin cancer, we wondered whether we might be able to reduce their interest in tanning by warning them about the effects of the sun on the impressions they make. As you may know, most attempts to get people to protect their skin from the sun have used threats about the risk of cancer. But, if people are getting too much sun because they want to look better, might it not be better to warn them about the risks to their *appearance* rather than their health?

In a second study (Jones & Leary, 1994), we had university students read one of three essays about tanning. One stressed the health risks involved in tanning (i.e., you'll get skin cancer), one stressed the risks to one's appearance (i.e., your skin will wrinkle, age, and sag prematurely), and one was a control essay that didn't mention any risks at all. Overall, the essay that discussed the effects of the sun on appearance was most effective in promoting safe-sun attitudes. Unfortunately, it was least effective with those students who needed it most—those who were most motivated to maintain an attractive appearance. In addition to demonstrating a novel approach to inducing people to avoid excessive exposure to the sun, this study suggested that people are sometimes more motivated to take care of themselves to make better impressions than to be healthy per se (Hayes & Ross, 1987).

Likability

It goes without saying that people generally prefer warm, likable people to cold, despicable ones. Furthermore, although exceptions exist, the advantages of being liked usually outweigh those of being disliked. People who are liked and accepted reap a cornucopia of social rewards, including friendship, social support, companionship, help, romance, and status. For these reasons, people usually want to be perceived as likable, or at least as not dislikable. In fact, **ingratiation**—the strategy of conveying an impression of being likable—is perhaps the most basic and ubiquitous of all self-presentational strategies (Jones, 1990).

In every culture, certain characteristics are so widely valued that, all other things being equal, people want to be seen as possessing those characteristics. A few years ago, my students and I surveyed students to get a sense of the kinds of impressions they generally did and did not want others to form of them.

The adjectives that they mentioned most often, which are shown in Table 5.1, will not surprise you. They represent characteristics that are valued and devalued by most people in our culture (or at least among the groups with which our students identified). Importantly, most of the impressions they wanted to make involved attributes that would result in *liking*—such as being perceived as friendly, fun, sincere, funny, caring, and easy to talk to. And, the impressions they did not want to make were ones that would lead others to dislike them, such as boring, conceited, obnoxious, superficial, self-centered, and mean.

TABLE 5.1 Impressions American Students Typically Do and Do Not Want to Make

Impressions People Want to Make	Impressions People Do Not Want to Make
Friendly/nice	Boring
Intelligent	Conceited
Attractive	Stupid
Fun	Obnoxious
Outgoing	Superficial
Sincere	Self-centered
Funny/humorous	Unattractive
Caring	Mean
Easy to talk to	

Men and women differed only slightly in the impressions they wanted others to form; both men and women listed friendly, intelligent, attractive, and fun as their top four desired impressions (although, consistent with sex role stereotypes, women listed friendly first, whereas men listed intelligent first). They also agreed in their top three undesired impressions; neither men nor women wanted to be perceived as boring, conceited, or stupid.

Some gender differences emerged, however. Women listed interesting, kind, considerate, and honest among the top 15 impressions they wanted to make, but these impressions did not appear high on men's lists. In contrast, men indicated they wanted to be perceived as athletic, personable, and easy-going; whereas, the women did not mention these impressions to the same degree.

One of the most potent determinants of liking is perceived similarity. We are likely to evaluate people more positively the more similar they are to us. In laboratory experiments, for example, subjects' liking for a stranger is a direct function of how similar they think the stranger is to them (Byrne, 1971; Palmer & Kalin, 1985). In real-life settings, people's choices of friends are affected strongly by perceived similarity (Davison & Jones, 1976; Kandel, 1978). People are also more attracted to dates who share similar attitudes (Byrne, Ervin, & Lamberth, 1970).

Given the potency of the **similarity-attraction effect,** we should not be surprised that people who want to make a "good" impression will manage their impressions so that they will seem similar to the target. If you'll think about beginning a conversation with a stranger (on an airplane, for example), you'll see that the early part of such a conversation consists mostly of seeking common ground. You ask questions about where the person is from, where he or she is going, about hometowns, occupations, families, interests, and so on. In part, this is simply to find a basis for conversation. But, in addition, it provides crucial information that allows each interactant to tailor his or her impressions to the other person. We'll get along much better if we have reasonably favorable impressions of one another, and establishing a basis of similarity is one way to foster favorable impressions.

People who want to be regarded favorably often agree with others more than they otherwise would. Research suggests that conveying that one has similar opinions to a target (**opinion conformity**) is perhaps the most common tactic people use when they want others to like them, and this is true not only in the United States, but in other cultures as well (Pandey, 1986). Again, by appearing similar to the target, the likelihood of making a good impression is increased.

Pressures to appear similar to other people underlie a great deal of conformity. People often conform to others' attitudes, values, preferences, and behavior because they realize that they will make a better impression on others if they share their opinions and act like them. As much as anyone, politicians recognize the importance of appearing similar to their constituents. In elections, voters prefer candidates whose positions are similar to their own (Brent & Granberg, 1982). And, because most Americans are middle class, politicians often want to be seen as middle class, as having middle-class values, and as doing middle-class things (Greenfield, 1992).

This use of self-presentational similarity was used by George Bush during the 1988 presidential campaign. One stumbling block in Bush's way to the White House was the public's perception that he was out of touch with the average American. He was wealthy and well educated, with an estate in Maine and a circle of rich and powerful friends. To counter this image and to show that Bush was just a regular guy, the campaign staff made a concerted effort to convey the image that Bush was similar to middle-class Americans. For example, Bush was photographed playing horseshoes rather than golf or tennis. He mentioned publicly that he liked to unwind with a beer and a bag of pork rinds, and campaign strategists discouraged photographs of the Bush mansion in Maine.

However, after he was elected, Bush dropped his working-class self-presentations. "It turned out that his favorite snack was not pork rinds but popcorn, and beer gave way to vodka martinis (on the rocks with lots of olives) and white wine. Bush once again strapped his watch to a striped-cloth band that had been banished during the campaign as too preppy" (Duffy & Goodgame, 1992, p. 34). What is unclear is whether such attempts to project middle-class impressions are effective or whether they backfire because they leave the public with the impression that the candidate is someone who must impersonate real life.

Although self-presentations of similarity tend to be the rule, exceptions may occur. For example, people may emphasize their dissimilarity when their goal is to alienate or avoid another person (Rosenfeld, 1966). Similarly, they may do so to maintain a sense of autonomy or to show others that they are not easily swayed (Gergen & Taylor, 1969). Furthermore, excessive opinion conformity may backfire if the person is perceived as insincere (Gould & Penley, 1984).

Competence

I doubt if any culture exists in which it's better to be stupid, incompetent, and uninformed rather than intelligent, competent, and knowledgeable. People who are viewed as knowledgeable and competent generally fare better within their social groups. They tend to have higher status, exert more influence over others, and have better jobs.

Self-Promotion

In light of this, we shouldn't be surprised that people often try to be perceived as competent, knowledgeable, or skilled, a self-presentational tactic known as **self-promotion** (Jones & Pittman, 1982). People use a full range of self-presentational behaviors to self-promote, not only verbal claims regarding ability, but nonverbal behaviors (e.g., demonstrating the ease with which one performs a particular task) and the staging of performances (e.g., waiting until others are watching to perform a feat of skill).

Perhaps the most clearcut way to demonstrate one's knowledge, competence, or skill is to perform well on diagnostic tasks. Viewed in this way, one primary reason that people try to do a good job is so others will perceive them as competent (Baumeister, 1989). As Baumeister (1982a, p. 19) put it, "Task performance can become a mere tool in the service of self-presentational goals." Although people are motivated to succeed and achieve for many reasons (e.g., for self-satisfaction, because the task is inherently important, to receive higher pay), one reason is to be regarded as a successful, competent, effective, or productive person. Research has shown that people expend greater effort on tasks when the self-presentational stakes are high (Palmer, Welker, & Giacalone, in press).

Because performance on most tasks results from a combination of ability and effort, people sometimes realize that they can give an impression of having high ability by downplaying how much effort they exerted on a task. For example, people who are afraid of being perceived as incompetent may reduce how hard they try. That way, if they do the task poorly, their poor performance can be attributed to lack of effort rather than to low ability (Pyszczynski & Greenberg, 1983). In addition, even if they perform well, claiming that one didn't work very hard at a task makes the person look even more competent.

In one study, subjects who rode on an exercise cycle rated their effort lower when they performed alongside another person who appeared to find the task easy than when they rode the cycle alone (Hardy, Hall, & Prestholt, 1986). Presumably, when subjects performed with someone who appeared to have little difficulty on the cycle, they also wanted to appear fit and downplayed their reported effort.

People who want to be perceived as competent run two self-presentational risks. First, they sometimes face the **self-promoter's paradox** (Jones & Pittman, 1982). This paradox involves the fact that, because people who are truly outstanding do not need to explicitly present themselves as competent, engaging in self-promotive self-presentations is often taken as evidence that the person is, in fact, not actually competent. We sometimes refer to people who do this as "full of hot air."

A second difficulty self-promoters confront is the **likability-competence tradeoff.** Even when it enhances others' perceptions of one's competence, self-promotion often causes others to like the person less. One study showed that subjects who tried to convince another person that they were highly competent were subsequently liked less well (Godfrey, Lord, & Jones, 1986). There are several reasons for this: people don't like others who brag about themselves, the target may be made to feel inferior by the self-promoting person, and people who are trying to impress others with their intelligence often dominate the conversation (Godfrey et al., 1986).

Concerns with appearing competent can also affect people's reactions to receiving help from other people. People are reluctant to accept assistance from others if doing so implies to others that they are incompetent, helpless, or dependent. We often speak of someone being too "proud" to accept help, but pride often has little to do with it. For example, people are more willing to seek help from another person if the context allows them to save face (Tessler & Schwartz, 1972). Furthermore, people are more likely to accept help that is offered than to request help. Presumably, having to actually ask for help presents a greater self-presentational threat (Broll, Gross, & Piliavin, 1974). People also feel better about taking help if they can reciprocate it sometime in the future (Baumeister, 1982a; Gross & Latané, 1974). Reciprocation allows the person to demonstrate that he or she is not generally helpless.

Playing Dumb

Although people generally want to be perceived as competent, they sometimes infer that a particular target would prefer that they *not* possess certain skills or knowledge. As a result, they may present themselves as less intelligent, competent, or skilled than they actually believe themselves to be. In everyday language, we say that people sometimes *play dumb*.

When people hear the phrase "playing dumb," they often think of a woman downplaying her knowledge to impress a man. Do women really pretend to be inferior to men? Studies published in 1950 and in 1975 suggest that the answer is "yes." Approximately half of the women in both studies said they had pretended to be inferior to men (Dean, Braito, Powers, & Britton, 1975; Komarovsky, 1950). Contrary to stereotypes, however, Dean et al. (1975) found that men were just as likely to play dumb as women. The domains in which men and women played dumb were somewhat different: men pretended inferiority in art more than women, whereas women feigned intellectual inferiority more than men, but the overall percentages were quite similar. In fact, men are more likely to play dumb in certain contexts. For example, men may play dumb in front of their bosses more than women (Dean et al., 1975; Gove et al., 1980).

People play dumb for a variety of reasons. One is that the person knows the target prefers that he or she not know something, as when the adolescent talking to his or her parents feigns less knowledge about drugs or sex than he or she really has. A second reason that people pretend to be less knowledgeable or competent than they really are is to avoid onerous chores. If people can self-presentationally minimize their competence, others won't ask them to do things or to help others do them. Third, people may feign less skill than they have when they are competing against someone and want their opponent to underestimate their true ability. By downplaying one's competence, the person hopes to catch the opponent off guard and, perhaps, lead him or her to exert less effort.

A fourth reason people play dumb is to make the other person feel superior. This could arise either because the person wants the target to feel good (as when parents let their children occasionally win at games), because the person thinks he or she will make a better impression by not knowing something (nobody likes a know-it-all), because the target might feel threatened if the person knew more than he or she did, or because the person wants the target to feel responsible for helping him or her (people who know how to do something are often obligated to help those who don't).

Pandey (1986) suggested that self-degradation may be particularly common in traditional societies, such as India, where lines of status and authority are more clearly delineated than they are in the United States. Unlike self-enhancement, self-depreciation will not threaten persons in positions of authority but will induce a sense of social responsibility.

Effort and Exertion

Our culture places nearly as much emphasis on effort as it does on ability. We are quite willing to excuse another person's poor performance as long as we think the person tried as hard as he or she could. Because we value effort, people often want others to perceive that they are working hard. I'm sure you know students who talk about how much they study or people who often mention how hard they work. In athletic contexts, people who appear to exert a great deal of effort may be viewed more positively than those who don't (Rejeski & Lowe, 1980); we often hear coaches and sports announcers say with admiration that a certain player gave 110 percent during the game.

Not only do people talk about exerting effort for self-presentational reasons, they really try harder when trying hard will make a desired impression. For example, people work harder and exert more effort when other people are watching than when they are alone. Joggers, for example, run faster when they're being observed than when they think they are exercising alone (Worringham & Messick, 1983), and weight lifters lift more weight when others are watching (Meumann, 1904, cited in Forsyth, 1987).

Behavioral researchers have wrestled for many years with trying to understand why people sometimes perform better when others are present (the **social facilitation effect**). Although several explanations of social facilitation have been offered, the self-presentational perspective suggests that people perform better in the presence of others because they are motivated to make a good impression (Bond, 1982; Sanders, 1984).

Ironically, although people typically work harder when others are watching, they tend to work less hard when they are part of a group than when they work alone (Geen, 1991). When people work as part of a group, their personal input to the group's outcome is often not clear. When others can't tell how hard a given group or team member is working, each person has less incentive to work at full capacity, and **social loafing** occurs. The most effective way to reduce social loafing is to make each individual's contribution to the group's performance individually identifiable (Williams, Harkins, & Latané, 1981; Williams,

Nida, Baca, & Latané, 1989). By making each person's contribution public, impression motivation is increased, and social loafing declines (Karau & Williams, 1993).

Some football coaches use this principle to increase the performance of their players. Although the performance of certain members of a football team, particularly the quarterback, are quite visible, other players, such as linemen, may get the sense that neither the fans nor the media pay close attention to their individual performances in a game. Because this sense of unidentifiability may lead to social loafing, some coaches have movies taken of every player on every play of a game, and these movies are viewed by the entire coaching staff and team the next week. Anecdotes suggest that making linemen's play more public increases their motivation and performance on the field (Williams et al., 1981).

Virtue

Exemplification involves self-presentations that convey an impression of virtue (Jones & Pittman, 1982). Often, exemplification involves fostering public images associated with moral virtues, such as honesty, integrity, and generosity. At other times, people exemplify by demonstrating other virtues such as conscientiousness, dedication, and self-sacrifice.

People are most likely to present such images when their targets value the virtue in question. The most obvious example involves members of the clergy. The effectiveness of a minister, priest, or rabbi depends heavily on his or her ability to maintain a consistent image of piety, morality, and selflessness. Another example involves the hard-working employee who wants everyone at work, particularly the boss, to know how dedicated he or she is to the company. Some people exemplify by parading virtues such as a healthful lifestyle, showing others how abstemious and health conscious they are. Parents often engage in exemplifying self-presentations, presenting images of themselves to their children that are far more "good" than the parents really are.

When I talk about people engaging in exemplification, I am not implying that their self-presentations are false. Many religious leaders really are devoted, selfless, and pious; many employees are dedicated; some people are exceptionally health conscious, and many parents lead exemplary lives. However, this does not counteract the fact that people often want to be sure that others *perceive* them in these ways. One's piety, dedication, honesty, or ethics may not be immediately obvious to other people unless the person engages in strategic self-presentation.

People must sometimes consciously and deliberately impression-manage so that other people will perceive their characteristics, motives, and feelings accurately.

The exemplifier faces three difficulties. First, more than most other self-presentational strategies, exemplifying self-presentations must be supported by consistently exemplary behavior. Whereas ingratiators do not necessarily jeopardize their images of likability by a single unfriendly outburst, and self-promoters do not appear globally incompetent if they fail once, a single incident can permanently damage one's image of being of high integrity.

Second, exemplifiers who act contrary to their self-presentations not only show that they lack the virtue in question, but are disliked for being hypocritical. Interestingly, however, the exemplifier who behaves in a nonexemplary manner may be regarded no less favorably than the person who admits that he or she is sometimes not virtuous. The fallen exemplifier tends to be regarded as pitiful, hypocritical, and lacking self-insight; the professed cheater is disliked for being selfish and exploitative (Gilbert & Jones, 1986).

Third, to be effective, exemplification cannot cross over into self-righteousness (Jones & Pittman, 1982). There's often a fine line between being virtuous and being obnoxious about it. We've all been turned off by people who make too big of a deal about how hard they work, how pious they are, how nutritiously they eat, or how far they jog.

Specific Target Values

So far, we have discussed images that are valued widely in our culture—images involving attractiveness, similarity, likability, competence, effort, and virtue. Of course, particular targets may value specific things. As a result, people convey different impressions of themselves to different targets and even to different classes of targets. Several studies have demonstrated that people's self-presentations are quite sensitive to the values and preferences of the people with whom they are interacting.

In one study (Gergen & Taylor, 1969), ROTC cadets were told that they would be placed in a situation that emphasized either their competence at a decision-making task or their ability to get along with other people. The subjects were then given the opportunity to describe themselves to the person with whom they would be interacting. When subjects thought their competence was under scrutiny, they presented themselves in a self-enhancing manner. But when subjects thought that interpersonal ability was most important, they presented themselves more modestly.

Another study (Zanna & Pack, 1975) asked female subjects to describe themselves to a man whom they believed preferred either traditional or nontraditional women. When the man was described in a socially desirable fashion, the women tended to present images of themselves that were consistent with the kind of woman they thought he liked. However, when the man was described in an undesirable fashion, the women's self-presentations were unaffected by his preferences; they simply were not motivated to present themselves in a way that he would like.

People sometimes present themselves differently to men and women, presumably because they assume that men and women value different things. For example, both sexes are more willing to discuss behaviors that are consistent with their sex role with same-sex than other-sex friends (Snell, 1989). Women are more motivated to be perceived as competent by other women than by men (Leary et al., 1994).

When the Target's Values are Bad

Fortunately, because targets generally reward those who make socially desirable impressions, people usually behave in ways that lead others to conclude that they are friendly, intelligent, attractive, and fun (see Table 5.1). Sometimes, though, people believe that targets will respond most favorably to antisocial, socially undesirable, or dangerous images. In such cases, people may do things that are dangerous to themselves or others simply to make an impression on a target.

A case in point involves images of bravery and recklessness. In some circles, being brave and adventuresome, if not downright reckless, is greatly admired. As a result, people do things to demonstrate that they possess such attributes. For example, many people (adolescents and young adults in particular) drive at excessive and unsafe speeds to convey such images. In the extreme case, tests of daring such as "chicken" (in which two drivers speed toward one another to see who swerves first) and "Russian roulette" (in which players take turns pointing a loaded gun at their heads and pulling the trigger) are essentially self-presentational games. People participate in such potentially deadly "games" to convey that they are daring.

More commonly, people sometimes try risky activities that they do not have the ability or experience to perform safely because they do not want to be perceived as cowardly or as not being a

(Continued)

"good sport." Have you ever done something that you knew was rather dangerous because not doing it would convey that you were "chicken?"

Lest I be accused of picking on young people, I should note that adults often don't take adequate precautions with everyday activities because they don't want to be perceived as too cautious. Many people resist wearing seat belts in automobiles, helmets on bicycles and motorcycles, and life preservers in boats because they think such devices convey an impression of excessive cautiousness. Similarly, many people seem reluctant to wear protective gear (such as safety goggles, gloves, and helmets) when operating dangerous machinery because of the impression it might convey. This concern develops at a young age; my 8-year-old son resists wearing knee and elbow pads when he rollerblades because of what the other kids will think.

Experience suggests that men are much more likely than women to suffer self-presentationally caused injuries. Not only are men more likely to do dangerous things in the first place, but I suspect that they are also less likely to take adequate precautions while doing so. I assume that this is because men are more highly motivated to be perceived as brave, adventuresome, and reckless than women.

The Self-Presenter's Dilemma

People who are playing to a target's values often face the **self-presenter's dilemma:** the more important it is for an individual to impress a target, the more likely the target is to be skeptical of the truthfulness of the individual's self-presentations. If you know that someone has a great deal to gain by making a certain impression on you, you are more likely to wonder whether their self-presentations are authentic. (This has sometimes been called the "ingratiator's dilemma," but it occurs in cases other than ingratiation.)

People seem to realize this, and adjust their self-presentations accordingly. One tactic people use to increase the credibility of their self-presentations is to balance self-presentations that play to the target's values with other presentations that don't. For example, people may conform with another's opinion on important issues, but disagree on trivial issues (Jones, 1964). In this way, their agreement may seem authentic rather than ingratiatory. Similarly, people may present themselves in a self-enhancing fashion on attributes that the target values highly, but in a self-effacing fashion on attributes that are less important to the target. Such a tactic should make the positive self-presentations more believable than if the person self-enhanced on all dimensions.

Another way of skirting the self-presenter's dilemma is to utilize secondhand self-presentations. People are sometimes more likely to believe information they hear secondhand. Thus, you are more likely to believe positive information about me if you hear it from somebody else rather than directly from me. Similarly, when a target is likely to suspect the truthfulness of one's compliments, the person can compliment the target to a third party who is likely to convey it to the target (Jones & Wortman, 1973).

Yet another tactic is to structure the encounter so that the target *asks* about the attribute in question. If a person presents information about him- or herself in response to a question, the target is less likely to perceive that he or she is bragging or being manipulative (Jones & Wortman, 1973).

Impression Importance

Some impressions are more *important* than others. For example, people presumably think it's more important to be perceived as honest than tidy. Although tidiness is nice, most of us would prefer an honest, messy person to a dishonest, tidy one.

Although no research has examined the relative importance of self-presentations, a study by Williams, Saiz, and Munick (1991) is relevant to this issue. These researchers asked respondents to rate each of 300 traits according to how important each was "in describing what a person is really like." The ten most important traits were (in order): honest, dependable, friendly, loyal, reliable, responsible, self-confident, understanding, trusting, and selfish. Presumably, because people regard these characteristics as highly informative in telling them what someone is really like, people should be highly motivated to control others' impressions on these dimensions.

The ten least important of the 300 traits were (in order): retiring, superstitious, commonplace, slow, formal, slipshod, hurried, quick, mild, and awkward. In most cases, people may be less concerned about how they are perceived on these dimensions.

The Multiple Audience Problem

Multiple audience problems arise when people find themselves in the awkward position of wanting to present different impressions to two or more people in the same social encounter. Although multiple audience problems can arise for a number of reasons (see Fleming & Rudman, 1993), they commonly occur when a person interacts with two or more targets who value different impressions.

Adolescents sometimes confront this problem when they interact simultaneously with their parents and their friends. The impressions they want to make on their parents differ from how they want to be viewed by their friends. (Even Madonna played down the masturbation scene in her "Truth or Dare" concert when her father was in the audience.) In fact, different friends may value such different impressions of us that we sometimes find it awkward to interact with two friends at the same time. In the movie, *Grease,* John Travolta found himself with a multiple audience problem when interacting with both Olivia Newton-John (to whom he wanted to appear tender and loving) and his buddies (who expected him to be a roughneck hoodlum).

A variation of this multiple audience problem occurs when two targets value the same impression, but the person cannot easily convey the same impression to both simultaneously. For example, imagine finding yourself in an interaction that includes two people whom you've been dating recently. They each value your displays of friendliness and familiarity, yet you would find it awkward to be friendly, familiar, and chatty with both.

Because multiple audience problems are so distressing, people work hard to avoid them. We usually try to keep people apart to whom we want to present different impressions of ourselves, a tactic known as **audience segregation.** By keeping different targets away from one another, people can avoid the awkwardness of trying to present disparate images of themselves to two or more targets simultaneously.

Of course, people cannot always keep targets segregated, but little research has examined how people resolve multiple audience problems when they occur. One tactic is to convey messages that will be understood by some targets, but not by others. If communicators can reference knowledge that is shared with one target but not another, they can send messages that are interpretable by one but not the other. Friends, for example, can include clues in their messages that will not be understood by strangers (Fleming, Darley, Hilton, & Kojetin, 1990).

People also use **distancing behaviors** when they face a multiple audience problem. Distancing behaviors are used to communicate lack of commitment to a behavior one is performing, as when people roll their eyes, grimace, or stick out their tongues to convey disgust for what they are saying or doing (Fleming & Rudman, 1993).

The Boss' Illusion

Although people regularly tailor their self-presentations to the targets' values, targets often have difficulty determining whether others' self-presentations accurately reflect their personal characteristics or are fabricated to please the target. In one study (Baumeister et al., 1989), subjects were told to present themselves favorably to another person, to present themselves unfavorably, or were given no instructions about the impression they should try to make. Results showed, first, that subjects' self-presentations clearly influenced how the other person subsequently described him- or herself. When subjects presented themselves positively, the other person's self-descriptions were more favorable than when subjects presented themselves unfavorably. This self-presentation matching effect has been shown in other studies as well (Gergen & Wishnov, 1965).

Importantly, subjects did not realize that the other person's self-descriptions had been influenced by their own positive or negative presentations. Rather than recognizing that the other person's self-descriptions were influenced by their own self-presentations, subjects took the other person's descriptions at face value. For example, when subjects presented themselves unfavorably, the other person likewise described him- or herself less positively. But rather than seeing this as a reaction to their own self-presentation, subjects then interpreted the other person's modesty as a sign of low self-esteem!

In businesses and other work organizations, this effect is known as the **boss' illusion** (Baumeister, 1989). Not surprisingly, employees sometimes present images of themselves that they think the boss will value. If the boss him- or herself is a devoted family person, employees may present themselves similarly. If the boss comes across as casual and informal, employees may adopt a casual, informal image. But bosses have no way to tell whether the impressions they have of their employees are accurate (maybe the employee really is a casual, devoted family person) or are designed to please the boss. Indeed, unless the employee is obviously sycophantic, the boss is unlikely to even question his or her impressions. The result is that bosses often have the illusion that their employees are more similar to themselves than they really are.

The Experimenter as Target: Self-Presentational Biases in Research

Researchers who study human behavior must deal with possible biases in their research that researchers in the natural sciences do not. Unlike atomic particles, mollusks, sunspots, and viruses, the actions of human subjects may be influenced by their concerns with the experimenter's impressions and evaluations of them. Because of their self-presentational motives, subjects do not always behave "naturally" in psychological studies, leading researchers to draw incorrect conclusions (Christensen, 1981; Page, 1981; Stone, 1989).

Most commonly, research subjects want to be perceived positively. I suspect that most subjects would prefer that the researcher perceive them as likeable, intelligent, competent, and psychologically adjusted rather than dislikable, ignorant, foolish, petty, and maladjusted. Thus, they may not respond accurately to the researcher's questions if accurate answers might make the researcher form unfavorable impressions of them.

Other subjects try to make a good impression by looking cooperative and helpful. Subjects may try to figure out the study's research questions or hypotheses, then respond in ways that are consistent with them (Orne, 1962). If subjects can actually discern how they "should" behave, the data will confirm the hypotheses whether or not they are actually true. Interestingly, subjects may only do this when doing so makes a good impression (Sigall, Aronson, & Van Hoose, 1970).

Researchers typically do several things to reduce the effects of subjects' self-presentational motives on the outcome of a study. When possible, they assure subjects that their responses are fully anonymous, thereby removing any motivation for subjects to be less than fully honest. They often try to conceal the purpose of the study so that subjects won't try to confirm the experimental hypotheses. Researchers also try to remove themselves from the experimental setting as much as possible (by using written or tape-recorded instructions, for example) so that subjects won't be as concerned about what the researcher thinks of them. Despite all of these precautions, researchers often worry that their results are contaminated by subjects' self-presentations.

Summary

People tailor their self-presentations to the values of the particular individuals with whom they are interacting at a given time. Not only do they try to convey different impressions to different people, but they also may wish to make different impressions on the same target at various times. Certain impressions are so widely valued that people try to convey those impressions on a regular basis. For example, people usually want to be perceived as attractive rather than unattractive, likable rather than unlikable, and competent rather than incompetent. In addition, people assume that targets like those who try hard and who possess certain virtues.

People who are playing to a target's values sometimes confront the self-presenter's dilemma. The more important it is for the person to impress the target, the more likely the target is to question the truthfulness of the person's self-presentations. People must also sometimes face the multiple audience problem in which they must present different images to two or more targets simultaneously.

When subjects who are participating in behavioral research try to convey impressions that they think the researcher will value, the validity of the data is compromised. As a result, behavioral researchers try to minimize the influence of subjects' self-presentational motives on the outcomes of their studies.

CHAPTER

6

Current Social Image

CHAPTER OUTLINE

I've sometimes wondered how Richard Nixon felt when he ventured out in public in the years following Watergate. How was he affected by the knowledge that his image in most Americans' eyes remained irreparably tainted by the events that led to his resignation of the U.S. Presidency in 1974? How did knowing that people still viewed him unfavorably affect how he felt, what he did, what he said, and the ways in which he managed his impressions?

As people construct their public identities, they take into account what people know or are likely to find out about them. For example, their current social images constrain the range of impressions they even try to make. Given the country's preexisting impressions, Nixon found it difficult to convince most people that he was an honest, law-abiding citizen no matter what he did. In addition, people's current images in others' eyes sometimes compel them to manage their impressions in particular ways. Knowing that, despite his protestations, he was widely regarded as a "crook," Nixon seemed to go out of his way to display attributes unrelated to the Watergate scandal, such as his extensive knowledge of foreign affairs; he conveyed the image of an elder statesman with an extensive knowledge of international relations. In this chapter, we examine how people's self-presentations are affected by how they think they are already regarded by other people.

Constraints

Some of my students returned from spring break in Florida one year with stories of having adopted new identities while they were on vacation. As they met new people—on the beach, in bars, at parties—they fabricated new persona, presenting whatever images of themselves struck them at the time. Not only did they fabricate new hometowns, families, colleges, and life histories, but they even tried on different personalities. One normally extraverted woman pretended to be painfully shy, while another characteristically reserved woman tried being outrageous and flirtatious. She even wore wild clothes that were quite different from the clothing she wears on campus. Apparently, this was great fun, and none of their new acquaintances ever realized that my students were not who and what they appeared to be.

Such self-presentational freedom is rare in social life. Typically, the impressions we try to make are constrained by the information that others have or are likely to get about us. We usually find it very difficult to present ourselves in ways that are inconsistent with the information that other people have. If others know that I grew up in a middle-class family in Baltimore, what could possibly be gained from claiming I lived in a wealthy neighborhood in Hollywood? If a job interviewer has our academic transcripts showing we were poor students, how can we claim otherwise? Our behavioral history constrains us to act as we've acted in the past. Once people have or are likely to obtain information about us, we recognize that the probability of making an alternative impression is low. When others do not have such information, however, we are freer to make whatever claims we wish about ourselves.

This effect was demonstrated in an experiment conducted by Barry Schlenker. Schlenker (1975) gave subjects bogus feedback indicating that they had scored either low or high on a test of social sensitivity. Subjects then thought that they would work as a group on a task that required the same skills that were measured by the test they had taken. Some subjects were told that the other group members would learn how well they performed on this task, whereas others thought no one (not even the experimenter) would know how well they had performed.

When asked to describe themselves to the other group members, subjects presented themselves consistently with how they had performed on the earlier test only when they thought that the other group members would learn of their performance on the upcoming task. When others would know about their scores on the upcoming task, subjects who performed well on the earlier test described themselves as more socially sensitive than those who thought they had performed poorly. However, subjects who thought their later performance would not be known by the group presented themselves favorably *regardless of how well they had performed on the test* (see also Baumeister & Jones, 1978; Greenberg & Pyszczynski, 1985). As Schlenker (1975) observed, "secret information known only to the individual can be ignored when selecting a public image" (p. 1036).

PRINCIPLE:

People tend to present themselves in a self-enhancing way unless they think others have or are likely to obtain independent information that would contradict or discredit overly positive self-presentations.

Of course, people sometimes misjudge what a particular target knows about them. The result is usually a full-fledged self-presentational catastrophe. Not only does the truth about them come to light, but they come across as deceitful and manipulative. In one instance reported in the media, a woman reacted indignantly when a magazine offered to pay her to pose nude. "I would never under any condition pose naked for anyone," she claimed. "It's not in my character." Unfortunately, a news reporter had, in fact, obtained nude pictures of her. A person whose self-presentational claims are blatantly discredited in this way can rarely salvage the situation. This woman's response was typical: "Where did you ever——uhhhh!" (Overheard, 1991).

Although people generally convey impressions that are consistent with their current images in others' eyes, even public information can be ignored if the people believe that the target regards the source of the information as untrustworthy. Sometimes other people have information about us that they realize is of questionable accuracy because it is based on hearsay, comes from biased sources (such as our enemies), is ambiguous, or is otherwise invalid. When people think that a target questions the accuracy of an information source, they may present themselves however they desire without fear that their self-presentations will be repudiated (Schlenker, Miller, & Leary, 1983).

The degree to which a person's self-presentations are constrained by others' knowledge obviously depends on how well others know him or her. In a highly mobile society in which people's lives are private and quite segmented, people have considerable self-presentational freedom. However, in close-knit societies in which virtually everyone lives his or her entire life in the same small village, self-presentational constraints are much greater. When everyone knows everyone else in a variety of contexts, certain kinds of self-presentation are restricted.

Baumeister, don Juan, and the Effects of Personal History

When I was in college in the early 1970s, most of the students I knew read one or more books by Carlos Castaneda. Castaneda received his Ph.D. in anthropology from UCLA in 1973 for interviewing an old Mexican sorcerer he called don Juan. Castaneda claimed that he had been don Juan's apprentice for over 10 years and reported the lessons he had learned in a series of popular books. Although considerable evidence exists that don Juan was a hoax (de Mille, 1980), Castaneda's books sold millions of copies. I've been amazed at how many people of my age group say that they were affected by Castaneda's writings.

Roy Baumeister was among those of us who were captured by don Juan's teachings. In particular, Baumeister was intrigued by don Juan's admonition that Castaneda should "erase" his personal history. According to don Juan, what others know about us encumbers or constrains what we can do. In *Journey to Ixtlan,* don Juan tells Carlos, "If you have no personal history, no explanations are needed; nobody is angry or disillusioned with your acts. And above all no one pins you down with their thoughts" (Castaneda, 1972, p. 12). This aspect of don Juan's teachings struck Baumeister as a neglected fact of social life: people are victims of their own behavioral history and of others' preexisting expectations for them (personal communication, June 14, 1992).

Much of Baumeister's research has focused on how preexisting public impressions affect people's behavior. As a graduate student working with Edward Jones, he showed how others' knowledge constrains people's self-presentations while at the same time impelling them to compensate for that information (Baumeister & Jones, 1978). Later, he showed that people with low versus high

(Continued)

self-esteem deal with this "dilemma of reputation" in different ways. People with high self-esteem seem to be less constrained by others' impressions of them than people with low self-esteem, who seem less willing to take the risk of trying to contradict others' expectations (Baumeister, 1982b).

He also found that, because people feel trapped by others' expectations, they sometimes try to diminish their reputation in others' eyes when they think others' expectations for them are too high (Baumeister, Cooper, & Skib, 1979). Recently, he has shown that knowing that others will learn information about them counteracts people's general tendency to ignore negative information about themselves (Baumeister & Cairns, 1992).

Roy Baumeister has made many important contributions to our understanding of self-presentation and self-processes more generally (Baumeister, 1986, 1991). For some reason, I find it gratifying that his initial interest sprung, in part, from the mythical teachings of don Juan.

Self-Presentational Successes

Typically, people who are sure that others already regard them positively refrain from trying to convey additional positive impressions of themselves. Rather, they opt instead to convey an impression of modesty. Subjects present themselves in a self-enhancing fashion when they think others are unaware of their successes but modestly if they think others know or will learn how well they have performed (Ackerman & Schlenker, 1975; Baumeister & Jones, 1978).

Modest self-presentations make a great deal of sense if others already hold a favorable impression of the individual. Not only do people respond favorably to slight modesty (Schlenker & Leary, 1982a), but little is to be gained by trying to make an increasingly positive impression on those who are already impressed. Others are likely to form unfavorable impressions of people who trumpet their successes. If others do not already hold a favorable impression of the person, however, they may take the person's modest self-presentational claims at face value, concluding that he or she is, in fact, not very good (Schlenker & Leary, 1982a). Alternatively, they may come to believe that the person is simply insecure (Schlenker, 1980).

However, modest self-presentations may backfire if others interpret one's modesty as nonchalance. Appearing to be indifferent about one's good qualities may convey to others that they are not worth the person's self-presentational effort. Shrugging off compliments, for example ("So? It's no big deal."), may make one appear indifferent to others' opinions. In addition, apparent indifference about one's successes may convey that one is so successful and confident that he or she has come to ignore success; the person comes across as smug rather than modest. I've personally felt that way toward researchers I know who seem to experience no pleasure when they have a manuscript accepted for publication in a scholarly journal. Any researcher who shrugs off having his or her work published is very used to success, has lost the capacity for joy, or is managing his or her impressions. Paradoxically, then, people may interpret extreme modesty as a sign of arrogance (Pin & Turndorf, 1990).

Self-Presentational Failures

Despite people's best efforts, things sometimes happen that threaten their images in others' eyes: a public failure undermines one's image of competence or success; other people learn previously secret information regarding one's weaknesses or transgressions; the person behaves in a manner that is out of character (because of rage, passion, or drunkenness, for example); other people intentionally humiliate the individual; or the individual fails to control his or her body in ways that make a bad impression (by clumsily tripping, being publicly flatulent, or failing to zip one's fly, for example). Social images and their accompanying reputations are fragile things that can be damaged in large and small ways by a variety of everyday occurrences.

Events that clearly (and, sometimes, irrevocably) damage a person's image in others' eyes are called self-presentational predicaments. **Self-presentational predicaments** are situations in which events have undesirable implications for the images people have claimed or desire to claim (Schlenker, 1980). In this section, we examine the causes of self-presentational predicaments, explore people's emotional reactions to such events, and discuss the self-presentational tactics people use to repair the damage that predicaments cause.

Categories of Self-Presentational Predicaments

There is no shortage of ways in which we can make bad impressions on others and convey impressions of ourselves we did not want to convey. It takes only a second for an interaction to derail as we look incompetent, foolish, clumsy, impolite, immoral, egocentric, inconsiderate, forgetful, or some other undesired way. Several theorists have developed taxonomies of predicaments (see Edelmann, 1987; Sattler, 1966; Weinberg, 1968), but the richest description comes from the work of Rowland Miller. (Miller was a student of Barry Schlenker, and, thus, is another branch on the self-presentational family tree.) Miller (1992) asked university students to describe their last embarrassment. Analyses of these descriptions yielded four major categories of embarrassing circumstances.

Individual Behavior

The first category involved incidents that were precipitated solely by an individual's own actions. Miller identified three distinct types of predicaments caused by a person's own behavior. **Normative public deficiencies** involve violations of norms or expectations. These predicaments include physical pratfalls and inept performances (such as falling down the stairs or dropping one's tray of food in the cafeteria), cognitive shortcomings (such as calling one's boyfriend or girlfriend by the wrong name or forgetting to return a borrowed item), loss of control over one's possessions or body (such as stalling one's car in traffic, ripping one's pants, or being noticeably flatulent), and failures of privacy regulation (such as being seen in one's underwear by strangers or walking in on someone in the bathroom).

A second category of predicaments induced by the individual's behavior involved **abashed harm-doing.** These are situations in which the person is embarrassed by harming others, such as breaking someone else's possession or spilling a drink on someone.

Behaviors that lead to mere conspicuousness constituted a third type of individual embarrassment. People sometimes feel embarrassed when they are the center of attention, particularly if they don't know how to respond in the situation.

Interactive Behavior

The second major category of embarrassing circumstances involves situations in which people are embarrassed because of their association or interactions with other people. For example, awkward interactions are embarrassing. When people do not know how to respond, they may become embarrassed. People may feel embarrassed meeting an ex-boyfriend or ex-girlfriend on the street simply because they don't know what to say. A second class of interactive embarrassment involves **team embarrassment** in which the person was with other people who did something embarrassing. In this case, the individual him- or herself did not provoke the predicament but was associated with other people who were making a bad impression. We've all felt embarrassed by things that other people did when we were with them.

Audience Provocation

Audience provocation constituted the third category of embarrassing circumstances. I suspect that we've all been purposefully embarrassed by other people. When asked to describe their most recent embarrassment, nearly one fifth of the subjects in Miller's (1992) study described an audience-provoked predicament. We are embarrassed when people divulge our secrets and transgressions to others, when they make us the butt of their jokes, or when others tease or insult us. Being teased is a particularly common source of embarrassment during early adolescence but decreases during high school (Kauffman & Anderson, 1992).

Bystander Behavior

Finally, some cases of embarrassment arise from simply witnessing another person's embarrassing actions. I suspect we've all experienced **empathic embarrassment** (also called **vicarious embarrassment**) when another person tried to tell jokes that fell flat or when another student became embarrassed in front of the class.

Stigma

A special type of predicament is created by the existence of a physical or psychological stigma. Most people possess certain characteristics that, if publicly known, might lead others to regard them as deviant, flawed, limited, or otherwise undesirable. These so-called **marks** may involve past behaviors (the person is an ex-convict or spouse abuser, for example), physical characteristics (the person is deformed or disabled), personal character (the person is known to have an uncontrollable temper), psychological difficulties (the person was treated for schizophrenia), group membership (the person belongs to a disreputable group), occupation (the person is a prostitute or pornography dealer), or even ancestry (the person's father was a mass murderer). Most of us possess at least minor marks—mostly minor problems and indiscretions that would likely change some people's opinions about us for the worse if they were public knowledge.

When others become aware of a person's discrediting mark, they often react negatively, and the relationship or interaction between the people becomes derailed. When a mark leads other people to draw negative inferences about the marked person's abilities, personality, characteristics, or desirability, the mark becomes a **stigma,** and the person is said to be **stigmatized** (Goffman, 1963; Jones et al., 1984). People not only evaluate stigmatized persons unfavorably, but they also behave differently toward them. Because of this, stigmatized individuals engage in a number of self-presentational tactics to minimize the impact of their stigma on others' reactions toward them.

Concealment

Understandably, people usually prefer to hide their discrediting marks from other people. Some marks are easily concealed, whereas others are not. One may find it relatively easy to keep others from learning that he or she is HIV positive, spent time in prison, or is an alcoholic, for example. In contrast, people would find it more difficult to conceal the fact that they have disfiguring acne, committed a highly publicized crime, or stuttered badly.

People who try to conceal their marks often experience stress from the fear of detection. Furthermore, when others find out about the mark, they sometimes resent not having been told earlier, particularly if they are close friends (Jones et al., 1984). Thus, the marked person must decide the best time to disclose that he or she possesses the mark.

Some writers have suggested that an important step in deciding to tell others about one's marked condition is self-acceptance. People find it much more difficult to disclose marks to other people when they don't fully accept themselves. For example, one critical factor in gays' decisions to "come out of the closet" is accepting one's own homosexuality. Although self-acceptance is undoubtedly involved in decisions to include one's mark in one's self-presentations, self-acceptance alone is not enough. No matter how accepting marked people are of their own condition, they are reluctant to disclose it to others if such disclosure is likely to result in ridicule, criticism, or rejection. In a study of factors that predict gay men's and lesbians' willingness to disclose their sexual orientation to others, the best predictor of respondents' openness about their sexual orientation was not their own self-acceptance but how they thought other people felt about homosexuals (Franke & Leary, 1991).

Admission and Destigmatization

Often, stigmatized people purposefully convey their stigma to others. Rather than exerting the effort to hide it, they find it easier to simply acknowledge the mark, then take steps to either insure that it doesn't loom too large in the minds of other people or to try to destigmatize their condition altogether (Goffman, 1963).

The simplest type of destigmatization is simply to deny that the mark should be regarded negatively. By publicly downplaying the stigma, a person can convey the impression of having grace in the face of adversity. Occasionally, marked people use self-deprecating humor about their difficulties to show they have come to terms with their disabilities (Jones et al., 1984). If the person successfully conveys that he or she does not regard the mark as a stigma, he or she may even gain credit for maintaining composure, optimism, and humor in spite of the mark.

Another type of destigmatization involves admitting the negative mark but arguing that it is beyond the person's control and, thus, people should not form negative impressions of the person because of it. People seem to feel more justified acting negatively toward those whose stigma is perceived as controllable than those whose stigma is not controllable (Farina, Holland, & Ring, 1966; Rodin, Price, Sanchez, & McElligot, 1989).

A third type of destigmatization involves turning a stigma from a liability to a benefit. People can reframe their stigmas to glorify them. Physical limitations may be romanticized, for example, as long as they are not grotesquely disfiguring (Jones et al., 1984). Injuries and scars obtained in battle, for example, may be worn like badges of honor. At minimum, people can argue that their experience with the stigma has made them stronger, increased their empathy for other stigmatized people, or taught them other lessons.

Occasionally, members of a stigmatized group work together toward destigmatizing themselves. For example, the civil rights and black power movements were designed not simply to attain equal rights for blacks but to destigmatize dark skin, as exemplified in the phrase "black is beautiful" (Jones et al., 1984). Other examples include the Anti-Defamation League, the National Association for Retarded Citizens, and many gay rights organizations. Interestingly, many unmarked people may join to destigmatize a particular condition, as when whites join the civil rights movement or when heterosexuals argue for greater societal tolerance of homosexuality.

Compensation

People who have a known stigma sometimes try to compensate for it by conveying more positive impressions of themselves on other dimensions. In one study, normal subjects who thought another person believed they were mental patients performed significantly better on skillful tasks, presumably to dispel the impression they were mentally incompetent (Farina, Allen, & Saul, 1968). This is similar to the compensatory self-presentation effect that occurs after people have publicly failed (Baumeister & Jones, 1978).

Exploitation

Some stigma can be exploited for the marked person's benefit. Stigma that involve physical or mental limitations are particularly susceptible to exploitation. The marked person can advertise his or her condition, thereby eliciting sympathy, support, and other special treatment.

Stigmatized persons can also exploit their stigmas by using them to excuse other problems. By playing up their handicaps, people can blame their difficulties on their shortcomings or on others' prejudicial treatment of them.

Resignation

Finally, stigmatized people may realize that nothing can be done to either counteract or exploit their stigmas. In such cases, the person may resign him- or herself to the fact that others regard him or her unfavorably. Such a realization often leads to self-presentational resignation. If a person cannot change others' views of the stigma, why bother worrying about what they think?

Kowalski and Chapple (1993) demonstrated such an effect with the stigma of menstruation. Since earliest time, menstruating women have been stigmatized. In extreme cases, they have been isolated from other members of the community or thought to contaminate food, crops, and other people. Even in modern societies, menstruation is viewed as a taboo topic for discussion, and women learn to conceal the fact they are menstruating (Weideger, 1976).

In their study, menstruating and nonmenstruating women were told that a male interviewer either was or was not aware of their menstruating condition. Women who thought the man knew they were menstruating seemed to experience self-presentational resignation. They not only perceived that the man liked them less (thereby showing that they thought he viewed menstruation as a stigma), but they were less motivated to make an impression on him.

Embarrassment

As we all know from personal experience, making blatantly bad impressions on others can be very unpleasant. The hallmark of this experience is what we commonly call **embarrassment,** which is a feeling of mortification and chagrin that follows threats to one's public image (Edelmann, 1987; Miller, 1992; Schlenker, 1980). People who are embarrassed feel awkward, flustered, self-conscious, and otherwise ill at ease (Parrott & Smith, 1991).

Embarrassment has proven to be an intriguing emotional reaction. The embarrassed individual reports feeling nervous and tense with a sense of dread about having made a bad impression (Miller, 1986). In many ways, embarrassment seems like a type of anxiety (Leary, 1983c). However, embarrassment is clearly something other than intense anxiety per se. Part of the evidence for this comes from the fact that embarrassed people often blush, whereas when people are anxious or afraid, they do not blush—they blanch! The activation of the sympathetic nervous system that accompanies states of anxiety reduces the blood flow to peripheral veins, including those in the face. As a result, people who are frightened often look pale and have cold hands. Embarrassed people, on the other hand, show increased blood flow to the face paired with decreased blood flow to the extremities (Leary, Rejeski, Britt, & Smith, 1993). This is a highly unusual combination. We'll return to the matter of blushing later in the chapter.

The Function of Embarrassment

Embarrassment is universally unpleasant. I can't imagine anyone ever wanting to be embarrassed. Although embarrassment is a distressing experience—one we usually hope to avoid—it may actually serve an important function (Miller & Leary, 1992). Because people who make unfavorable impressions on others are derogated, ignored, shunned, punished, or ostracized, it is in the individual's best interests to maintain at least a minimally acceptable image in others' eyes. In fact, this is one reason that people impression-manage to begin with.

But people would not be appropriately circumspect about their public images unless a psychological mechanism existed to deter them from doing things that make the sorts of bad impressions that lead to rejection. Embarrassment may be precisely this kind of mechanism. Because embarrassment is aversive, people will usually try to avoid it, which means they will try to behave in ways that do not make undesired impressions. Furthermore, once they have made an undesired impression, they will try to remedy the situation to alleviate their feelings of embarrassment. In some ways, embarrassment has the properties of a drive state that promotes efforts to maintain and repair one's social image.

The capacity for experiencing social discomfort—including embarrassment—may have evolved because people who were distressed about others' impressions and evaluations of them were more likely to survive and reproduce than those who acted without regard for others' judgments (Miller & Leary, 1992). Early humans who were responsive to social pressures to be the "right" kind of person—competent, rule abiding, and socially desirable—were less likely to be rejected, ostracized, banished, or killed and, thus, more likely to survive and reproduce (Baumeister & Tice, 1990; Miller & Leary, 1992). I find the analogy between embarrassment and physical pain compelling. Just as we would be unlikely to survive without pain to deter us from harming our physical well-being, we would be unlikely to survive without embarrassment to deter us from harming our social well-being (Baumeister & Tice, 1990; Miller & Leary, 1992).

An Embarrassment Paradox

As we've seen, embarrassment arises most commonly when people are in a self-presentational predicament and believe they have conveyed undesired images of themselves. In light of this, let me pose a puzzling situation in which many people report they would be embarrassed, but yet the source of the self-presentational threat is not clear.

First, would it embarrass you to undress with a close family member of your own sex in the room? For example, if you are male, would it bother you to undress in the same room with your father or brother? If you are a woman, would undressing in the same room with your mother or sister bother you? Most people have told me that it would not embarrass them to undress in front of close family members of the same sex, or even close friends, for that matter.

Now, if you are not married, imagine for a moment that you are. Would it embarrass you to undress in front of your spouse? When I ask people this question, they look at me like I've lost my mind; "Of course not," they all say.

Fine. You wouldn't be embarrassed to undress in front of a same-sexed family member nor in front of your spouse. What if the same-sexed family member and your spouse were *both* in the room? Most (though not all) people I've asked tell me that they would feel embarrassed to undress in this situation. Why?

Some people have suggested that they would be embarrassed by the sexual connotation in the situation, but I don't follow that logic. There's nothing sexual involved, and both your family and spouse know that you have gotten dressed and undressed in front of the other before. In fact, it wouldn't bother you if your family knew you were changing clothes in front of your spouse in the next room, or if your spouse knew you were changing clothes in front of a same-sex family member. So why are many people embarrassed when both are present?

I have no idea.

Saving and Repairing Face

As we've seen, people try hard not to create self-presentational predicaments that will prove embarrassing. Despite their best efforts, however, everyone encounters situations that convey undesired impressions of themselves to others. Sometimes people can save face by pretending that the predicament did not occur at all. People may apply this "studied nonobservance" to their own behavior (as when they do not indicate that it was *their* stomach that rumbled) or to the behavior of others (as when one pretends not to notice that someone else has stumbled) (Goffman, 1955).

However, more often, self-presentational predicaments cannot be ignored. When people believe they have made an undesired impression on others, they typically take active steps to repair their image. Generally speaking, these **remedial tactics** or **face-saving behaviors** may involve one or more of the following self-presentational tactics: apologies, accounts, and compensatory self-presentation.

Apologies

When people apologize, they accept responsibility for what they said or did while asking to be pardoned (Schlenker, 1980). **Apologies** and expressions of remorse are nearly always expected in predicaments that harm other people, and the failure to apologize exacerbates the person's self-presentational predicament. Even children as young as three years old evaluate transgressors who apologize more favorably than those who don't (Darby & Schlenker, 1982).

Not all predicaments are equally distressing. The severity of a predicament is a function of two things. The more undesirable the impression that is created and the greater the person's apparent responsibility for the behavior that led to that impression, the more severe the predicament and the greater the person's embarrassment (Schlenker, 1980). For most minor predicaments, an apology alone will rectify the situation. If I clumsily bump into another person in a crowd, a simple "I'm sorry" is usually sufficient. The apology shows that I am not a bad person (I wasn't intentionally hurtful) and that, because I already regret my behavior, I do not need to be reprimanded or punished (Goffman, 1971; Schlenker, Weigold, & Doherty, 1991). However, for more severe predicaments—ones that convey a very negative impression of oneself—a perfunctory apology is rarely sufficient. Simply apologizing for molesting a child will not rehabilitate the person in others' eyes.

A study by Schlenker and Darby (1981) showed that the kinds of apologies people use are affected by both the severity of the offense and by the person's apparent responsibility for it. For example, when the consequences of one's behavior were minor, people said they would offer a perfunctory apology (such as simply saying "Pardon me"). However, as severity increased, subjects were more likely to say they were sorry, express feelings of remorse, explicitly ask for forgiveness, and offer to help the victim.

Elaborate apologies are clearly advantageous from a self-presentational perspective. People who offer more elaborate apologies are evaluated more favorably, liked more, blamed less, and more likely to be forgiven (Darby & Schlenker, 1982, 1989). This is true even when the infraction was very minor; thus, it seems best to err on the side of overapologizing rather than underapologizing.

Accounts

In addition to apologizing, people caught in self-presentational predicaments often offer accounts. An **account** is a verbal explanation for unexpected, unacceptable, or unsatisfactory behavior that is designed to rectify a self-presentational predicament (Gonzales, Pederson, Manning, & Wetter, 1990; Schlenker, 1980; Scott & Lyman, 1968). Put simply, accounts are self-presentational tactics designed to reduce the likelihood that others will draw undesirable inferences about the character or worth of an individual who is enmeshed in a self-presentational predicament (Gonzales et al., 1990). If I am late for our meeting, I am likely to provide you with an account for my tardiness. A person trying to account for his or her behavior has three general options: refusals, excuses, and justifications (Austin, 1956; Schlenker, 1980).

Defenses of Innocence

The ultimate account is a **defense of innocence** (also called a **refusal**) in which the person denies any and all responsibility for the event in question. Essentially, a defense of innocence says, "I didn't do it." If others accept this type of account as valid, the person's predicament is resolved.

Excuses

Often, however, people cannot deny all responsibility for a predicament-creating event, in which case they may offer **excuses.** People use excuses to reduce their perceived responsibility for an undesirable event. The intent is to reduce the negativity of the impressions others form by denying some or all responsibility for the action. One type of excuse—a **plea of ignorance**—occurs when people claim that they didn't intend or fully foresee the consequences of their behavior. After all, people usually can't be held fully responsible for things they couldn't or didn't foresee (although they might be criticized for not foreseeing something they should have).

Another type of excuse involves **mitigating circumstances** in which the person suggests that he or she did not have a normal amount of control over the event and, thus, couldn't really help it. When people claim that they behaved as they did because they were tired, under stress, drunk, or ill, for example, they are using mitigating excuses. Simiiarly, claiming that other people forced or pressured them to perform the behavior may absolve them of some responsibility.

Third, people may try to excuse their behavior through **diffusion of responsibility.** With this excuse, the person argues that responsibility for the event was shared by a number of people and, thus, he or she was not as responsible as might first appear. "Yes, I helped soap the car windows on Halloween, but seven other people did it too, so it's not all my fault."

Justifications

Whereas people use excuses to minimize how responsible they appear for bad events, they use **justifications** to characterize their behavior as more appropriate, desirable, or defensible than it might at first appear. With justifications, people accept personal responsibility for their behavior ("Yes, I did it."), but provide reasons why the behavior was not really all that bad. For example, people may use **direct minimization** in which they emphasize that the event was not as bad as it might appear (Schlenker, 1980). In defending his cheating on a test, a student might say, "It really didn't hurt anybody." Closely related to minimization is **claimed beneficence** in which people suggest not only that their behavior was not bad, but that it was possibly beneficial ("Yes, I forgot our date on Sunday night. But at least you got extra time to study for the test you had on Monday.")

People may also justify their behavior by comparing it to other actions that are even worse—**comparative justification.** Sometimes this sort of justification involves comparison with other people. The message is: "What I did wasn't nearly as bad as what other people do." ("Sure, I cheated a little on my income taxes, but that's nothing compared to what a lot of people get by with.") At other times, comparative justification involves comparison to one's own behavior at other times. ("Yes, I got drunk again, but not nearly as drunk as I usually do.") A third type of comparison is with a hypothetical scenario. ("Yes, I carelessly dropped the baby, but at least he didn't break any bones.") In each case, the attempt is to characterize the behavior as less negative by comparing it to even worse actions.

In **principled justification,** the person explains that, although his or her behavior resulted in negative consequences, it was justified by higher principles or goals. In victim derogation, for example, people justify having hurt other people by stressing that the victim deserved it. In victim benefaction, the action is justified by claiming that it actually helped the person who seemed to be hurt. Parents use this justification when they punish their children "for their own good."

Within seconds, Ernie's team of image consultants springs into action mapping out damage control for post-game interviews.

FIGURE 6.1
Athletes often provide accounts for performance during a game.
Reprinted by permission: Tribune Media Services.

I should point out that we usually speak of excuses and justifications in disparaging terms, but excuses and justifications are not necessarily deceitful. People can provide accounts that are either true or false. Excuses may be accurate (I really didn't mean to do it.), and justifications may be true (I really did do it for a good reason.). On the other hand, we sometimes use excuses and justifications that present a picture of the situation that we know isn't true.

Avoiding Accounts

In some instances, people think they can best protect their social images if they avoid giving an account altogether (Scott & Lyman, 1968). For example, individuals sometimes claim that they are invulnerable to accounting because of their power or position. Few dictators feel the need to account for their actions. In some cases, the person may even challenge others' right to ask for an account ("How dare you ask me where I was last night!").

In some cases, people avoid accounts by using **mystification.** In mystification, people explain that they cannot explain the reasons for their behavior. "If you knew the whole story, you'd understand why I did what I did," they say. "But I can't tell you the whole story."

Political Accounts

An important part of the life of politicians and public officials involves explaining their decisions to others. Not only do citizens in a democracy deserve to know why their elected officials made certain decisions, but such decisions have implications for the official's success and re-election. Of course, the need for accounting increases when the official's behavior puts him or her in a self-presentational predicament (McGraw, Timpone, & Bruck, in press).

Political predicaments seem to be of two kinds. First, politicians' public images are tarnished by policy decisions that are unpopular among their constituents (McGraw, 1990). Research suggests that principled justifications are more effective in reducing constituents' negative reactions to unpopular decisions than other kinds of accounts (McGraw, 1991; McGraw et al., in press). In the context of a political decision, a principled justification explains that a controversial decision was justified by higher principles. Attorney General Janet Reno justified her decision to authorize the FBI to batter the walls of the Branch Davidian compound in Waco, Texas, by explaining that children inside the compound were being abused. (Interestingly, the Justice Department's final report on the episode, in which 87 cult members died, was more of a "defense of innocence," finding no fault with the FBI's tactics; Periscope, 1993).

Not only may principled justifications increase acceptance of a controversial decision (and thereby improve the public official's image), but it may turn political loss into political gain if constituents are convinced that the official deserves credit for a beneficial decision (McGraw et al., in press). In contrast, excuses do not work well as accounts for politically controversial decisions (McGraw, 1990, 1991). The public is unlikely to accept the excuse that an official wasn't really responsible for a decision he or she made.

A second type of political predicament results from personal misconduct. Although research on this topic does not exist, I suspect that excuses are more effective in the case of personal misconduct than controversial decisions. A public official accused of sexual misconduct, corruption, or other ethical indiscretions is unlikely to change public opinion by trying to justify his or her

(Continued)

behavior. ("Yes, I sexually harassed 24 women, but there were many benefits.") Rather, they will try to excuse the behavior, either by denying responsibility altogether or by showing how they were not entirely responsible (I was under stress/I had a drinking problem/My marriage was in trouble/etc.).

Compensatory Self-Presentation

When others have information about us that would contradict the impressions we want to make, we sometimes try to compensate for the negative impression by presenting particularly positive impressions on some other dimension, one that is not related to the negative information people have about us. Research shows that when people realize that others have an unfavorable impression, they may try to compensate by presenting themselves more favorably in other areas (Baumeister, 1982a; Baumeister & Jones, 1978; Leary & Schlenker, 1980). For example, if you know that I am a lousy tennis player, I will probably not try to dispel you of that impression but instead tell you about the marathon I ran.

Similarly, when people face a self-presentational predicament because they violated some moral or legal code, they often go out of their way to do nice things for people. Although people may engage in prosocial behavior following a transgression for a number of reasons (such as to relieve their own guilt), evidence suggests that one reason is to repair the person's image in others' eyes (Tedeschi & Riordan, 1981). After people do something bad, they are understandably concerned about the inferences other people are drawing about them. By doing prosocial things, the harm-doer can convey that he or she is not such a bad person after all.

Self-presentational compensation serves two functions for the person who thinks others have an undesired impression of him or her. Most obviously, when compensatory self-presentation is directed toward the target who holds an unflattering view of the person, it serves to repair the person's damaged image.

However, compensatory self-presentation is sometimes directed toward targets who do not have a negative impression of the individual. For example, people who appear foolish in front of one target sometimes try to convey a particularly positive impression to *other* targets who did not witness the self-presentational predicament (Apsler, 1975). Having looked like a fool to one person, people can repair their damaged mood and self-esteem by making good impressions on other targets.

Nonverbal Embarrassment Displays

When people encounter self-presentational predicaments, they not only engage in verbal remedial behaviors to help them save face, but they tend to display a stereotypic set of nonverbal behaviors. This **embarrassment display** consists of three primary elements that occur across various cultures: facial blushing, gaze aversion, and nervous smiling (Edelmann & Iwawaki, 1987).

Facial Blushing

People who encounter self-presentational predicaments often experience an increase in blood flow to the face, neck, and ears, often accompanied by the visible reddening or darkening of the face that we call blushing.[1] The social blushes that arise from embarrassing circumstances can be physiologically and psychologically distinguished from facial flushing that occurs for nonsocial reasons (for example, flushes due to alcohol consumption, sexual arousal, physical exertion, and menopause).

If I ask you to recall the last time you blushed, it likely involved a situation in which you were concerned with others' impressions of you. In fact, Darwin (1892/1955) concluded that blushing "depends in all cases on . . . a sensitive regard for the opinion, more particularly for the depreciation of others" (p. 335). People often blush when they've appeared incompetent, immoral, foolish, or otherwise socially undesirable.

Although self-presentational predicaments such as these are the most obvious causes of blushing, people also blush in response to being complimented, praised, or honored (Leary & Meadows, 1991). Furthermore, people may blush even when others simply scrutinize or stare at them, such as when they speak before audiences or are the center of attention (one common cause of blushing is having others sing "Happy Birthday to You;" Leary & Meadows, 1991). People even blush when other people simply accuse them of blushing, even when they're not ("Aw, look; she's blushing.").

---

[1]Although blushing may be imperceptible in blacks, Native Americans, and other dark skinned peoples, all racial groups experience facial vasodilation in response to undesired social attention and self-presentational predicaments.

The fact that people blush in situations other than obvious self-presentational predicaments demonstrates that, contrary to the popular view, blushing is not simply a response to embarrassing predicaments. My view is that blushing is a reaction to **undesired social attention** (Leary et al., 1992). Although people often desire attention from others and find it rewarding, in some situations people do not want social attention. One set of situations in which people find social attention undesired and aversive involves self-presentational predicaments. People who have behaved in ways that others view as incompetent, immoral, foolish, or otherwise undesirable understandably find social attention aversive and would prefer to be ignored for the time being. Yet in these kinds of situations, people usually feel that everyone is looking at them (Silver, Sabini, & Parrott, 1987). Thus, people do not blush in self-presentational predicaments because they are embarrassed or ashamed, as has been widely assumed, but because they are the objects of undesired social attention (Leary et al., 1992).

Gaze Aversion

People who think they've made a bad impression on others tend to avert their gaze and avoid eye contact with other people (Edelmann, 1987; Modigliani, 1971). In fact, when embarrassed, people find it difficult to meet the gaze of other people even if they want to.

Nervous Smiling

The third component of the embarrassment display involves a silly, nervous grin (Edelmann, 1987). On the surface, this smile is quite paradoxical; after all, embarrassed people rarely feel like smiling. In fact, this nervous smile is easily distinguished from a genuine smile of happiness or amusement (Asendorpf, 1990). The smile itself is more of a self-conscious grin than a genuine smile, and the eyes appear vacant rather than bemused.

Nonhuman Appeasement

Why do people display this stereotypic pattern of behavior when they think they've made an undesired impression? Why should such a reaction have evolved? Part of the answer to this question may involve similarities between human embarrassment displays and the appeasement behaviors of other primates. When facing a physical or social threat from a member of their own species, many other primates, such as chimpanzees and baboons, engage in behaviors that diffuse the threat, thereby avoiding aggression and maintaining the individual's position in the group.

FIGURE 6.2
The appeasing grin of many nonhuman primates bears a striking resemblance to the silly, sheepish smile of people who feel embarrassed.

Three aspects of these appeasement behaviors are relevant to understanding human embarrassment displays. First, when a lower status primate is threatened by a higher status one, the lower status animal invariably averts his or her eyes, or at least looks at the dominant primate obliquely (van Hooff, 1972). In fact, gaze aversion is a central component of primate appeasement (Altmann, 1967). As we discussed on the previous page, people who find themselves in a self-presentational predicament typically avert their gaze in much the same way.

Second, under certain circumstances, appeasement and submission in nonhuman primates involves a vacant, mirthless grin. This grin, which Goodall (1988) called the "full closed grin," is easily distinguished from both friendly smiles of affiliation and aggressive teeth baring (van Hooff, 1972). As you can see in Figure 6.2, this appeasing grin is quite similar to the embarrassed smile in humans.

Third, although I've found no evidence that other primates blush (although their faces flush for other reasons), blushing and nonhuman appeasement share a common cause. A steady gaze from a more dominant animal is a primary elicitor of appeasement behaviors in nonhuman primates (Bolwig, 1978; Chevalier-Skolnikoff, 1973; Miller, 1975). As we saw, people often blush when others stare at them; in fact, blushing may be a response to undesired social attention.

Considered together, these similarities suggest that human embarrassment displays are loosely analogous to appeasement behaviors in nonhuman primates (Leary et al., 1992). They are behaviors that occur in socially threatening situations when one's image and social standing are in jeopardy. Traditionally, ethologists have viewed nonhuman appeasement as a way of averting aggression among conspecifics (Bolwig, 1978; Manning, 1972; Walters & Seyfarth, 1987). Displays of appeasement deter physical aggression among nonhumans, partly by leading the threatening animal to lose interest in the less dominant one. Once an animal appeases, the higher status animal usually breaks its gaze and wanders away (Bolwig, 1978; van Hooff, 1972).

Embarrassment displays seem to have similar effects. Obvious signs of embarrassment—such as downcast eyes, nervous grinning, and blushing—seem to placate other persons when the individual has performed behaviors that would otherwise result in unfavorable evaluations (Goffman, 1959; Semin & Manstead, 1982). Contrast two situations: one in which a person who performs an undesirable behavior (by belching in public, for example) appears nonplussed, against one in which the individual conveys that he or she is embarrassed. I think your impression will be more positive of the person who engages in an embarrassment display.

Summary

People's self-presentations take into account how they are perceived by other people as well as how they might be perceived by others in the future. What others know or are likely to find out about us constrains the kinds of images we can claim and leads us to regulate our impressions to compensate for our current social image. People who believe they are already conveying a desired impression often reduce the positivity of their self-presentations in a show of modesty, whereas people who experience a self-presentational predicament or possess a stigma usually try to compensate for it.

Embarrassment is the emotional experience that results from real or imagined self-presentational predicaments. Although it is unpleasant, embarrassment may motivate people to protect their social images and to engage in remedial behaviors when their images are damaged. People repair damage to their social images through nonobservance, apologies, accounts (e.g., excuses and justifications), and compensatory self-presentation. People in a self-presentational predicament also engage in nonverbal embarrassment displays (blushing, smiling, gaze aversion) that may be related to the appeasement behaviors observed in other primates.

CHAPTER

7

Instrumental Complementarity

CHAPTER OUTLINE

We are all amateur psychologists. Even without formal training in the principles of human behavior, most people have a basic understanding of what makes people tick, and they regularly use this knowledge to influence others to behave as they desire. Even though you may not know me personally, I suspect that you could easily figure out how to make me angry, how to get me to help you, or how to make me feel afraid of you. And, in part, you could elicit these reactions purely through your self-presentations. If you wanted to make me feel angry, you could give me the impression that you are rude, egocentric, and totally unconcerned about my welfare. To receive my help, you could show me that you are unskilled, weak, or ineffectual. To make me afraid, you could convey the impression of being violent, reckless, or unstable.

We saw in previous chapters that people tailor their self-presentations to specific social situations and to particular targets. In this chapter, we address the fact that people sometimes try to create impressions that will directly elicit certain reactions from other people. Making certain impressions will lead to certain responses, whereas making other impressions will lead to other responses. Through their self-presentations, people can subtly, yet directly, influence others to respond to them as they desire.

Complementarity

People are able to do this because one person's behavior constrains how other people are likely to react. People often naturally respond to others' behaviors in particular predictable ways. If you know that Anna told her friend that she was upset because she failed a test, you could probably make a general prediction about how her friend would and would not be likely to react. Anna's distressed behavior would quite naturally elicit certain supportive behaviors from her friend.

The **principle of complementarity** states that one person's actions "invite, pull, elicit, draw, entice, or evoke 'restricted classes' of reactions" from other people (Kiesler, 1983, p. 198). Because the person's behavior affects others' perceptions of his or her characteristics and motives, certain "complementary" responses become more likely and certain "noncomplementary" responses become less likely (see Carson, 1969).

Some behaviors encourage similar, correspondent behaviors from others. For example, most people respond to nurturant and cooperative overtures with further nurturance and cooperation and to hostility and distrust with hostile distrust of their own. Other behaviors encourage dissimilar, reciprocal behaviors. For example, people tend to react to others' dominant behaviors with submissiveness and to expressions of sadness with emotional support.

Armed with a naive understanding of complementarity, people can elicit desired reactions from other people by presenting themselves in particular ways. The average person knows precisely how to present him- or herself to lead other people to respond with sympathy, support, anger, rejection, fear, compliance, and numerous other responses. Of course, no single self-presentation reliably elicits a particular response 100 percent of the time. But people can notably increase their chances of getting others to respond as they desire by relying on their knowledge of complementarity.

PRINCIPLE:

People often present images of themselves that they think will evoke desired, complementary reactions from others.

Supplication: Looking Weak

Supplication refers to self-presentations designed to make others regard the person as helpless in some regard (Jones & Pittman, 1982). By advertising their weakness and dependency, people can prompt others to nurture, protect, help, and care for them. In addition, supplicating self-presentations can be used to avoid onerous obligations and to excuse one's poor performance.

The Need for Help and Support

The norm of social responsibility says that people should help those who cannot help themselves. As a result, we often feel obligated to help those who need our assistance whether we really want to help them or not and to offer our emotional support to those who are suffering. Knowing this, people can get others to help and support them through supplicating self-presentations. As a child, did you ever exaggerate your ineptitude at homework or a household chore to induce your parents to help you? Have you ever expressed your insecurities to others, hoping that they would help build up your confidence? Have you made sure other people knew how upset you were about something so that they would offer their support?

Some have suggested that people sometimes use depressive symptoms as supplicating self-presentations. This is not to say that people don't really get depressed. But why do they sometimes hide their unhappy feelings from some people, whereas at other times they let others see how depressed they feel? Research suggests that people convey impressions of being sad and discouraged when they want others to come to their aid or when they want to avoid certain kinds of demands on them (Hill, Weary, & Williams, 1986; Weary & Williams, 1990).

People may also supplicate to avoid criticism. Because social norms dictate that we should not attack or demean those who are inferior, publicly disparaging oneself should reduce the likelihood of criticism by others. Thus, people sometimes preemptively self-deprecate to discourage others from criticizing them (Baumgardner, 1991).

Figure 7.1
Self-presentations of incompetence or weakness can sometimes pay off.

Avoiding Aversive Tasks

In addition to getting help or support, people use supplicating self-presentations to avoid doing things they don't want to do. By demonstrating their incompetence, weakness, ignorance, or instability, people may convince others that they are not capable of doing certain things, thereby relieving them of responsibility for doing so.

Risks of Supplication

Despite the benefits of supplication, the person who uses a supplicating self-presentational strategy runs certain risks. One is that, even if the target offers help or emotional support, he or she may form an unflattering impression of the person—that he or she is incompetent, weak, lazy, or insecure, for example. Although people often publicly support those who self-deprecate, they privately hold unfavorable opinions of them (Powers & Zuroff, 1988). Furthermore, over time, the target may feel trapped and resentful, begrudgingly coming to the supplicant's aid. This is clearly true in the case in depression, for example. Although people are generally happy to help a friend who is down, over time people begin to resent and avoid those who are often depressed (Segrin & Dillard, 1992).

Because supplication carries these risks, people probably use supplication only as a last resort (Jones & Pittman, 1982). In fact, we've had a certain amount of difficulty getting subjects in our studies to self-deprecate even when doing so would have allowed them to avoid an onerous task (Kowalski & Leary, 1990).

Physical Illness

Have you ever "played sick?" At one time or another, most people have feigned or exaggerated illness or injury to get out of something they didn't want to do (such as going to school), to account for undesirable behavior (such as failing a test), or to elicit nurturing responses from other people (others are expected to take care of sick people). In a survey conducted at a major northeastern university, an average of one out of three students reported that they had fraudulently claimed they were ill while in college, usually to gain more time for a test or assignment (Caron, Whitbourne, & Halgin, 1992). Another study found that one out of five American workers calls in sick at least once a year because they really need time to rest and relax (Siegel, 1993), and this doesn't include the other times that people call in sick for other reasons (to work around the house, take care of ill children, go on a date, or whatever). Interestingly, this tactic may actually increase worker productivity in the long run because workers who don't relieve stress may perform with less efficiency and may even really get sick.

In some instances, people completely fabricate their reported illness or injury, whereas in other cases they simply exaggerate its severity. Either way, the fact that the person communicated his or her illness to others suggests a self-presentational motive. Why else would someone tell others he or she was sick?

The Sick Role

Self-presentations of illness are effective because of the **sick role**—a set of culturally-shared assumptions about people who are ill (Gordon, 1966; Parsons, 1951). Because the sick role stipulates that people who are ill or injured are exempt from normal social and occupational obligations, appearing sick can be used to avoid onerous activities or duties. We don't expect sick students to go to school, sick employees to go to work, sick lovers to have sex, or sick friends to play tennis. Thus, people can occasionally escape school, work, sex, or sports simply by telling others they don't feel well.

The sick role also includes the assumption that people cannot be expected to perform up to their normal levels of ability when they are ill. Thus, self-presentations of illness can be used to excuse poor performances in class, in athletics, at work, and even in social life. Again, the claim of illness may be either true or false. Either way, it can shield the person from the normal implications of undesirable behavior.

Hypochondriacs—people who obsess about their health—may use self-presentations of illness for their social benefits, including as an excuse for poor performance. In one study, subjects who scored high on a measure of hypochondriasis reported having a greater number of physical symptoms when they thought that their score on a test of social intelligence might be affected by their health. In contrast, hypochondriacs who took a nonthreatening test did not overemphasize their symptoms (Smith, Snyder, & Perkins, 1983). Because their poor health, whether real or imagined, can serve as an excuse for poor performance, hypochondriasis can protect people from evaluation apprehension (Rezek & Leary, 1991). I need not be as worried about doing poorly if I and others can blame my performance on illness. For some people, appearing to be in poor health has social and personal benefits.

A third aspect of the sick role is that sick individuals have a right to expect others to help care for them (Gordon, 1966). Thus, letting other people know you are sick is likely to elicit concern and nurturance. You may be one of those people who really enjoy being doted on when you don't feel well.

Self-presentational illness and injury are also common when people expect financial or other benefits from being sick or hurt. For example, in personal injury cases, people have a stake in continuing to seem injured until their legal claim is resolved. Because of this, some chronic pain clinics refuse to admit accident victims to their programs until litigation is over (Weissman, 1990). People have a disincentive to improve as long as they are motivated to appear injured so they will receive an insurance settlement.

Illness Validation

Of course, we all realize that others may fake or exaggerate illness. Because of this, we often require independent validation of a person's illness (Gordon, 1966). The most widely accepted validation is legitimization by a physician. A "doctor's excuse" is widely accepted as evidence that a person is ill. In fact, many people (some college professors included) will not accept illness claims that are not substantiated by a note from a medical professional.

In some cases, just a visit to a physician may provide validation because it demonstrates that the person was concerned enough about his or her health to seek medical help. Even if the physician can't find anything wrong, a trip to the doctor's office shows other people that the person truly didn't feel well. Most people don't go to the effort, inconvenience, and expense of going to the doctor unless they think they are sick or injured. This legitimizing function of seeking medical attention may partly explain why hypochondriacs make incessant trips to the doctor.

Visits to a physician, in themselves, serve a self-presentational function. People who claim to be sick and go to a doctor are perceived to be more ill than people who only claim to be sick.

Self-Presentations of Healthfulness

Before leaving self-presentations of illness, I should acknowledge that people who really are ill or injured sometimes want others to think they are not. An injured athlete may downplay the extent of his or her injury so he or she can stay in the game. A teenager may deny feeling sick so that his parents will let him go to a party. Some people may be embarrassed by their medical condition and, thus, hide it from others. Others may understate their degree of illness or disability because they don't want to be perceived as weak or incapacitated. Self-presentations of healthfulness may contribute to illness when people who are ill or injured fail to take proper care of themselves so that others don't detect their medical problem.

Psychological Stability and Instability

One Flew Over the Cuckoo's Nest was an extraordinarily popular book and movie. In the movie version, Jack Nicholson played R. J. McMurphy, a man who has been sent to a mental hospital. Throughout the movie, one is never quite sure whether McMurphy is really mentally disturbed or merely faking mental illness to avoid prison.

We are all familiar with cases of otherwise normal people who wanted others to think they were "crazy." Defendants accused of heinous crimes often plead "not guilty by reason of insanity," hoping that they will be sent to a psychiatric institution rather than to prison. Legal and medical experts have been discussing the problem of feigned insanity at least since the 18th century, and as early as 1806, defendants have successfully faked mental illness to avoid conviction (Geller, Erlen, Kaye, & Fisher, 1990).

In the case of the "Son of Sam" murders in the 1970s, David Berkowitz openly admitted that he feigned mental illness. After being arrested for killing six young people and wounding seven others, Berkowitz first maintained that he had been ordered to kill by a neighbor's demon possessed dog. Later, he admitted that he fabricated the story. "There were no real demons, no talking dogs, no satanic henchmen," he said. "I made it all up . . . to find some form of justification for my criminal acts against society" (Berkowitz Admits, 1979).

People have also tried to convince others they were crazy to avoid military service. Apparently such self-presentation tactics were used even in ancient times. In *The Odyssey,* for example, to avoid serving in the war with Troy, Odysseus sowed a field with salt, purposefully trying to appear crazy. The theme of malingering to avoid military service appears again in the popular television show *M*A*S*H* in which Corporal Klinger dresses in women's clothing, hoping to be discharged from the army.

In cases such as these, the person's motives may be transparent, leading us to conclude that he or she is not really mentally disturbed and that the irrational behavior is a self-presentational ploy. Laypeople and professionals alike draw a sharp distinction between "normal" people who pretend to be mentally ill and "disturbed" people who are truly experiencing psychological problems. However, the line between these two is not as sharp as may first appear.

Self-Presentation and Schizophrenia

Some have argued that what appear to be symptoms of psychological problems are sometimes self-presentational strategies designed to accomplish certain interpersonal goals. This is not to suggest that abnormal behavior is nothing but impression management or that all people who appear mentally disturbed are only managing their impressions. Far from it. Many people do experience severe emotional and behavioral problems over which they have little or no control. But many people who manifest behaviors that are widely regarded as indicative of psychopathology, even those who are so severely impaired that they are confined to a mental institution, may be managing their impressions to appear psychologically disturbed.

Evidence for this conclusion comes from studies in which patients diagnosed as schizophrenic were found to display either more or less psychotic symptomatology depending on their goals. In a classic study by Braginsky and Braginsky (1967), 30 long-term schizophrenics in a mental hospital were interviewed by a staff psychologist. The patients were given one of three explanations for the interview. Some were told that they were being interviewed so the staff could decide whether they should be placed on an open or closed ward. Given that open wards are more pleasant, being reserved for less disturbed patients, the researchers reasoned that patients in this condition would want to appear as well adjusted as possible so as to be assigned to an open ward.

Other patients were told that the interview was to determine their suitability for release from the hospital. Based on previous studies, the researchers expected these patients to want to be appear disturbed. If this seems surprising, keep in mind that long-term mental patients often come to doubt their ability to function in the outside world. Among the very poor and indigent, being within the protective, nondemanding confines of an institution may be preferable to the harsh realities of the outside world. Some have suggested that some of the underprivileged use mental institutions as a "resort" (Braginsky et al., 1969).

The findings showed that patients who thought they were being evaluated for the open ward displayed significantly fewer indications of psychological problems than those who thought their suitability for release was being assessed. They described themselves more positively and reported fewer medical and psychological problems. In fact, *no* patient who thought he or she was being evaluated for the open ward reported *any* severe problems, whereas half of those in the other condition did so. Furthermore, psychologists judged the patients being evaluated for the open ward as exhibiting less psychopathology and requiring less supervision.

The finding that diagnosed mental patients selectively present themselves as more or less disturbed depending on which image will most benefit them has been replicated by other researchers (Fontana & Gessner, 1969; Fontana & Klein, 1968; Watson, 1972; Wilcox & Krasnoff, 1967). Furthermore, the psychiatric literature contains case studies of instances in which people who at first appear to be severely disturbed are found to be managing their impressions to appear dysfunctional (Cain, 1964; Sadow & Suslick, 1961). However, Watson (1973) suggested that such patients are more likely to suppress impressions of abnormality when normalcy will result in desired outcomes than they are to actually fake psychoticism.

These findings raise questions about the traditional view of certain mental disorders. First, they suggest that some psychiatric symptoms may reflect self-presentational tactics rather than underlying psychopathology. Again, this does not mean that "true" mental disorder does not exist or that nothing is wrong with people who try to appear psychologically disturbed. People who try to maintain the image of being "crazy" so they can live in an institution clearly have difficulty living effectively in their normal environments. However, a self-presentational perspective suggests that the nature of the person's problem is sometimes different from that traditionally identified by psychiatrists and psychologists.

Second, the fact that some hospitalized mental patients, even those diagnosed as schizophrenic, can successfully manage their impressions calls into question the standard, textbook conceptualization of schizophrenia. Although some people are truly so disturbed that they have virtually no control over their behavior, some such patients are sufficiently in tune with their social worlds to engage in the complex cognitions required for successful impression management (Braginsky et al., 1969; Kelly, Farina, & Mosher, 1971; Sherman, Trief, & Sprafkin, 1975;

Watson, 1973, 1975). As two writers observed, schizophrenics are "more expert at producing certain reactions on the part of the staff, family, and society at large than the latter are at evoking desired patient responses" (Ludwig & Farrelly, 1967, p. 740).

Dissimulation on Personality Inventories

Psychologists are well-known for their personality scales. Behavioral researchers use personality inventories in their studies; clinical psychologists have clients complete measures of personality and psychopathology (such as the MMPI); personnel psychologists use personality tests to screen job applicants; and organizational psychologists frequently use personality measures as they help people become better managers or promote organizational development.

Although psychologists hope that the respondents' answers on such tests are accurate and honest, some have pointed out that people completing a self-report questionnaire are essentially engaging in an act of self-presentation. After all, self-report measures of personality simply ask respondents to describe themselves by answering a series of questions. Viewed in this way, taking a psychological test is a form of self-presentation that is not notably different from self-presentation in social interactions (Hogan & Jones, 1983).

Most commonly, people taking psychological tests try to appear healthier or better adjusted than they really are (**socially desirable responding** or **faking good**). For example, college students who serve as subjects in an experiment presumably do not want the researcher to think they are neurotic, unethical, or otherwise maladjusted. Similarly, job applicants are understandably motivated to present themselves as favorably as possible and, thus, may be inclined to answer questions untruthfully.

Less commonly, people sometimes want to look disturbed if doing so has benefits for them (**faking bad**). A criminal defendant who faces prison if he's psychologically stable or a mental institution if he's insane may respond to a psychologist's tests so as to appear psychologically troubled. In some cases, people who resent having to complete such questionnaires may respond in random or bizarre ways.

Obviously, the validity and usefulness of personality tests are compromised when people do not answer the questions as accurately and as honestly as they can. For many years, researchers and test developers have studied ways of increasing the truthfulness of people's answers and of determining whether a particular respondent was faking his or her answers.

One of the most widely used measures of self-report biases is the Marlowe-Crowne Social Desirability Scale (Crowne & Marlowe, 1964). The Social Desirability Scale asks the respondent whether he or she has ever engaged in each of 33 behaviors. Some of the behaviors are very common things nearly everyone has done, yet ones that some people might be inclined to deny. One such item says, "I like to gossip at times," and another states "I am sometimes resentful when I don't get my way." Other items involve relatively uncommon behaviors that are highly desirable, such as "I'm always willing to admit it when I make a mistake," and "My table manners at home are as good as when I eat out in a restaurant." People who are inclined to describe themselves in an unrealistically positive fashion on personality measures tend to deny the common but undesirable actions but claim to perform the uncommon but desirable ones. There is also a Social Desirability Scale for Children that includes items such as "I always finish all of my homework on time" and "I always do the right things" (Crandall, Crandall, & Katovsky, 1965).

Researchers have asked whether people who score high on measures of social desirability are managing their impressions to appear in a desirable light or whether such people *really* believe they possess exceptionally positive attributes. Paulhus (1984) suggested that both may be true, and developed the Balanced Inventory of Desirable Responding (BIDR) to assess these two tendencies separately. His research suggested that people may exaggerate their desirable attributes either because their personal view of themselves is positively biased or because they are trying to present a favorable image to other people.

When researchers develop a new scale, they usually want to show that scores on their scale are not related to scores on measures of social desirability. If scores on their scale correlate with a measure of social desirability (such as the Social Desirability Scale or the BIDR), we may suspect that scores on the new measure are contaminated by social desirability bias. That is, respondents may be answering the questions on the new scale in a way that will make them appear in a favorable light. Unfortunately, people even fake their answers on the Social Desirability Scale itself! Subjects obtain higher social desirability scores when they put their names on their responses than when they complete the scale anonymously (Becker, 1976).

Another way to determine a scale's susceptibility to faking is to have subjects complete an inventory under one of three sets of instructions. One group of subjects is told to answer the questions to give a good impression of themselves, one group is told to try to give a bad impression, and another group is told to answer as accurately and honestly as possible. If average scores on the measure differ across these three groups, we know that the scale is potentially vulnerable to faking. If the scores don't differ, we can conclude that subjects can't figure out how to fake their answers even when they want to. Unfortunately, many of the measures most commonly used by researchers in personality and social psychology are at least minimally susceptible to response bias (Furnham & Henderson, 1982).

Many of the personality inventories used by clinical and counseling psychologists include **lie scales** that are designed to detect whether or not a client is faking his or her answers. Some inventories include two such scales, one to detect "faking good" (trying to appear psychologically healthy or socially virtuous) and another to detect "faking bad" (trying to accentuate the extent of one's difficulties, anguish, or vulnerability) (Bagby, Gillis, & Dickens, 1990).

Intimidation: Looking Tough

I'm irked by people who get their way by being mean and disagreeable. If a person is willing to forego others' good will and doesn't mind living with the reputation of being a nasty son-of-a-bitch, he or she can pretty much get others to do whatever he or she wants. Realizing this, people sometimes foster an intimidating, threatening image to induce others to do their bidding (Jones & Pittman, 1982). The schoolyard bully, the gruff boss, and the stern parent may all be fostering images that elicit others' unquestioning compliance. The bully or gang member who displays his penchant for aggression is relying on an image of being physically violent, whereas the gruff and uncompromising boss relies on being socially unpleasant, but the effect is the same.

Intimidation for Compliance

Usually, self-presentational intimidation is used by persons with the greater power in an interaction (Jones & Pittman, 1982). Teachers may intimidate students, employers employees, sergeants recruits, and so on, but not vice versa. People hesitate to direct intimidating self-presentations toward those who have the power to retaliate. Even so, persons with less power may manage their impressions to intimidate others in certain circumstances. For example, people with less power can often get others to do what they want by threatening to "make a scene." Children do this to their parents when they throw tantrums in public places to get what they want. Similarly, patients in mental institutions can often get their way by intimidating the staff and being difficult.

One type of self-presentational intimidation commonly occurs during negotiations. Many negotiators believe that, by appearing tough and uncompromising, they will lower their opponents' aspirations and discourage them from asking for too much (Wall, 1991). Furthermore, negotiators must often maintain an intimidating image for their constituents as well; research shows that negotiators work harder to look tough when the parties on whose behalf they are negotiating are present (Carnevale, Pruitt, & Britton, 1979). Unfortunately, the complementary response to intimidation, toughness, and dominance is often countertoughness rather than submissiveness. Thus, negotiators often avoid this strategy when their opponent has the resources to retaliate.

From a self-presentational standpoint, some (but by no means all) instances of violence reflect intimidating self-presentations. In order for physical intimidation to succeed, people must occasionally back up their threatening posture with real aggression. Much seemingly senseless violence may serve this purpose. In fact, senseless, unprovoked aggression may be more effective self-presentationally than justified aggression because it shows that the aggressor is clearly not a person to be trifled with. Bullies, for example, tend to pick on their victims in relatively public settings where their peers can see.

Similarly, many violent prisoners admit that they started unprovoked fights with strangers to build their reputation for bravery, fighting ability, and recklessness. Toch (1992) found that one out of four of the violent men he studied used violence to promote his self-image:

> . . . a self-image promoter is a man who works hard at manufacturing the impression that he is not to be trifled with—that he is formidable and fearless. . . . His fights are demonstration matches, and they are designed to impress the victim and the audience. The impression left is presumed to govern future interactions with him. He is worried that if he does not follow this course of action he will be mistaken for a weakling or a coward (p. 135).

An extreme and unusual instance of self-presentational intimidation occurs when militant groups claim responsibility for attacks that they didn't commit. Typically, after a bombing or terrorist attack, dozens of groups claim responsibility for the attack. When the World Trade Center in New York City was rocked by a strong bomb in 1993, more than 50 groups called to claim responsibility. The purpose of such claims is to establish that the group is willing to resort to violence to achieve its goals and, thus, is a force to be reckoned with. Oddly, with the exception of the people who actually planted the bomb, these groups do not really resort to aggression. Yet, they believe it is useful to establish the image of being a group that does.

Not all self-presentational intimidation is bad. For example, people may adopt an intimidating persona simply to ward off possible attacks. When walking down a deserted city street alone, people may adopt an unfriendly expression, stare straight ahead, and walk purposefully. When the police conduct raids on suspects who are thought to be dangerous, they usually shout commands and threats, use a great deal of physical force, and brandish their weapons to convey an intimidating impression of strength and forcefulness (Felson & Tedeschi, 1993).

Retaliatory Aggression

As kids, we all learned that "Sticks and stones will break my bones, but words will never hurt me." Yet, people sometimes react to others' words with the same ferocity that they react to physical attacks. People are particularly likely to retaliate aggressively when others insult or demean them or, in self-presentational terms, when others indicate that they hold highly unfavorable impressions of them (Felson, 1978, 1982). For example, the most common cause of aggression among street gangs is a perceived insult to the honor of a gang or one of its members (Horowitz & Schwartz, 1974).

When people are insulted, they are confronted with the fact that another individual holds an unflattering view of them—that they are weak, incompetent, immoral, or otherwise unvaluable. Furthermore, insults convey that the insulter is in the position to deliver his or her evaluation of the individual and does not fear the target's reaction. The insulted party is then often motivated to try to restore his or her image in the eyes of both the insulter and any bystanders who may be present.

Furthermore, failing to respond to an insult often causes further damage to the person's image, conveying that he or she is weak, afraid, or simply unable to come up with an appropriate reaction. By retaliating, the offended party can reestablish that he or she is a forceful and assertive person who cannot be treated with disrespect. As Goffman (1967) observed, "in aggressive interchanges the winner not only succeeds in introducing information favorable to himself and unfavorable to others, but also demonstrates that as an interactant he can handle himself better than his adversaries" (p. 25). Unfortunately, because retaliation casts the insulter in a negative light, the original provocateur is inclined to respond to the counterattack. Unchecked, these reciprocal attacks can escalate into a conflict spiral.

Interestingly, people are most likely to retaliate against insults when third parties are present, particularly if they know that the bystanders value aggression (Bond & Venus, 1991; Felson, 1978, 1982). This suggests that aggressive retaliation is performed as much for the benefit of bystanders as for the insulter. We seem willing to swallow our pride and endure insults unless other people know we have been insulted.

A self-presentational analysis of retaliatory aggression suggests that people who are unusually sensitive to real or imagined attacks upon their public images may be particularly prone to violence. Toch (1992) identified such people as "self-image defenders" whose violence "arises in the form of responses to challenges, retaliations to slights, or reactions against aspersions to his advertised self-conception" (p. 141).

Self-Presentation and Crime

Although most of us have been rewarded since childhood for being good, honest, law-abiding persons, evidence suggests that some people benefit from being viewed as criminals. When the attention, respect, and approval of one's parents and peers depend on the impression of being tough and antisocial, people will manage their impressions so as to be viewed as "criminal." For some working class people (particularly men), being criminals is a major portion of their social identities. They *want* others to view them as tough, reckless, and disrespectful of the law (Hogan & Jones, 1983; Toch, 1992). These self-presentational strategies range from mere antisocial posturings to outright criminal behaviors.

This sort of deviant self-presentational tactic may seem odd until we realize that most people have, at one time or another, wanted others to see them as a risk-taker, reckless, or unconcerned about breaking rules. For example, when adolescents use alcohol or illegal drugs, they often do so because they don't want their peers to regard them as a "goody two-shoes." Many normal, otherwise law-abiding people go along with dangerous or illegal activities because they don't want others to think they are excessively cautious or overly concerned about doing things that aren't right.

Of course, the images that criminals want to present to their peers and to other criminals are quite different from those they want to convey to law enforcement personnel. When they appear before parole boards, for example, convicted criminals often try to give the impression that they are, if not rehabilitated, at least moving in that direction. Members of parole boards are aware that felons engage in impression-management during parole interviews, yet they do not readily distinguish between prisoners who strategically present fraudulent images and those who convey an unrealistic image simply because they do not have a great deal of self-insight (Radelet & Roberts, 1983).

Sexual Interest

In our society, norms discourage people from explicitly conveying their sexual interest in people they do not know well, and this is probably more true of women than of men. People often use subtle behaviors to express their sexual interest in others—behaviors that can be denied if the other person takes offense. As a result, conveying sexual intent is a tricky affair in which people must send and receive subtle, often ambiguous cues (Grammer, 1990).

Some behaviors clearly connote sexual interest (Abbey & Melby, 1986). For example, if a woman asks a man back to her apartment, then changes into a see-through nightgown and puts a pornographic movie on the VCR, he probably wouldn't be too far wrong to assume she was interested in some form of sexual activity. However, many behaviors that connote sexual interest are ambiguous, opening the way for misunderstanding and awkwardness. If she asks him back to her apartment, dims the lights, and puts on soft music, should he infer she is interested in sex?

The possibility for misunderstanding is compounded by two patterns. First, men and women sometimes interpret nonverbal behaviors differently, with men having a lower threshold for perceiving behaviors sexually. Kowalski (1993) asked male and female university students to indicate the degree to which each of several behaviors would indicate that a woman was interested in sex. When the behaviors were high in sexual connotativeness (such as the woman undressed him or removed her blouse), men and women did not differ in their inferences of her sexual interest. However, when the behaviors were more mundane (such as the woman simply had a drink with him or held his hand), the men were more likely to infer sexual interest than the women.

Second, because norms discourage women from appearing too interested in sex, they may try to seem less interested than they really feel. Muehlenhard and Hollabaugh (1988) found that 39 percent of the women they surveyed reported saying "no" to a man's sexual advances when they really meant "yes." The women's reasons for doing so were often self-presentational; a primary reason was the fear of appearing promiscuous. Such a self-presentation is risky, of course, because it may lead men to disregard what a woman says when she *really* means no (Kowalski, 1992).

Role Modeling

A great deal of research over the past 30 years has demonstrated that role modeling is one of the most potent ways to influence other people's behavior. Put simply, people often imitate what they see other people doing. The consequence of this is that people can sometimes get others to behave in certain ways through impression management.

The effects of self-presentation on role modeling are perhaps most obvious when parents use self-presentations to instill certain virtues in their children. By presenting themselves to their children in certain ways, parents hope to lead their children to develop similar characteristics. I suspect that most parents try to present themselves to their children in a somewhat idealized fashion—as more honest, considerate, and strong than they really are, for example. If the child imitates the model provided by the parent's self-presentations, he or she will develop socially desirable patterns of behavior.

During military battles, officers may try to promote courageous behavior in their soldiers by purposefully engaging in displays of courage. During the American Civil War, officers sometimes refused to take cover so as to model bravery. For example, afraid that his men would retreat under the Southern artillery barrage during the Battle of Gettysburg, Brigadier General Carl Schurz walked calmly up and down the ranks smoking a cigar. Though effective in impressing the troops, such self-presentations were sometimes deadly. Military leaders have been killed when they purposefully took cover in a leisurely fashion so as not to appear hasty or concerned to their soldiers (Linderman, 1987).

Impression Management and Career Advancement

Whether they admit it or not, many people use impression management to advance their careers and occupational opportunities (Gould & Penley, 1984). In business settings, certain impressions are more likely to result in jobs, promotions, and pay raises than others. Feldman and Klich (1991) described several self-presentational tactics that some people use to pursue career advancement.

Many people believe that merit alone is not sufficient to be hired and promoted, so it is essential to convey an image of being competent, powerful, and effective. Employees try to project such images through the style and color of their clothing, the layout of their offices, and the use of props. Image consultants who advise people on how to create a more promotable image advise everything from using small appointment calendars so that one's schedule always looks busy, to leaving folders labeled "CONFIDENTIAL" on one's desk, to having the *Wall Street Journal* delivered at work instead of at home so everyone sees that one reads it.

One way to give one's employer the impression that one is a valuable employee is to provide evidence from outside sources that one is well-known, connected, or in demand. For example, people can show that they are valuable employees by getting job offers from other organizations. Some managers regularly apply for jobs they don't really want hoping that an offer will improve their image (and salary) in their employer's eyes. Becoming involved in professional or civic organizations is another way to demonstrate one's importance or worth, particularly if one serves in a leadership capacity.

If you have ever prepared a resume, I'm sure you thought a great deal about the self-presentational implications of what you put on it. By selective editing, phrasing one's previous job experiences and responsibilities in certain ways, and by assuring that the resume "looks" right, people can present an image that increases their chances of getting a particular job. Of course, some people are not above actually misrepresenting themselves on a resume. Similar issues involving impression management arise when people interview for jobs.

People interested in career advancement often foster inauthentic relationships with their employers and co-workers. For example, no matter how much they hate the boss, most people act like they like and respect him or her. Other people pretend to agree with their bosses more than they really do (Gould & Penley, 1984). People also work to be seen as a "team player" who will do anything for the good of the organization. Even when a conflict exists between what is good for the organization and what is good for the individual, employees often try to show they will give all for the organization.

Self-presentational maneuvers such as these do, in fact, enhance career opportunities. Gould and Penley (1984) found that employees who used self-presentation as a career strategy—by making supervisors aware of their accomplishments or presenting themselves as a person who "gets things done"—received more frequent salary increases than those who did not.

Opponents of the use of self-presentational strategies in the workplace argue that deliberate self-presentations of these kinds are manipulative and unethical. Advocates insist, however, that because ability is not sufficient to succeed in the business world, employees are entitled to "package" themselves in ways that advance their careers.

Summary

The principle of complementarity states that one person's behavior will elicit a restricted range of behaviors from other people. Given this, people can influence others to behave in certain desired ways by presenting particular impressions of themselves. People adopt supplicating self-presentations when they want others to help or support them and avoid onerous tasks and obligations. Similarly, self-presentations involving physical injury and illness relieve people of certain duties, excuse poor performances, and induce others to take care of them. People sometimes manage their impressions to show that they are either more or less psychologically disturbed than they really are.

Intimidating self-presentations are used to convey a threatening impression, either to increase others' compliance or to retaliate against attacks. Much aggression seems to involve a self-presentational component. People also use self-presentation to seek sexual partners, to lead others to imitate them, and to advance their careers. In each case, conveying certain impressions of oneself often leads to predictable reactions from others.

CHAPTER

8

The Private Self

CHAPTER OUTLINE

The concept of the self has had a checkered history in psychology. In their discussions of human development and social interaction, early psychologists and sociologists—such as William James, Charles Horton Cooley, and George Herbert Mead—placed a great deal of emphasis on the individual's self. However, the concept of the self was virtually banished from mainline behavioral science during the heyday of behaviorism. To many researchers, the idea of a self sounded too much like an invisible soul or essence to have any scientific value whatsoever. For many years, the study of the self was kept alive primarily by humanistic and existential psychologists such as Carl Rogers and Abraham Maslow.

During the past 25 years, however, the self has regained a position of prominence among mainline social, personality, and developmental psychologists. Look at just a sampling of the many psychological constructs currently being investigated that make reference to the self:

self-awareness
self-completion
self-concept
self-consciousness
self-consistency
self-control
self-disclosure
self-efficacy
self-esteem
self-fulfilling prophecy
self-handicapping
self-monitoring
self-perception
self-schema
self-verification
and, of course, self-presentation.

In looking back at the explosion of research on self-processes during the past 25 years, Baumeister (1987) observed that "the self must be ranked with dissonance and attribution as one of the fundamental issues that has concerned social and personality psychologists" (p. 163). Today, many theorists and researchers would argue that a full understanding of human behavior is impossible without reference to the self.

The Self

Part of the self's difficulty as a scientific construct arises because of confusion about what the term "self" actually means. When we say that a person has a self, we simply mean that he or she has the capacity for self-reflection (or what Mead [1934] called "self-reflexivity"). The **self** is the cognitive structure that allows people to think consciously about themselves. Just as we can think about objects and events in the external world, we can also think about ourselves.

This capacity for self-relevant thought is essential for many of the things that we regard as being human. Without a self, we could not consciously plan for the future because planning requires thinking about oneself. Nor could we worry about personal problems that were not immediately present, agonize over past misfortunes, consciously consider alternatives, or think about death. We wouldn't even recognize ourselves in a mirror! Each of these acts requires self-thought.

Research evidence suggests that, with the exception of certain great apes (such as chimpanzees), other animals do not have this ability to consciously contemplate themselves, at least not to the same degree. Even lower monkeys can not learn to recognize their own reflections in a mirror (Gallup, 1977), which is a rather low level type of self-thought. In fact, some have suggested that human beings did not develop this capacity for self-reflection until relatively recently in evolutionary history (Jaynes, 1976).

The fact that most animals, perhaps as well as early humans, have gotten along pretty well without a self shows that a self is not essential for survival. In fact, much if not most of what we do each day is done without self-awareness (that is, without using our self). For example, we perform most routine tasks without any conscious thoughts about ourselves. We can balance our checkbook, jog, make love, and mow the lawn without thinking about ourselves. In actuality, such tasks are often accompanied by self-reflection as we worry about our bank account being overdrawn, think about how slowly we are running, wonder how a sexual partner perceives us, or wish we were napping instead of mowing, but we can easily perform these tasks without thinking consciously about ourselves.

We can perform even more complex behaviors, such as conversing with other people or driving a car, without consciously thinking about ourselves. I'm sure you've had the experience of driving down the highway and suddenly becoming aware that your conscious thoughts had been turned off, yet you had driven successfully and safely for several miles. We can get by reasonably well much of the time without the self, although we do need our selves to do many things that are distinctively human.

You should be able to see that the self is intimately involved in self-presentation. We could not consciously and deliberately try to affect others' impressions of us if we could not think about ourselves, specifically about how we were being regarded by other people. Thus, a person without a self, or one whose self was not currently active, could not consciously impression-manage. For example, young children do not develop the capacity for deliberate self-presentation until their self begins to develop, usually after age two (Buss, 1980; Lewis, Sullivan, Stanger, & Weiss, 1989). Among adults, the fact that alcohol seems to interfere with self-reflection helps to explain why people who are intoxicated don't worry as much about how they're coming across as they normally do (Hull, 1981).

Even though a person must be self-aware to engage in deliberate impression management, certain self-presentational behaviors may be performed so frequently that they become habitual and no longer require self-awareness (Schlenker, 1980). Many manners fall into this category of behavior. Initially, we are motivated to use good manners because other people would form a negative impression of us if we didn't. At first, we must consciously remind ourselves to wipe our feet as we come in the door, say "please" and "thank you," and keep our elbows off the table. However, over time, we begin to practice manners without consciously thinking about them.

A similar example involves daily grooming. Most mornings, I stumble into the bathroom to shave, shower, and dress without any thoughts of impression management. (I may have other self-relevant thoughts, however, such as "I hate getting up," "I feel like hell," or whatever.) Even so, many of these behaviors are self-presentational. When I was little, my parents had to remind me to comb my hair, then later I had to consciously remind myself. Now, I do it pretty much without thinking.

The Self-Concept and Phenomenal Self

The Self-Concept

When people are thinking about themselves (that is, when their self is active), how they present themselves to other people is affected by whatever they are thinking about themselves at the time. The **self-concept** consists of the set of beliefs that a person holds about him- or herself. Just as we have beliefs about things in the external world (including other people), we also have beliefs about ourselves. These include beliefs about our physical bodies (our appearance, health, level of fitness, and so on), our personal characteristics (such as our personality, intelligence, and abilities), our social relationships (including our relationships with family members, friends, co-workers, and even enemies), the roles we play (student, accountant, teacher, salesperson, or whatever), the beliefs we consciously hold (such as our religious convictions, attitudes, and philosophy of life), our personal histories, and even our possessions (we recognize that we own certain books, cars, clothing, stereo equipment, and so on).

The self-concept has been compared to a person's "theory" about what he or she is like (Epstein, 1973). Like a theory, the self-concept not only contains facts that we believe are true about ourselves but also untested hypotheses. Your assumptions about how you would respond in new situations are essentially hypotheses that you have derived from the theory you hold about yourself.

The self-concept is also like a theory in the sense that people use it to interpret their experiences. Two scientists who hold different theoretical orientations may interpret the same experimental observation in two very different ways. Similarly, two people with different self-theories may interpret the same event differently. If your self-theory (i.e., your self-concept) says you are intelligent, you may attribute a poor test grade to the teacher's unfairness or to the fact you didn't study enough. On the other hand, if your self-theory says that you have the intelligence of a baboon, you might interpret a poor test score as a reflection on your intelligence.

The Phenomenal Self

People's self-concepts are very complex. Thus, when we are thinking about who we are and what we are like, we can be consciously aware of only a very small portion of the self-concept at a particular time. Think how long it would take for you to write down every fact and assumption about yourself that you could. The portion of one's self-beliefs that is present in conscious awareness at any particular time is called the **phenomenal self** (Rhodewalt, 1986). The phenomenal self includes both contents of the self-concept that the person is thinking about at the time ("I'm not a very interesting person.") as well as thoughts about momentary states ("Boy, am I tired.").

The self-concept influences people's behavior primarily through the phenomenal self. That is, beliefs about oneself that are stored in memory have little direct effect on behavior until the person thinks about them. Much research has shown that people tend to behave consistently with their internal attitudes, morals, and self-concepts only when they are thinking about themselves (and the phenomenal self is activated) (Buss, 1980; Duval & Wicklund, 1972). In contrast, when people are blocked from thinking about themselves, they often behave very uncharacteristically (Diener, 1980).

What this means is that people's self-presentations will be affected by their self-concepts to the extent that they are consciously self-aware. Furthermore, the images they convey to other people are likely to be affected by whatever is in the phenomenal self at a given time. The parts of oneself that are not part of the phenomenal self will not be represented in one's self-presentations to others.

The Self in Self-Presentation

As I noted earlier, some people have viewed self-presentation as inherently deceptive. In fact, Buss and Briggs (1984) criticized impression management explanations of behavior because they argued that such models emphasize "pretense" in which people "portray a character different from themselves" (p. 1322). Similarly, Bednar et al. (1989) equated impression management with "pretending" to be what others want us to be.

Without denying that people sometimes present public images that are inconsistent with how they see themselves (that is, images that are inconsistent with their self-concept and phenomenal self), their self-presentations are as likely to be accurate and honest as they are to be deceptive and duplicitous (Schlenker, 1980; Tetlock & Manstead, 1985). In fact, they often consciously and deliberately manage their impressions so that other people will see them *as they see themselves* (Gergen, 1968; Jones & Pittman, 1982; Schlenker & Weigold, 1992). This point may strike you as odd: Why would people need to *try* to appear to be someone or something that they, in fact, actually are?

The primary reason is that other people often can not infer much about us simply from observing our behavior. Much of the time, our behavior is so constrained by the roles we play and by the norms of the situation that it reveals little personal information about us. As a result, if we want others to know something about us, we sometimes must deliberately behave in ways that disclose information about our personalities, abilities, attitudes, interests, personal histories, moods, intentions, reactions, or whatever. Furthermore, even when our behavior could potentially convey something about us to others, we may use self-presentation to increase the "legibility" of our reactions (DePaulo, 1992). For example, people sometimes exaggerate their emotional expressions to assure that others accurately decipher what they are feeling. Because people's expressions are often ambiguous, they sometimes engage in impression management to be sure that others are interpreting their reactions correctly.

A third reason that we sometimes must be tactical to convey accurate impressions is that we do not have unlimited time to disclose information about ourselves. As a result, we must select which information we will emphasize about ourselves in a particular social context. Thus, self-presentation often involves selectively presenting information about oneself that is essentially true (Schlenker & Weigold, 1992).

One's self-concept also has another, less direct effect on self-presentation. The self-concept provides a subjective indicator of the likelihood that we will be able to successfully project a particular image. In most cases, we are more likely to successfully convey impressions that are consistent with our self-concepts than impressions that are not consistent with our self-concepts. I'm more likely to think I can convey the impression of being athletic if I think I am, in fact, athletic than if I think I'm not athletic. Because failing to successfully present a particular image is often worse than not trying in the first place, believing that one lacks the ability to make a particular impression may deter people from trying to do so.

Self-Esteem

Few psychological constructs have spread so widely into everyday usage as self-esteem. **Self-esteem** refers to a person's evaluation of him- or herself. Coopersmith (1967) defined self-esteem as "the evaluation that the individual makes and customarily maintains with regard to himself; it expresses an attitude of approval or disapproval and indicates the extent to which the individual believes himself to be capable, significant, successful and worthy." Whereas the self-concept involves beliefs or thoughts about oneself, self-esteem refers to the person's evaluations and feelings about those beliefs. Two people with the same self-concept may have different self-esteem; one C student may feel very good about being a C student, whereas another C student's self-esteem may be deflated by that fact.

Traditionally, researchers interested in self-esteem have focused on how people generally tend to feel about themselves. People show some degree of consistency in how they evaluate themselves across different situations and over time. Some people tend to have relatively high self-esteem, whereas others' self-esteem tends to be lower. A person's general, characteristic level of self-esteem is called **trait self-esteem.**

You should be aware that the term "low" self-esteem is really a misnomer. Very few people can be accurately described as having truly low self-esteem (Tice, 1993). When asked to rate themselves, most people rate themselves as "neutral" or better. So-called "low self-esteem" people are really "moderate" in how they evaluate themselves, and only a few severely disturbed people truly see themselves as generally undesirable. Thus, keep in mind that the terms "low self-esteem" and "high self-esteem" should be viewed as relative rather than absolute.

Even though people have a characteristic level of trait self-esteem, their evaluations of themselves also fluctuate as they go from one situation to another. A student may experience low self-esteem in gym class, for example, but feel very good about herself in algebra class. A person's level of self-esteem in a particular situation at a particular time is called **state self-esteem.**

The relationship between self-esteem and self-presentation has been studied in terms of both trait self-esteem and state self-esteem. Self-esteem appears to be related to self-presentation in two discrete ways: (a) low and high self-esteem people have different self-presentational motives, and (b) they differ in their self-presentational confidence.

Impression Motivation

People have a basic need to maintain their self-esteem—that is, to evaluate themselves positively and to feel good about themselves (Brown, 1993; Leary & Downs, in press; Steele, 1988). As a result, people do a great many things to maintain and enhance their self-esteem, some of which involve self-presentation.

State Self-Esteem and Self-Presentation

One way in which people maintain their self-esteem is to obtain approval from others. Because their feelings of worth are based partly on others' evaluations of them (Cooley, 1902; Shrauger & Schoeneman, 1979), people may seek others' approval as a way of increasing low self-esteem and/or maintaining high self-esteem. Presenting particular desirable impressions is one way of gaining approval (Jellison & Gentry, 1978), so we might expect that people who want to increase self-esteem are more motivated to impression-manage than those who do not have a need to increase self-esteem.

An experiment by Schneider (1969) showed this to be the case. In his study, subjects took a test of what they thought was an important ability, then received low scores, high scores, or no scores on the test. Presumably, subjects who received low scores suffered a decrease in state self-esteem. Subjects were then interviewed by an interviewer. Half of the subjects thought the interviewer would reveal his evaluation to them, whereas the others were told that they would not learn how the interviewer evaluated them. As Schneider predicted, subjects who received low scores on the initial test and who expected feedback from the interviewer presented themselves more positively than subjects who received low scores but did not expect feedback. Because their self-presentations would help enhance their damaged self-esteem only if they received the interviewer's evaluation, subjects self-enhanced only in that condition. Furthermore, subjects who received low test scores and expected feedback from the interviewer conveyed more positive impressions than those who received high scores and expected feedback, presumably because they were more highly motivated to impression-manage.

Trait Self-Esteem and Self-Presentation

Schneider's study focused on the effects of transient changes in state self-esteem that were produced by receiving low or high test scores. As we noted, people can also be classified as having generally high or low trait self-esteem. Who do you think is most likely to try to convey positive impressions of themselves—people with high self-esteem or people with (relatively) low self-esteem (which, as I noted, is usually not low, but moderate)? This is a more difficult question than it may first appear.

Based on Schneider's (1969) study, we might expect that persons with low trait self-esteem impression-manage more readily than those with high trait self-esteem. This is because people with lower self-esteem presumably are more motivated to receive positive evaluations from others that would raise their self-esteem. Because making good impressions is one way to enhance others' evaluations, low self-esteem people should be more motivated to impression-manage than highs, who don't need to impression-manage to increase self-esteem.

However, this tendency could be counteracted by the fact that people often want other people to see them as they see themselves. Research suggests that people sometimes want self-verifying feedback from others—feedback that is consistent with how they see themselves. Receiving feedback that is discrepant from one's self-concept can be unsettling because it implies that the person does not really know him- or herself very well. As surprising as it may seem, research shows that people do attempt to verify their self-views, even if those views are negative (Swann, 1983, 1987). If self-presentation serves self-verification motives, people with high self-esteem should work harder to make positive impressions on others than people with low self-esteem, who should prefer that others not perceive them as favorably. Thus, we have good reason to predict that low self-esteem people are more motivated to present themselves positively than highs (because they need approval more badly), and we have good reason to predict that low self-esteem people are less motivated to present themselves positively than highs (because they want to receive self-verifying feedback).

The apparent conflict between these two positions can be resolved in two ways. First, people apparently possess *both* the motive to self-enhance and the motive to self-verify. Swann, Pelham, and Krull (1989) showed that people prefer positive feedback over negative feedback regardless of their level of self-esteem. However, when dealing only with attributes on which they regard themselves unfavorably, people prefer to receive negative feedback. Put differently, people usually prefer to receive positive feedback, but there are good reasons to accurately perceive one's shortcomings (Swann, Griffin, Predmore, & Gaines, 1987).

A second resolution to this question was offered by Baumeister, Tice, and Hutton (1989). They suggested that both low and high self-esteem people are motivated to impression-manage, but the nature of their motivations differ. Specifically, people with high self-esteem are primarily motivated to make favorable impressions (acquisitive self-presentation), whereas people with low self-esteem are motivated to avoid making unfavorable impressions (protective self-presentation) (Arkin, 1981; Tice, 1992). Whereas high self-esteem people are motivated to succeed to look good, low self-esteem people are motivated to avoid failure so they won't look bad. As Baumeister et al. (1989) put it, low self-esteem "entails a self-presentational orientation based on protecting oneself from failure, embarrassment, rejection, and humiliation, whereas high self-esteem entails a self-presentational orientation based on enhancing one's prestige and reputation for competence" (p. 553). Both low and high self-esteem people want to feel good about themselves and to have others regard them as positively as possible. But their approach to these goals is different.

Baumeister et al. (1989) suggested that scores on standard measures of trait self-esteem more directly measure self-presentation than the person's own self-evaluations per se. After all, the way that people score high on self-esteem scales is by indicating that they possess desirable attributes or otherwise feel positively about themselves. High scores reflect highly positive self-presentations on the scale.

As we noted above, people who are labeled "low self-esteem" rarely have low self-esteem at all but score toward the middle range of self-esteem scores. From a self-presentational standpoint this makes sense. A person who is concerned with not making a bad impression will not want to endorse either positive *or* negative attributes. Endorsing positive attributes is risky because the person may be seen as braggardly or will later fail to live up to his or her claims. Endorsing negative attributes automatically makes a bad impression. As a result, people concerned about failure and embarrassment would be expected to describe themselves in an average, middle of the road, noncommittal manner—not too good, not too bad—which is precisely what people with so-called low self-esteem do.

Self-Presentational Confidence

Self-esteem may be related to self-presentation in yet another way. To the extent that self-esteem is associated with self-confidence, a person's self-esteem may affect whether he or she tries to execute certain self-presentational behaviors, particularly those that entail some degree of social risk. People with high self-esteem are more willing to present positive impressions of themselves because they are confident that they can successfully sustain positive images in the future. Their favorable self-view leads them to expect approval and respect from others. People with low self-esteem, in contrast, may lack confidence that they can maintain positive images in others' eyes. Instead of respect, they may expect disinterest or disapproval (Baumeister, 1982b).

Persons high in self-esteem take greater self-presentational risks than those low in self-esteem. Schlenker, Weigold, and Hallam (1990) found that high self-esteem persons became more self-aggrandizing as social evaluative pressures increased; low self-esteem persons became more self-presentationally cautious under such circumstances. Baumeister (1982b) found that persons high in self-esteem were more likely than lows to try to counteract negative information that other people had about them. In contrast, persons with low self-esteem appeared reluctant to try to disconfirm others' preexisting impressions. Presumably, high self-esteem people are more confident that they can successfully refute others' negative impressions.

The Imposter Phenomenon

Many seemingly successful people go through life seeing themselves as imposters. Although they receive objective, external evidence that they are successful and know that other people perceive them as intelligent and talented, **imposters** believe that their successes are largely accidental and that, in time, others will learn of their true ineptitude (Clance, 1985). From a self-presentational standpoint, imposters believe that they have unwittingly constructed a highly favorable public image that they will be unable to maintain in the future. As a result, they live in fear of situations that might expose their "true selves" to other people.

Not surprisingly, imposters worry more about being evaluated than nonimposters. For example, university students who scored high on the Imposter Phenomenon Scale were more anxious about exams in their courses than students who scored low on the scale even though the two groups of students did not differ in how well they actually did on the exams. Imposters also felt worse and suffered greater loss of self-esteem if they did poorly on their exams (Cozzarelli & Major, 1990).

Desired and Undesired Selves

When you think about yourself, I suspect that you think as much about the kind of person you want to be as about the kind of person you are. You may think about being a better student, being a thinner person, having more money, or whatever. We all have ideas about the kinds of people we would like to be, as well as of the kinds of people we do not want to be. These ideas of what we would and would not want to become are called our **desired and undesired selves** (Markus & Nurius, 1986; Ogilvie, 1987).

Psychologists have often used the term "ideal self" to refer to this representation or idea of how one would like to be. However, the term "ideal self" is misleading for our purposes because it suggests that people strive to achieve some lofty, if not unreachable, state of being. In reality, most of us are more reasonable than to strive for our "ideal" self. For this reason, I prefer to think in terms of desired and undesired, rather than ideal selves.

Just as impression management is affected by people's beliefs about the kinds of people they are (i.e., their self-concepts and phenomenal self), it is also affected by their perceptions of the kinds of people they want to be. Even when they are trying to be accurate, people's self-presentations tend to lean in the direction of their desired selves and away from their undesired selves (Leary & Kowalski, 1990; Schlenker, 1985).

People's desired and undesired selves affect their self-presentations in at least two ways. First, people's desired and undesired selves presumably reflect their own values. They want to be a certain kind of person because they value certain characteristics. If I want to be patient, it's because I place a high value on patience. When people value certain characteristics, they usually want to convey to others that they possess those characteristics. Thus, if I value patience, I will want others to see me as a patient person and will manage my impressions to convey an image of patience. As impatient as I may feel with my 5-year-old in the mall, I will not want to *look* impatient to other people.

Second, impression management can be used to actually help the person move closer to his or her desired self (Baumeister, 1982a; Tedeschi & Norman, 1985). When people successfully present a particular image of themselves to others, they sometimes begin to internalize that image. If I act patient often enough, I may actually become more patient. Research shows that people who are induced to describe themselves as extraverted, not only later rate themselves as more extraverted, but actually behave in a more outgoing fashion in subsequent interactions (Fazio, Effrein, & Falender, 1981; Tice, 1992)! Because self-presentations can become self-fulfilling, people who want to move toward their desired selves or away from their undesired selves may present public images that approximate their desired selves (Pin & Turndorf, 1990). We'll return to how self-presentations become internalized later in this chapter.

PRINCIPLE:

When people are self-aware and not motivated to deceive others, their self-presentations are influenced by their phenomenal self (and, thus, self-concept), self-esteem, and desired and undesired selves.

Self-Presentational Dilemmas

The ideal social encounter, from an individual's self-presentational perspective, is one in which all factors point the person toward constructing the same image. When the person's self-concept and desired self, the roles and norms operating in the immediate situation, the target's values, and the person's existing image in others' eyes all converge toward the same image, the person's self-presentational task is easy. Not only is the choice of an appropriate image easy, but the person should feel fairly confident that he or she can convey the desired image.

A problem arises, however, when two or more of these factors point to different impression-management tactics, particularly if the desired images are mutually exclusive. Although any pair of factors may collide, our interest here is in dilemmas that involve a conflict between the person's private self (such as one's self-concept or desired/undesired self) and features of the social context (such as norms, roles, the target's values, or others' perceptions of the individual).

One of the most common and personally troubling self-presentational dilemmas occurs when the image that would have the desired effect on a target is discrepant from the person's own self-concept. As we saw in Chapter 5, people often tailor their impressions to the target's values. But when an individual recognizes that he or she does not possess attributes that the target values, or possesses qualities that the target will view negatively, a self-presentational dilemma occurs.

Everyday life is replete with examples of such dilemmas: a student disagrees with the grouchy teacher (Should she express her true opinion or falsely agree?); a sports fan finds that her date hates sports (Should she feign less interest in sports than she feels?); the job interviewer asks about the applicant's familiarity with computers (Should the applicant express more confidence about his computer ability than he really feels?); the sexual egalitarian's co-workers start telling sexist jokes (Should he take a stand, remain silent, or join in?). In each case, an entirely truthful self-presentation (one that is consistent with the person's self-concept) would likely result in a less positive impression and in less favorable social or material outcomes for the presenter than a presentation that is tailored toward the targets' values. Yet, most of us are so socialized to be truthful that we have difficulty telling bold-faced lies about ourselves. So what do we do?

Authentic, Deceptive, and Exclusionary Self-Presentation

People who find themselves in such dilemmas tend to respond in one of three ways that I call authentic, deceptive, and exclusionary/evasive self-presentation.

Authentic Self-Presentation

First, people may respond in a principled or authentic fashion, presenting themselves consistently with their private self-images regardless of what the target values. In some cases, people are more or less forced to be authentic because others have information that would discredit inauthentic impressions (Schlenker, 1975). At other times, people in a self-presentational dilemma present authentic images as a matter of principle.

Authentic self-presentations that conflict with others' values do not always pose a liability. People who stand up for their beliefs in the face of social pressure are sometimes liked better than those who conform to others' values (Braver, Linder, Corwin, & Cialdini, 1977), but the conditions under which this effect is most likely to occur have not been investigated.

Research suggests that, if people realize that a target will respond unfavorably to certain information about them, they may be better off disclosing this information early rather than later in the interaction. In two studies, subjects rated others who revealed negative information about themselves (that they were expelled from school or got a girlfriend pregnant) more positively if they introduced this information early rather than later in the encounter (Archer & Burleson, 1980; Jones & Gordon, 1972). Presumably, people perceive those who withhold such information as shady or dishonest.

Deceptive Self-Presentation

A second resolution to self-presentational dilemmas is outright self-presentational deception or fabrication. People may project a public image that they know is inconsistent with how they "really" are but conforms to the target's values. Such dissimulation ranges from small exaggerations to absolute lies.

Three factors seem to determine the degree to which people stretch their self-presentations beyond the bounds of truthfulness. The first involves the person's view of the seriousness of the deception. People find it easier to tell white self-presentational lies that have no obvious consequences for others than to misrepresent their identities in ways that harm other people. Also, some people regard lying as a more serious offense than others.

Second, people are more likely to make false claims the less likely others are to detect the deception (Baumeister & Jones, 1978; Schlenker, 1975; Tesser & Moore, 1986). Third, the perceived incentive of self-presentational deceit has an effect. People will dissimulate more readily, the more they stand to gain (Tesser & Moore, 1986).

Of course, people differ in their willingness to self-presentationally fabricate—to present images of themselves they know are not true. Two general classes of variables underlie the tendency to fabricate—insecurity and manipulativeness. One reason people present false images of themselves is that they think that others will ridicule or reject them if they know how they "really are." People with low self-esteem consider themselves deficient in certain respects and may try to hide their true selves and convey what they view as more acceptable impressions. Persons who think more highly of themselves, in contrast, do not need to create a false impression. As a result, they proudly let others see the "real" them without lying about their personal characteristics or feelings (Elliott, 1982).

People who have a manipulative streak are also more willing to fabricate self-presentations. Such persons are often called **Machiavellian** because they espouse the philosophies of the Florentine philosopher and statesman, Niccolo Machiavelli (1469–1527). In *The Prince,* Machiavelli advocated that political leaders use guile and deceit to seize and maintain power. According to Machiavelli, the effective leader must use impression management to hide his unscrupulous actions and to appear to be acting in the state's best interests. As he observed, "All men will see what you seem to be; only a few will know what you are . . ." (Machiavelli, 1513/1966, p. 63). Machiavelli did not advocate lying as a matter of course, but only when telling the truth would not serve one's interests adequately.

In the 1960s, researchers began to study people who endorse Machiavelli's philosophy, even developing a scale to measure a person's tendency to be Machiavellian. The Machiavellianism Scale consists of statements taken directly from Machiavelli's writings as well as others made up by researchers (Christie & Geis, 1970). Some sample statements endorsed by persons high in Machiavellianism include:

- Never tell anyone the real reason you did something unless it is useful to do so.
- The best way to handle people is to tell them what they want to hear.
- It is wise to flatter important people.
- Anyone who completely trusts anyone else is asking for trouble.

People who score high in Machiavellianism tend to live in calculated, strategic manners. They are more likely to lie and cheat when such behaviors will help them achieve their goals (although they are no more devious in general). Christie and Geis observed that Machiavellians have a "utilitarian rather than a moral view of their interactions with others" (1970, p. 3).

As you would expect, Machiavellians are more likely than non-Machiavellians to use fabricated self-presentations when it is in the best interests to do so. For example, they can appear to be more deferential and ingratiating when appearing that way will help them achieve their goals (Blumstein, 1973). They also are more selective in the amount and type of information they disclose about themselves depending on the social situation (Dingler-Duhon & Brown, 1987; Jones, Nickel, & Schmidt, 1979). Contrary to what you might think, Machiavellians do not lack morals, however. Rather, they endorse an unconventional ethical system that can best be described by the oxymoron "absolute relativism." That it, they are absolutely steadfast in their belief that there are no absolute moral laws that apply in all situations (Leary, Knight, & Barnes, 1986).

In one sense, all of this deviousness pays off for the Machiavellian person. Studies have shown that "high Machs" are more effective in interpersonal settings. They are better at negotiating and bargaining than the average person (Christie & Geis, 1970) and are better able to stand up against social pressure (Geis & Christie, 1970). They are more successful when debating emotional topics (partly because they are better at keeping their cool; Geis, Weinheimer, & Berger, 1970) and are better at lying without being detected (Exline, Thibaut, Hickey, & Gumbert, 1970; Geis & Moon, 1981). Observers in one study could not differentiate truthful from lying high Machs but could tell when low Machs were lying (Geis & Moon, 1981). In a role-playing study, subjects who scored high in Machiavellianism playing the part of courtroom lawyers were more successful in leading witnesses to say things in support of their clients; furthermore, judges allocated less blame to the clients of high than low Mach "lawyers" (Sheppard & Vidmar, 1980).

In a study of Machiavellianism in children, Machiavellian 10-year-olds were more successful at getting other children to eat crackers that had been soaked in bitter tasting quinine than other kids (Braginsky,

1970). Despite the fact that they lied more to get the other kids to eat the crackers, adult observers rated the Machiavellian children as more honest and innocent than the non-Machiavellian children!

Exclusionary and Evasive Self-Presentation

In addition to authentic and deceptive self-presentation, a third, less obvious tactic is also commonly used to resolve self-presentational dilemmas. When people do not think that accurate self-presentations on a certain dimension will be well-received, they may try to withhold, as much as possible, information that is relevant to that dimension. This self-presentation tactic involves the attempt to exclude or edit particular self-relevant information from the images one conveys (**exclusionary self-presentation**) or to behave in ways that evade the necessity of ever broaching the issue (**evasive self-presentation**).

Exclusionary and evasive forms of self-presentation may be the preferred ways of dealing with self-presentational conflicts between the private self and external contingencies. Rather than boldly taking the authentic high road or pragmatically stooping to blatant deception, people often try to skirt the issue, withholding information about themselves that might undermine the impression they desire to create.

My students and I studied the use of exclusionary tactics in two experiments. In the first (Lamphere & Leary, 1988), respondents who viewed themselves as either extraverted or introverted learned that a subject with whom they would interact either preferred people who were extraverted or preferred people who were introverted. Thus, some subjects faced a self-presentational dilemma that pitted their private self-concepts against the target's values. Subjects then rated themselves on cards that would ostensibly be shown to their partners. To allow subjects the option of *not* mentioning their standing on the introvert-extravert dimension, subjects were told they could then *choose* which of the cards they wanted to show their partners.

Not surprisingly, self-perceived extraverts presented themselves as more extraverted than self-perceived introverts, which reflects the effects of the self-concept on their self-presentations. Furthermore, subjects presented themselves as more extraverted to targets who ostensibly preferred extraverts than to targets who preferred introverts, thereby reflecting the influence of the target's values.

Most interesting, however, analysis of the cards subjects elected not to show their partners showed that subjects used an exclusionary tactic to make the desired impression. When their targets preferred introverts, extraverts withheld more cards that would have shown them to be extraverted than when the target preferred extraverts. Furthermore, subjects showed more cards overall when they thought they were the kind of person the target liked. Thus, subjects presented less information about themselves when their self-concepts were inconsistent with the target's values.

In a second experiment (Spivey & Leary, 1990), subjects who had rated themselves as particularly lighthearted learned that their conversation partner preferred people who were serious, preferred people who were jovial, or did not learn about the target's preference. Subjects then described themselves to the target on a questionnaire that included items that were relevant and not relevant to the dimension of joviality-seriousness. To allow subjects the option of engaging in exclusionary self-presentation, subjects were told that they could leave items blank if they wished.

Evidence of exclusionary self-presentation was shown by the fact that, when their self-conceptions were inconsistent with the target's preferences, subjects who scored high in fear of negative evaluation rated themselves on fewer adjectives related to joviality. The self-presentations of low fear of negative evaluation subjects were unaffected by partner preference presumably because these subjects were relatively unconcerned with others' evaluations of them.

That subjects adjusted their self-presentations in these two studies to match characteristics valued by the target is neither surprising nor novel. As we saw in Chapter 5, many studies have demonstrated that self-presentational behaviors are affected by targets' values. However, these two studies provided a more detailed analysis of the tactics people use to balance the pressure to convey accurate impressions (i.e., those consistent with the self-concept) against targets' preferences. Rather than attempting to project an image that was blatantly inconsistent with their self-views, subjects withheld information that was inconsistent with the impression they wanted the target to have of them. Subjects were less willing to convey information about themselves when their self-concepts were different from the kinds of people the target ostensibly liked. This exclusionary tactic allows individuals to present desired impressions of themselves without resorting to lying.

One special type of exclusionary self-presentation involves the personal *secret*. Most of us have secrets that we keep from most, if not all, other people because the information might unfavorably affect how they would perceive us. People conceal information about behavioral indiscretions (e.g., the time they shoplifted or cheated on tests), traumatic events (e.g., they were an incest or rape victim), and personal failures (e.g., they flunked out of college or were fired from jobs). Although we do not always hide our secrets for self-presentational reasons (parents may hide financial difficulties from their children to keep the children from worrying, for example), secrets may often be considered examples of exclusionary self-presentation.

Keeping Secrets Can Be Hazardous to Your Health

James Pennebaker and his colleagues have demonstrated that keeping personal secrets can, over time, be hazardous to a person's health. For example, one study found that people who suffered a traumatic event early in life and who never disclosed it to anyone were much more likely to experience physical illness and psychological distress in early adulthood than people who had discussed their traumas with others. They also showed that widows and widowers who discussed their spouse's deaths with others were more healthy than those who didn't (Pennebaker, 1990).

Pennebaker's research also showed that, when people were given the opportunity to express their deepest thoughts and feelings about a personal trauma, they subsequently became healthier. Not only did they visit the doctor less frequently, but analyses of blood samples showed that their immune function actually improved! Apparently, keeping personal secrets can generate a great deal of stress.

Unfortunately, although people often feel better after revealing their personal secrets, such disclosures may sometimes have negative interpersonal consequences. In many cases, we may be advised *not* to reveal certain things about ourselves. Fortunately, Pennebaker (1990) showed that simply expressing traumatic events in writing can reduce stress and improve health even if no one else ever learns about them.

Effects of Self-Presentation on the Self

We have been talking in this chapter about the effects of the self on the kinds of impressions people try to make. Before leaving our discussion of the self, we must acknowledge that, conversely, the process of self-presenting can cause changes in the self-concept.

Internalization

When people behave in a particular way, their self-concepts sometimes change in line with their behavior. Simply inducing people to describe or present themselves in particular ways can cause their views of themselves to change. For example, subjects who are induced to present positive images of themselves later rate themselves more positively than subjects who are induced to present less favorable impressions (Gergen, 1965; Jones et al., 1981; Kowalski & Leary, 1990; Rhodewalt & Agustsdottir, 1986). Similarly, subjects who are induced to respond in an introverted fashion subsequently rate themselves as being more introverted than subjects who are induced to respond like an extravert (Fazio et al., 1981; Tice, 1992), and subjects induced to describe themselves as sociable subsequently both rate themselves as more sociable and behave more sociably in a subsequent interaction (Dlugolecki & Schlenker, 1985).

When people's self-concepts change in response to their overt behavior, we say that they have *internalized* their self-presentations. At least three different processes may underlie internalization. First, people sometimes learn something new about themselves after seeing how they respond in certain situations. The central premise of self-perception theory (Bem, 1972) is that people infer their personal characteristics (such as their attitudes and personalities) from observing their own behavior and the conditions under which it occurs. After presenting themselves in a particular way, people may conclude that they *are* the way they presented themselves.

Furthermore, behaving in a certain way can lead people to think about aspects of themselves they hadn't thought about before (Jones et al., 1981). Behaving in a certain way can lead them to scan their self-concept in a biased fashion that causes them to think about information that is consistent with their self-presentation.

Third, when people present a new image of themselves—one that is not currently part of their self-concept—they may receive affirming feedback from other people (signification). When starting a new job, many people experience a sense of unreality in which they feel like they are just playing a part. They are presenting the image of being a bank manager, professor, police officer, or whatever, but don't really *feel* like one yet. However, as other people begin to respond to the person's new image, the new identity becomes internalized.

Determinants of Internalization

Of course, our self-concepts do not change each time we present a different image of ourselves to other people. Certain conditions increase the likelihood that a person will internalize his or her self-presentations.

Choice

People are more likely to internalize a particular self-presentation when they feel they had a high degree of choice in presenting that image (Schlenker, 1986). In part, this is because people are less likely to infer their own personal characteristics from their behavior when they know they were "forced" to behave in a particular way (Bem, 1972). People are likely to internalize a self-presentation if they think that their behavior was truly reflective of who they are, which is unlikely if the person had little choice (Schlenker, 1986).

Discrepancy from Self-Concept

A single self-presentation will not dramatically affect a person's self-concept if that presentation is highly discrepant from how the person has always seen him- or herself. Put differently, the presented image must be within the person's "latitude of acceptance"—among those images that *could* be true at least under some circumstances (Rhodewalt & Agustsdottir, 1986). This may be the reason that people are more likely to internalize positive self-presentations than negative ones (McKillop, Berzonsky, & Schlenker, 1992). People are more likely to view themselves neutrally or positively than negatively (Baumeister et al., 1989).

One implication of this is that people are more likely to internalize their self-presentations when they are *uncertain* of how they stand on relevant characteristics. The less certain one's self-concept, the more open it is to change from all sources, including one's own behavior. People with low self-esteem, for example, seem to be less certain of who they are (Campbell, 1990). As a result, their self-concepts change more after they present themselves in particular ways than do the self-concepts of high self-esteem people (Kowalski & Leary, 1990).

Publicness

People are also more likely to internalize their self-descriptions if their descriptions are public rather than private. Dianne Tice (1992) asked subjects to portray themselves as either emotionally stable or as emotionally responsive. Furthermore, some subjects engaged in these emotional self-presentations in front of another person, whereas other subjects did so anonymously. When later asked to rate their "true selves" on a measure of emotionality, subjects who presented themselves to other people showed greater evidence of internalizing their self-presentations.

In a second study, Tice (1992) asked subjects to portray themselves as either introverted or as extraverted. Subjects described themselves either as another person watched or while they were alone. Again, subjects' ratings of their "true selves" were more congruent with their self-presentations in the public than private condition. More surprisingly, when they later interacted with a confederate, subjects who had described themselves as extraverted actually *behaved* in a more extraverted fashion by sitting closer to the confederate and talking more. Furthermore, this effect was stronger for public than private self-presentations.

The results of these studies show that public self-presentations are more likely to lead to changes in the self-concept than the same behaviors performed in private. In fact, Tice (1992) questioned whether private behavior leads to changes in the self at all. Some degree of real or imagined observation by others may be necessary for producing internalization (see, however, McKillop et al., 1992).

Affirmation from Others

Finally, people are more likely to internalize self-presentations when others respond to those presentations in approving or affirming ways (Gergen, 1965; Schlenker, 1986; Schlenker & Weigold, 1992; Upshaw & Yates, 1968). If I present myself as stoic and others seem to accept my self-presentations at face value, I'm more likely to conclude that I *really am* stoic.

Dysfunctional Effects of Self-Presentation on the Self

The effects of self-presentation on self-concept change may create problems when people have, for one reason or another, presented an undesirable image of themselves. For example, if people convey to others that they are weak, dependent, helpless, depressed, or unstable, they may actually internalize these kinds of self-presentations, begin to see themselves as having a problem, and create a cycle of maladaptive behavior. People who are asked to present themselves in a depressed manner actually become more depressed than people who present themselves in an undepressed manner (Kelly, McKillop, & Neimeyer, 1991). They also recall more depressive episodes from their past, which leads to further depression!

Furthermore, consider what happens when people present themselves unfavorably and other people seem to accept their negative self-presentations at face-value. On one hand, the person who has successfully conveyed an undesirable image and reaped the social benefits may feel good about having accomplished his or her social goals. But on the other hand, successfully presenting oneself negatively may lead a person to believe he or she really possesses the undesirable attributes (Jones, Brenner, & Knight, 1990).

Even favorable self-presentations can have undesirable effects on a person's self-concept. When people present what they realize are unrealistically favorable images of themselves, they are less likely to believe the favorable feedback they receive from others (Bednar, Wells, & Peterson, 1989). Even if other people really do like and accept them, they may think that others' reactions are based on a sham. For this reason, people sometimes do not believe the authentic social feedback they receive from other people. This may be partly responsible for why some people feel like imposters. Knowing that they tactically presented positive impressions of themselves, they may wonder whether others are responding to who they are or to who they appear to be.

Summary

The self is the cognitive structure that is responsible for self-related thought. Without a self, people could not think consciously about themselves and could not engage in deliberate self-presentation. People's self-presentations are affected by three aspects of the private self, specifically their self-concept, self-esteem, and desired and undesired selves.

People generally present images of themselves that are consistent with their self-concepts. In most instances, people want others to see them as they really are. Furthermore, people avoid conveying impressions that are inconsistent with their self-concepts because they feel unable to sustain false impressions over time. Although people with low and high self-esteem are equally concerned with their social images, their approach to self-presentation differs. High self-esteem people usually try to convey positive impressions of themselves, whereas low self-esteem people try to avoid making bad impressions. Self-presentations are also affected by people's desired and undesired selves. People also usually try to present images that are consistent with their ideal selves.

When people think the impressions that will best meet their goals in a particular situation are inconsistent with their private selves, they experience a self-presentational dilemma. When facing a self-presentational dilemma, people may opt to be authentic, to convey deceptive impressions, or to engage in self-presentational evasion or exclusion. People who score high in Machiavellianism are more likely to fabricate their self-presentations than people who score low.

The impressions people try to make can affect how they see themselves. People are most likely to internalize their self-presentations when they had a great deal of choice in presenting the image; it was not highly discrepant from their self-concept; the self-description was public; and they received affirming feedback from other people.

CHAPTER

9

Worrying about Impressions

CHAPTER OUTLINE

People have many good reasons to be concerned with what others think of them. Their social lives, friendships, romantic relationships, job success, self-esteem, and mood are all affected by how they are perceived and evaluated by other people. Given the consequences, people can not afford to ignore how they are regarded by others. At the same time, however, being concerned about others' impressions can have serious drawbacks. Excessive self-presentational concerns can make people miserable, interfere with their social lives, and lead them to behave in ways that are not always in their best interests. In this final chapter, we examine the causes and consequences of people's self-presentational worries.

Self-Presentation and Social Anxiety

People are anxious about many things ranging from going to the dentist to walking down a dark street at night to thinking about dying. Interestingly, studies show that the most common causes of anxiety involve not threats to a person's health or physical well-being but difficult social situations. People often become nervous when they talk to people in positions of authority (a boss or teacher, for example), deal with potential romantic partners, go to parties where they don't know many people, or give speeches in front of a large audience. In fact, one national survey showed that more people are afraid of speaking in front of large groups than of any other single stimulus (Bruskin Associates, 1973). Feelings of anxiety in social situations are so common that most people don't even stop to ask themselves the intriguing question, "What is so worrisome about social encounters that people often become nervous before and during them?"

One morning in 1978, I happened to see a television appearance by Philip Zimbardo, a noted social psychologist, who was being interviewed about a book he had written on shyness. I was intrigued by the interview because, although shyness has many implications for interpersonal behavior, behavioral researchers had virtually ignored the topic. At the time, I was a graduate student thrashing around for a topic for my dissertation research, so I bought a copy of Zimbardo's book the same day (Zimbardo, 1977). As I read the book, it dawned on me that shy people's anxiety and inhibition in social encounters were a direct consequence of their concerns with the impressions others form of them. Thus, I immediately began to design research to examine the self-presentational aspects of shyness, as well as to work with Barry Schlenker on a theoretical model of social anxiety.

According to the self-presentational theory (Leary, 1983c; Schlenker & Leary, 1982b), people experience **social anxiety** when they are motivated to make desired impressions on other people but doubt that they will be able to successfully make those impressions. The relationship between self-presentation and social anxiety can be seen in the following formula:

$$SA = M \times (1 - p)$$

where:

SA is the amount of social anxiety an individual experiences in a particular social situation,

M refers to impression motivation—the degree to which the individual is motivated to make a desired impression on others,

and p is the subjective probability of making the desired impression—the person's estimate of the likelihood of making the impression he or she desires (Leary, 1983c).

As can be seen in this formula, social anxiety is a function of two things: impression motivation (M) and the perceived probability of self-presentational success (p). If a person does not care how he or she is regarded in a particular situation—that is, if M is zero—the person will not experience any social anxiety. (If M = 0, then SA = 0 regardless of the value of p.) However, as impression motivation (M) increases, the amount of social anxiety will increase, assuming that the value of p is not 1.00. Thus, social anxiety is directly related to the degree to which a person is motivated to manage his or her impressions in a particular situation.

However, no matter how motivated people are to make an impression, they do not feel anxious if they are certain that others will form the desired impression of them. In other words, if the subjective probability of making the desired impression (p) is 1.00—absolute certainty—the person should not feel socially anxious. (If p = 1.00, then 1 – 1 = 0, and SA = 0.) But given that some degree of impression motivation exists (that is, M is not zero), social anxiety should increase as the person increasingly doubts his or her self-presentational efficacy (and p goes down).

The worst possible situation from a self-presentational standpoint is one in which the person is exceptionally motivated to make a desired impression (that is, M is sky-high), but something has happened to make the person believe that he or she has no chance of making that impression (that is, p = 0). For example, imagine how you would feel if, while you were being interviewed for your "dream job," you realized that your responses to the interviewer's questions had led the interviewer to perceive you as incompetent, shallow, boring, and unfriendly.

PRINCIPLE:

People experience social anxiety when they are motivated to make desired impressions on others but doubt that they will successfully do so.

Some researchers have misinterpreted the theory as suggesting that social anxiety arises when people think they will make *negative or unfavorable* impressions on others. This interpretation is incorrect for two reasons. First, as we saw in earlier chapters, people sometimes want to make negative, socially undesirable impressions. For example, they may want to appear intimidating to induce compliance, helpless to obtain support, or incompetent to avoid unpleasant responsibilities. In cases such as these, people may become anxious when they do not think they will make *undesirable* impressions. People's assessments of their self-presentational effectiveness can be made only relative to the impressions they want others to form; whether those impressions are positive or negative, as judged by others or by social norms, is irrelevant. Admittedly, in most instances the impressions people want others to form of them are positive, socially desirable ones, but this need not be the case.

Second, people may feel socially anxious even when they know they are making good impressions if they do not think they are being perceived *favorably enough* to accomplish their goals. A job applicant in an interview, a political candidate in a debate, or an adolescent on a first date may each think others view them positively, yet feel anxious because they do not think they are being viewed as positively as they would like (positively enough to get the job, to win the election, or to get a second date, for example). It is not true that people must think they are regarded unfavorably in order for them to feel socially anxious.

Situational Antecedents

The self-presentational approach to social anxiety helps us understand why certain situations make people feel socially anxious, as well as why some people tend to be more socially anxious than others. According to the theory, people should experience greater anxiety the more motivated they are to make impressions and the less certain they are that they will do so. As a result, any situation that makes people motivated to make an impression or that leads people to doubt they will make that impression should make them feel socially anxious. Furthermore, people who are unusually motivated to impression-manage or, for whatever reason, tend to think they won't make the impressions they want, will tend to be more generally anxious than people who have fewer self-presentational concerns.

Impression Motivation

In Chapter 3, we discussed three factors that motivate people to control others' impressions of them: the goal-relevance of impressions, the value of desired goals, and discrepancies between one's desired and current image. Because they heighten impression motivation, such factors are associated with increases in social anxiety. For example, people are more motivated to impression-manage when the consequences of their self-presentations are important or valuable. At one extreme are situations in which people believe they have absolutely nothing to gain or lose as a result of making certain impressions on others. In such situations, impression motivation should be near zero and social anxiety should not occur. At the other extreme are situations in which the person thinks that very valuable outcomes are contingent on him or her making the "right" impression. When the person's goals are valuable or important, self-presentational motivation is high, and social anxiety is more likely.

For example, because people know that first impressions are particularly important, they are more motivated to make desired impressions the first few times they meet a particular person. As a result, people feel especially anxious when they meet new people or interact with strangers (Leary, 1983c).

People are also more motivated to be perceived in particular ways by those who have power over their lives. Thus, people feel more socially anxious when dealing with their employers or with other powerful people than with people on whom they are not dependent.

Impression Efficacy

According to the self-presentation model, social anxiety also increases with the degree to which people doubt they will make the impressions they desire. Thus, events that reduce a person's sense of impression efficacy should heighten social anxiety. In support of this, research has shown that subjects' anxiety in experimental conversations is related to how good of an impression they thought they had made on others (DePaulo, Epstein, & LeMay, 1990; Leary, 1986; Maddux, Norton, & Leary, 1988; Pozo, Carver, Wellens, & Scheier, 1991). Similarly, subjects who thought they possessed a trait that was associated with making good impressions were more relaxed and less shy than subjects who doubted that they possessed this trait (Leary, 1980).

People are more likely to doubt that they will make desired impressions on other people when they do not know what impression they should try to make. In the initial study that tested the self-presentation model (Leary, 1980), subjects who were told how to make a desired impression on another person reported feeling less anxious than subjects who were not told how to make a desired impression. In everyday interactions, people feel socially anxious when they are uncertain about the kinds of impressions they should make or about how to effectively make those impressions. This explains why encounters involving strangers, ambiguity, or novel roles often evoke considerable anxiety. In each case, uncertainty leads the person to question whether he or she can make the desired impression, and anxiety results. Without a "script" about how to behave, people are likely to have doubts about their impression efficacy. One implication of this is that people will feel more comfortable about new situations the more they can find out about what is likely to happen and about how they should act (Leary, Kowalski, & Bergen, 1988).

For ethical reasons, I have hesitated to experimentally induce social anxiety by leading subjects to think they made undesired impressions on other people. However, in one experiment, I attempted to *decrease* social anxiety by lowering subjects' self-presentational concerns. The reasoning behind the study was that, if people feel anxious because they are worried about the impressions they will make, social anxiety should be lower when a person's self-presentational difficulties can be attributed to situational impediments. A person interacting under very difficult circumstances need not be as concerned about making undesired impressions. Not only will other people have difficulty forming clearcut impressions to begin with, but others may be likely to attribute the person's self-presentational problems to the difficult situation. For example, if I think I am coming across poorly while giving a talk in front of a large audience, I may begin to feel nervous. But if I am giving my talk in a room located beside a noisy construction site (with hammers banging, jackhammers blasting away, concrete mixers groaning, and workers yelling), I may be less concerned about coming across poorly because the audience is likely to attribute my difficulties to the distractions.

To examine people's reactions in such a situation, I conducted an experiment in which subjects interacted with another person in the presence of moderately loud, distracting noise (Leary, 1986). Some subjects were told that we expected the noise to be distracting enough to interfere with the other person's ability to form accurate impressions of them, whereas other subjects were told that the noise would not interfere with the other person's ability to form accurate impressions. (In fact, the noise was equally loud in both conditions.) As predicted, subjects who were told that the noise would be distracting had lower pulse rates (indicating lower anxious arousal) than those who were told that the noise was expected to have little effect. In addition, subjects who tended to be highly socially anxious were particularly comforted by the supposedly distracting noise. The self-presentational interpretation of these findings is that the presence of a situational impediment that ostensibly interfered with interpersonal behavior released subjects from the negative implications of a mediocre or substandard self-presentational performance.

The results of this study may shed light on a puzzle I have wondered about: the popularity of singles bars. Many people who go to singles bars complain about them. "You can't really get to know anybody there," they say. "It's crowded and loud; people are superficial, and it's just a meat market." If that's the case, why would people go to such a place? Could it be precisely because it's crowded and loud, people are superficial, and it's just a meat market?

With everything in the situation working against effective impression management, no one needs to be too concerned about rejection. If a person "scores" and meets someone to spend time with, great. But if not, the person need not feel too badly about it. After all, the place is crowded and loud, people are superficial, etc.

In brief, research has supported the notion that social anxiety is associated with self-presentational concerns. Experimental manipulations designed to raise or lower self-presentational worries are associated with changes in self-reported anxiety and physiological arousal, and self-reported anxiety correlates with the degree to which people are worried about others' impressions in a particular context.

Trait Social Anxiety

Although virtually everybody feels socially anxious now and then, some people experience social anxiety more often than others. Some individuals are bothered by pangs of social anxiety only rarely, whereas other people are anxious a great deal of the time. People who are particularly likely to feel anxious in social encounters are said to be high in **trait social anxiety.** (Trait social anxiety is also called dispositional social anxiety or social anxiousness.)

Psychologists have developed several self-report scales to measure trait social anxiety (see Leary, 1990b, for a review of these measures). Although differences exist among them, all of these measures ask subjects how often or intensely they feel nervous in social situations. For example, a few items from the Interaction Anxiousness Scale (Leary, 1983b) are:

- I often feel nervous even in casual get-togethers.
- I usually feel uncomfortable when I am in a group of people I don't know.
- I usually feel nervous when I speak to someone in a position of authority.
- I seldom feel anxious in social situations (reverse scored).

People who are so high in trait social anxiety that their lives are severely affected are called socially phobic. **Social phobia** is a psychiatric classification reserved for people who show "a persistent fear of one or more social situations . . . in which the person is exposed to possible scrutiny by others and fears that he or she may do something or act in a way that will be humiliating or embarrassing" (American Psychiatric Association, 1987, p. 241).

The self-presentational approach suggests that some people are higher in trait social anxiety than other people because they are more motivated to make impressions on other people and/or are less likely to think they will do so. According to this view, social phobics are people who are extraordinarily concerned about others' impressions of them (Leary & Kowalski, in press).

In support of this model, socially anxious people score higher than people low in trait social anxiety on measures that are associated with impression motivation. For example, socially anxious people score higher in public self-consciousness; that is they are more aware of others' impressions of them (see Chapter 3). In addition, they tend to be more concerned about being perceived unfavorably and being evaluated negatively (Buss, 1980; Hope & Heimberg, 1988; Leary, 1983b; Leary & Kowalski, 1993).

In addition, people who score high in social anxiousness report thinking more about the impressions they're making on others in laboratory conversations than subjects low in social anxiety (Leary, 1986). Socially anxious and shy people also consistently think that they are making less favorable impressions on other people than subjects low in social anxiety (Bruch, Hamer, & Heimberg, in press; Leary, 1986; Leary & Kowalski, in press). In one study, socially anxious subjects assumed they had made a worse impression on other people than less anxious subjects even if the other person had only glanced at them (Leary, Kowalski, & Campbell, 1988)!

Socially anxious people also tend to have lower self-esteem than less anxious people (Leary, 1983b; Leary & Kowalski, 1993; Zimbardo, 1977). The reason for this should be clear. Because people tend to assume that others see them pretty much as they see themselves, people with lower self-esteem are likely to conclude that others hold less positive impressions of them than people whose self-esteem is higher. Thus, low self-esteem per se does not lead to social anxiety but is mediated by the person's assumptions about how he or she is regarded by others.

Appearance and Physique Anxiety

Children learn to worry about their appearance at an early age. As VanderVelde (1985) pointed out, "every child learns that such bodily features as size, weight, strength, complexion, or looks are used with often painful accuracy by peers, classmates, teachers, and coaches to determine the pecking order in social and athletic activities. Bodily 'flaws' become social liabilities and ever-present potentials for rejection and humiliation" (p. 532). Even as adults, people sometimes worry about their appearances and become anxious or depressed when they don't think they look as good as they would like. We've all seen people worry about their bad complexions, their facial features, the extra pounds they gained, or other bodily features that they believe make an undesired impression on others.

One aspect of appearance that is particularly distressing to many people is their physique—that is, their body's form and structure. Of primary concern in our culture is the amount of body fat one has. (We often talk about people being concerned with their weight, but it seems to me that we're not really worried about how much we weigh. Rather, we're concerned about how fat we look.) Many people become absolutely distraught when they think they've gained (or failed to lose) weight.

Other aspects of physique that people find distressing include musculature; men, in particular, worry about looking too scrawny. Women, on the other hand, tend to worry about being overweight and about the size of their breasts. Some women think their breasts are too big, but most women who are dissatisfied with their breasts wish they were larger. Each year, approximately 100,000 American women undergo cosmetic surgery to change the size of their breasts (Findlay, 1988).

Although many people worry about their physiques at one time or another (often when it's time to go to the beach or swimming pool), some people are so chronically concerned that we could label them **physique anxious.** People who are physique anxious feel particularly nervous or uncomfortable when others seem to be evaluating their bodies and report thinking more negative thoughts about their bodies. They also tend to be more worried about others' evaluations generally and are more likely to be high in trait social anxiety (Hart, Leary, & Rejeski, 1989).

In American culture, weight and appearance are considered more important aspects of a woman's social image than a man's. As a result, female college students tend to score higher on measures of appearance and physique anxiety than male students (Dion et al., 1990; Hart et al., 1989). For example, twice as many college women consider themselves overweight than can be regarded as even slightly overweight on the basis of objective body measurements. One study showed that 70 percent of the female respondents surveyed thought they were overweight, and that respondents wanted to lose an average of 14 pounds each (Miller, Linke, & Linke, 1980)! In contrast, most men considered their weight to be essentially "normal." Such gender differences presumably occur because the societal ideal for women currently specifies an unrealistically low body weight, whereas the ideal for men does not.

Behavioral Responses

When people doubt they will make the kinds of impressions they desire, they not only feel socially anxious, but they often behave differently. Much of the behavior of socially anxious and shy people can be understood as attempts to make the best out of a bad self-presentational situation.

Avoidance, Withdrawal, and Inhibition

In the extreme case, people may avoid altogether situations in which they doubt they will make desired impressions. For example, many people do everything they can to avoid speaking before large groups, and other individuals shirk social engagements that pose a self-presentational threat. Avoiding such situations serves two functions for people: it reduces their level of anxiety, and it preempts the possibility of making undesired impressions.

Of course, people cannot always avoid threatening social situations. People who become uncomfortable in a social encounter may socially withdraw while remaining physically present. For example, an employee who feels out of place at the boss' party may be unusually quiet and reserved. Research shows that people who score high on measures of trait social social anxiety generally talk less in conversations (Leary, 1983c).

The interesting question is *why* people withdraw when they are socially anxious. Contrary to what you might think, social withdrawal is *not* a typical response to anxiety. When people are anxious or afraid for nonsocial reasons—for example, when they're afraid of experiencing physical pain—they actually prefer to interact with other people (Schachter, 1959). They only withdraw from other people when they are anxious for self-presentational reasons.

From the standpoint of self-presentation theory, withdrawal is a reasonable response to self-presentational worries. If you don't think you'll make the impression you desire, continuing to interact carries quite a risk. Better to pull back and be quiet than to plunge ahead and potentially make a complete fool of yourself. Rather than reflecting helpless resignation or a fearful retreat from a difficult interaction, this quiet, passive interaction style is socially adaptive.

Recent research suggests that this tendency for socially anxious people to remain quiet in social situations can have implications for the effectiveness of small groups. The quality of a group's decisions depend in large part on the active participation of all group members. As the saying goes, two (or three or four) heads are better than one. But if some group members are afraid to contribute their ideas out of fear of being perceived negatively, the group can not benefit from their ideas and expertise. Furthermore, not only do socially anxious people not contribute their own ideas, but their quietness seems to reduce the participation of other group members (Camacho & Paulhus, 1993).

Innocuous Sociability

Unfortunately for the socially anxious person, being quiet and withdrawn can create additional self-presentational problems. In our culture, excessive quietness, withdrawal, aloofness, and shyness often do not make good impressions. To counteract this, people who feel socially anxious often adopt an interpersonal style that I call **innocuous sociability**. By being innocuously sociable, people who are worried about the impressions they are making can remain engaged in an interaction in a manner that presents little additional risk to their social identities. For example, socially anxious individuals tend to agree more with other people, both by nodding their heads (Pilkonis, 1977) and by verbally agreeing (Leary, Knight, & Johnson, 1987). They also tend to use more back-channel responses—the sounds that people make to indicate that they are actively listening to others during conversations (such as "uh-huh," "oh," and "hummmm") (Natale, Entin, & Jaffe, 1979). They also seem to smile more (even though they feel uncomfortable and not much like smiling) and look at others more (Cheek & Buss, 1981; Pilkonis, 1977).

Together, these kinds of innocuously sociable behaviors serve as useful self-presentational tactics for the person who is worried about the impressions others are forming. First, innocuous sociability helps to keep the focus of the conversation on other people and off oneself. Nodding, back-channeling, and smiling encourage others to dominate the conversation. More importantly from a self-presentational perspective, innocuous sociability conveys an impression of quiet friendliness and interest. Without contributing much to the conversation, the individual who nods, back-channels, and appears interested can remain engaged in a social encounter without doing anything that might damage others' impressions of him or her. In fact, these kinds of behaviors can actually create a mildly positive impression—that of someone who, though quiet, is interested in getting to know other people.

Viewed in this manner, the behavior of shy people is a rational and somewhat strategic response to self-presentational difficulties. The individual who doubts his or her ability to make desired impressions can make the best of a bad self-presentational situation by being quiet, yet innocuously sociable.

Protective Self-Presentation

So far, we have seen that people who are worried about their impressions tend to withdraw as much as possible, limiting their behaviors to those that are innocuously sociable. What do they do, however, when they must disclose information about themselves to other people? When people do not think they will make the impressions they want to make, they often adopt a **protective self-presentation style** (Arkin, 1981). Rather than attempting to make a good impression (acquisitive self-presentation), the socially anxious person tries to avoid making a bad impression (protective self-presentation) (Shepperd & Arkin, 1990).

One protective self-presentation strategy is simply to convey as little information about oneself as possible. As I noted above, socially anxious people talk less during interaction than less anxious people. Doing so will usually not make a good impression on other people, but it also will not make a bad impression.

Other evidence that social anxiety is associated with protective self-presentation comes from studies that have examined self-presentational behaviors directly. I have data showing that socially anxious people present themselves as more typical—that is, as closer to the average of all subjects' ratings—than subjects low in social anxiety. Such a tactic is a safe one: if I come across as pretty much like everybody else, I'm not likely to make a particularly good impression, but I'm not likely to make a bad one either. Another study showed that socially anxious people generally present themselves more cautiously than lows (Leary, 1986).

Paradoxically, this seemingly safe, protective style of self-presentation can sometimes backfire. On occasion, the self-protective behaviors of socially anxious people are associated with less liking and greater discomfort in the people who interact with them (Meleshko & Alden, 1993). Thus, their self-presentational worries may lead them to behave in ways that cause others to form less positive impressions!

Big Time Social Anxiety

For those of us who worry when we think even one person thinks poorly of us, it is hard to imagine what it must be like to know that much of the country thinks you are an ineffectual, uninformed buffoon. Such was the plight of Dan Quayle during his tenure as Vice-President of the United States. From the time of his nomination in 1988, George Bush's choice of Quayle as his running mate was mired in controversy. Quayle was widely regarded as a political lightweight who had a penchant for saying stupid things.

For the first half of the Bush-Quayle administration, Quayle was the most mocked figure on late night television, only to be replaced by Iraqi President Saddam Hussein during the Persian Gulf War. In 1991, Quayle's popularity rating was only 19 percent, and most voters thought he should be dropped from the Republican ticket for the 1992 campaign. T-shirts were peddled emblazoned with "Keep Bush Alive" (The Quayle Handicap, 1991).

Much of Quayle's image problems revolved around his tendency to say things that were innane, if not entirely nonsensical. After the San Francisco earthquake, he observed that, "the loss of life will be irreplaceable." He was widely ridiculed for botching the motto of the United Negro College Fund when he said, "What a terrible thing it is to lose one's mind." (The motto is "A mind is a terrible thing to waste.") He also got flak for correcting a student's correct spelling of potato. All public figures commit verbal gaffes from time to time with little or no fallout, but for Quayle, they reinforced the public's negative perception of him.

Although admitting that the widespread criticism of him was difficult, Quayle had no option other than to continue his vice-presidential duties, many of which involved public speaking. However, we should not be surprised that his behavior showed telltale signs of self-presentational concern, social anxiety, and protective self-presentation. After all, he was obviously motivated to project certain desirable images, yet had every reason to doubt that he was successfully doing so.

Although Quayle was once self-confident and easy going, after the beating he took in the press, he became excessively cautious, stiff, and uncomfortable in public appearances. He began speaking very slowly and cautiously, presumably monitoring his words more carefully. As one political observer noted, "He looks like he's not playing to win—but merely not to lose" (Rx for the Veep, 1991)—an apt description of a person who is engaging in protective self-presentation.

Attention and Memory

In Chapter 3, I suggested that people can monitor the impressions they are making on different levels. In some instances, people are in a state of impression focus where impression monitoring dominates their thoughts. People who are concerned about the impressions they are making are likely to be in such a state as they wonder about how others are perceiving them ("What is he/she thinking?"), castigate themselves over self-presentational flubs ("Boy, that was a stupid thing for me to say."), plan how to improve their image ("What should I talk about?"), or simply agonize over how awful the situation is or how badly they feel.

Being preoccupied with one's self-presentations in such situations makes a certain degree of sense. If there is some good reason to make the "right" impression (whatever that might be), but things seem to be going awry, we can't fault people for being impression-focused. Unfortunately, devoting excessive attention to one's impressions can divert a person's cognitive resources from other tasks. When people are excessively preoccupied with their self-presentations, they pay less attention to what is going on around them. Self-presentational concerns use mental resources that would otherwise help them deal with their social environment (Baumeister, 1989; Baumeister, Hutton, & Tice, 1989). As a result, a person's behavior can become disrupted.

One consequence is that people who are thinking about their social images are less likely to remember information they hear than people who are not impression-focused. Most of us have had the experience of being introduced to someone, then finding only moments later that we couldn't recall the person's name. What happened? Most likely, we were thinking about other things, including how best to respond, and didn't encode the person's name into memory. Although we might say we "forgot" the person's name, the truth is that we never really learned it to begin with.

Research has documented that people who are under social scrutiny have more difficulty paying attention to what is happening around them. For example, Kimble and Zehr (1982) had subjects interact with another person who either could or could not see them. Subjects who could be seen by the other person remembered less information than those who could not be seen, presumably because they were more preoccupied with the other person's impressions. Furthermore, a study by Baumeister et al. (1989) suggested that the more people think consciously about making a particular impression, the less they remember about a social interaction. Similarly, another study showed that subjects high in social anxiety had difficulty remembering what happened while they were being scrutinized by other people, whereas subjects low in social anxiety were not affected by being scrutinized (Lord, Saenz, & Godfrey, 1987).

Many students experience a similar effect when they take tests. When people experience **test anxiety,** they find it difficult to recall things they have learned. In part, this is because they are thinking about how poorly they are doing on the test and the disastrous consequences of failing, and this anxious self-preoccupation interferes with their ability to think about the test questions themselves (Wine, 1971). Many, if not most instances of test anxiety are self-presentational in that the person is concerned about others' impressions and evaluations of him or her.

This kind of cognitive disruption is also responsible for the **next-in-line effect.** When people are waiting to "perform" in a social situation, they often have difficulty remembering information that is presented just before they are to perform (Bond & Omar, 1990; Brenner, 1973). For example, imagine that you are in a group of 10 strangers, each of whom is to say a few words about him- or herself to the group. Chances are, you'll have more difficulty remembering what was said by the person who immediately preceded you than by the person who follows you. The reason is that you are so busy thinking about what you are going to say—how you are going to present yourself—that you literally do not have enough mental capacity to listen to and remember what the other person is saying.

If the next-in-line effect occurs because of self-presentational concerns, we would expect socially anxious people (who are more worried about the impressions they make) to show a stronger effect than low socially anxious people. Bond and Omar (1990) showed that this was the case. In their study, subjects took turns reading words aloud, then were tested for how many words they remembered. Subjects high in social anxiety remembered 26 percent of the words that followed them, but only 11 percent of those that immediately preceded them. In contrast, subjects who were low in social anxiety remembered virtually the same number of words both before and after they spoke. Further analyses showed that subjects' social anxiety was inversely related to their memory of the words that immediately preceded them; the more anxious a subject felt, the fewer words he or she remembered.

Choking under Pressure

Choking under pressure refers to inferior performance that occurs despite "individual striving and situational demands for superior performance" (Baumeister, 1984, p. 610). People choke when the pressures of performing lead them to perform far below the level of which they are capable. Two distinct processes—both of them related to self-presentational concerns—underlie choking (Baumeister, 1984; Baumeister & Showers, 1986; Martens & Landers, 1972).

First, when people become worried about how they are being perceived by others, they sometimes begin to pay conscious attention to behaviors that are normally mindless, habitual, and automatic. Have you ever noticed how unnaturally you walk when you know others are watching you?

Experienced athletes need not think consciously about the execution of routine movements. In fact, if they do, their performances are likely to be impaired. When they begin to worry about how they are doing, they may start thinking about these otherwise habitual movements, and they may choke (Baumeister & Steinhilber, 1984). That's why football coaches sometimes call a time-out just before the other team is to attempt a crucial field goal. The hope is that the kicker will begin to think about the kick and will choke.

The second cause of choking is physical tension. Many actions are difficult to perform when one is physically tense or, worse, trembling from anxiety. People find it more difficult to shoot a free throw, play the piano, sing, or swing a golf club when they are tense. Yet, as we've seen, concerns with others' impressions often lead to social anxiety, which is accompanied by bodily tension.

Self-Handicapping

People who are concerned about others' impressions may use yet another strategy to protect their public images—**self-handicapping.** The term "self-handicapping" has been used in two different ways by researchers, so we will be careful to specify which type of self-handicapping we are referring to—behavioral self-handicapping or self-reported handicapping (Leary & Shepperd, 1986).

Behavioral Self-Handicapping

Berglas and Jones (1978) defined self-handicapping as "any action or choice of performance setting that enhances the opportunity to externalize (or excuse) failure and to internalize (reasonably accept credit for) success" (p. 406). When people self-handicap, they set up an impediment that would be expected to reduce the probability of them performing well but that provides them with a plausible excuse for failure. The student who fails to get enough sleep before an exam, the golfer who never practices, the underachiever, and the problem drinker may all represent cases of self-handicapping (Jones & Berglas, 1978). In each instance, the presence of the self-created impediment insulates the individual to some degree from the implications of failure.

People who are uncertain about their performances on upcoming tasks self-handicap in a variety of ways. For example, subjects threatened by the prospect of failure sometimes choose to take drugs that will debilitate their performance prior to performing (Berglas & Jones, 1978; Gibbons & Gaeddert, 1984; Kolditz & Arkin, 1982; Tucker, Vuchinich, & Sobell, 1981). These findings have led some to speculate that some people abuse drugs and alcohol as a self-handicapping strategy (Berglas,

1985; Jones & Berglas, 1978). By consuming alcohol or drugs, the self-handicapper can reduce his or her personal responsibility for intellectual, social, or other failures.

Other studies show that people don't try as hard on tasks on which success is uncertain (Harris & Snyder, 1986; Pyszczynski & Greenberg, 1983; Snyder, Smoller, Strenta, & Frankel, 1981) and don't practice as much for threatening tasks (Rhodewalt, Saltzman, & Wittmer, 1984). By exerting less than full effort, people can blame failure, if it occurs, on lack of practice or effort rather than on lack of ability. People can also use this tactic even when they expect to succeed so that success will be attributed to superior ability (Tice & Baumeister, 1990).

People also self-handicap by electing to perform evaluative tasks under less than ideal circumstances. For example, people may choose to perform difficult tasks in a distracting environment so that they can blame poor performance on the distractions (Rhodewalt & Davison, 1986). People in competitive situations may also offer to give their opponents some advantage ("That's okay; I'll take the side of the court with the sun in my eyes."). Berglas (1985) recounted the tale of Deschapelles, a renowned chess champion who, when he became worried about beating challengers, insisted that they take a one piece advantage plus the opening move. In this way, losing a match could be attributed to his gracious willingness to handicap himself, and a win would be seen as an even greater triumph.

Although the fact that people sometimes self-handicap is beyond doubt, experts disagree regarding precisely why people self-handicap. In their original study of self-handicapping, Berglas and Jones (1978) interpreted self-handicapping as a means by which people protect their own self-esteem. However, Kolditz and Arkin (1982) suggested that self-handicapping could be used for self-presentational reasons. People may set up impediments to their performances to protect their images in other people's eyes should they fail. In their experiment, subjects were told that they were participating in a study of the effects of two drugs on intellectual performance. Subjects then took one of two tests. One test was composed of seemingly insoluble test questions, whereas the other consisted primarily of soluable questions. All subjects then received feedback indicating that they had performed "exceptionally well" on the test.

Subjects were told they would take one of two drugs, then complete a second test that was very much like the one they had just taken. Some subjects were told that their tests would be scored by the researcher (thereby making their performance public), whereas other subjects were told that their tests would be sent to a pharmaceutical company in another city for scoring (and, thus, the researcher wouldn't know their scores). Subjects were then given the choice of taking one of two bogus drugs: Actavil—which supposedly enhanced verbal ability—or Pandocrin—which supposedly disrupted verbal ability. Subjects made their choice either in the presence of the researcher or in totally private and anonymous conditions.

The primary finding was that subjects were most likely to choose Pandocrin, the drug they thought would interfere with their performance on the test, when they had worked unsoluable problems, thought the researcher would score their tests, and made their drug choice in public. Three-fourths of the subjects whose scores and drug choices were public chose the debilitating drug, whereas *no* subjects whose scores and drug choice were private chose Pandocrin. The self-presentational interpretation of these data is clear. Subjects were most likely to self-handicap by choosing a drug that would impede their performance on the second test when the researcher would know how well they performed, as well as which drug they took. These are precisely the conditions in which self-handicapping would be most useful as a self-presentational strategy.

The notion that people use behavioral self-handicapping for self-presentational purposes is also supported by the fact that people who score high in public self-consciousness self-handicap more than those who score low in public self-consciousness (Shepperd & Arkin, 1989). As you may recall from Chapter 3, public self-consciousness involves the tendency to think about the public, observable aspects of oneself, including the impressions one makes on others. The fact that people who think more about their public selves tend to self-handicap more readily suggests that impression motivation is involved in some cases of self-handicapping.

Self-Reported Handicaps

Of course, people who are worried about others' impressions can not always arrange real handicaps in advance of a threatening evaluation. Not only do real behavioral handicaps reduce the likelihood of doing well, but they would often require dire actions. (What long distance runner would purposefully sprain an ankle before a race?) However, even when people do not behaviorally self-handicap, they can usually *claim* that they are operating under a handicap. These verbal claims are called **self-reported handicaps** (Leary & Shepperd, 1986).

For example, people report experiencing more anxiety while taking a test when they are told that anxiety is a viable explanation for poor performance on the test (Smith, Snyder, & Handelsman, 1982). Similarly, socially anxious men report feeling more anxious when they believe that anxiety can account for a poor social performance (Snyder & Smith,

1986; Snyder, Smith, Augelli, & Ingram, 1985). Because people know that anxiety can interfere with how well they do, they can claim to be handicapped by it.

People also report that they are handicapped by traumatic events in their past. People sometimes advertise their past adversities so others will know they are operating with an ongoing handicap. Essentially they are saying, "Don't expect too much from me. My parents were divorced/I was sick a lot as a child/I was abused/my mother was an alcoholic/etc." In a laboratory demonstration of this effect, subjects reported having experienced more traumatic events in their lives when they thought that a traumatic personal history served as a plausible reason for performing poorly on a test (DeGree & Snyder, 1985).

Other-Enhancement

Another way that people can protect their images when they fear failure is to give others an advantage over them. Whereas behavioral self-handicapping involves constructing an impediment to one's own performance, **behavioral other-enhancement** involves enhancing the performance of a competitor (Shepperd & Arkin, 1991). By providing their opponents or competitors with tools, resources, or other advantages that promote better performance, people hope that their own relatively poor performance will be attributed to the opponent's advantage. Other-enhancement has a second self-presentational benefit as well. In addition to providing a reason why the person did not perform as well as the opponent he or she helped, the person who uses other-enhancement scores points for being unselfish and cooperative.

Often, self-handicapping and other-enhancement occur together. For example, a tennis player may offer her opponent use of her more expensive racket ("Here, try mine; see how you like it"), which may both advantage her opponent (other-enhancement) and disadvantage herself (self-handicapping). I've seen college professors give up their research space to younger, untenured faculty, arguing that "they need it worse than I do." Although such a gesture is undoubtedly helpful to younger faculty, the professor now has a good reason why the younger professor is doing more or better research than he or she.

Self-Presentational Worries and Health Risks

Much of the time, being concerned with others' impressions works in people's best interests. In some cases, however, self-presentational concerns can lead people to engage in behaviors that are clearly harmful to themselves or others. As we mentioned in an earlier chapter, concerns with others' impressions can be hazardous to your health (Leary, Tchividjian, & Kraxberger, 1994).

Safe Sex

One particularly important example of how worrying about one's impressions can be harmful involves safe sex. Although health professionals have long advocated using condoms as a means of preventing pregnancy and sexually transmitted diseases, the importance of condom use increased markedly with the spread of the AIDS virus during the 1980s. Even with the spread of this deadly disease, however, many people continue to take inadequate precautions against pregnancy and STDs. This is evidenced by the fact that approximately 1,000,000 teenage girls become pregnant annually in this country (Fielding & Williams, 1991) and over 12,000,000 Americans contract some form of STD each year (Sexually Transmitted Diseases Up, 1993).

Research suggests that the failure to use condoms is not usually due to lack of information about pregnancy, STDs, or condoms. Rather, one primary reason many people do not use condoms is self-presentational: put simply, people are often embarrassed about acquiring and/or using condoms (Leary et al., 1994).

One primary impediment to using condoms is concern about what others will think when one gets them at a drugstore or health center. Thirty percent of the respondents in one study reported being embarrassed when buying condoms (Hanna, 1989; Clinkscales & Gallo, 1977). Importantly, one study showed that embarrassment over obtaining condoms was greater than that for acquiring other forms of contraception such as contraceptive pills or foam, which, of course, do not protect against AIDS (Herold, 1981).

Even if a person acquires condoms, self-presentational concerns can deter people from actually introducing them into a sexual encounter. I've talked to college students who had unprotected sexual intercourse even though they had a condom in their possession at the time! Bringing up the topic of condoms with a sexual partner can raise a number of self-presentational concerns. When with a new sexual partner, some people worry that having a condom will imply that they had anticipated having sex or, worse, had actively worked to seduce the other individual. Women may be particularly afraid to produce a condom because they will appear sexually experienced (if not promiscuous) and certainly too bold. Furthermore, some people think that suggesting that they and their partners use a condom may convey a lack of trust (Catania et al., 1991).

"Seven days at sea . . . but thank God no one's seen us yet."

FIGURE 9.1
People's self-presentational concerns sometimes take precedence over their health.

Unfortunately, self-presentational worries about condoms are common among gay men. In one study of the reasons gay men give for having anal intercourse without using a condom, Gold, Skinner, Grant, and Plummer (1991) found that one reason was a fear of making a negative impression. One gay respondent indicated that bringing up the need for a condom would make his partners think he was "a bit of a wimp." Over one-third of the respondents indicated that such concerns had led them to have unprotected anal intercourse.

The effects of self-presentational concerns on the failure to use condoms are perhaps the most potentially disastrous we will discuss in this book. Not only is the risk involved exceptionally serious, but the failure to use a condom potentially creates a health risk for others as well as oneself and may contribute to the spread of a deadly and untreatable disease.

Willingness to Seek Medical Attention

Another consequence of self-presentational worries for health is the failure to seek medical attention. Some medical examinations create self-presentational anxieties because they involve parts of the body that people consider private, such as the sex organs and rectal area. Many individuals are embarrassed by medical examinations of these parts of their bodies, and some may postpone seeking medical attention because of their social discomfort. Studies of cervical screening exams (Sansom, MacInerney, Oliver, & Wakefield, 1975) and mammography (Lerman, Rimer, Trock, Balshem, & Engstrom, 1990) showed that embarrassment regarding these procedures deterred some women from being tested. Although women are encouraged to have annual Pap tests to detect cervical cancer at its earliest stages, few have gynecological exams that often. Women's discomfort seems to arise from three sources: they fear that the exam will reveal previously undetected pathology, the exam itself may be physically uncomfortable, and, most relevant to our discussion, they find the exam to be embarrassing and interpersonally awkward (Domar, 1986; Millstein, Adler, Irwin, 1984; Wheeless, 1984). Studies show that most women experience a certain degree of social anxiety, humiliation, or awkwardness during gynecological exams; and men and women alike report similar reactions to rectal examinations, such as those conducted to test for colon cancer, hemorrhoids, and prostate problems. In addition, some women, albeit a lower percentage, report being embarrassed by breast exams (Lerman et al., 1990).

Attempts to reduce women's anxiety during gynecological exams by having physicians explain the procedures as they occur have not generally reduced anxiety or discomfort (Domar, 1986). From the self-presentational perspective, this should not be surprising. Although not understanding aspects of a pelvic exam may indeed be anxiety producing, purely educational interventions do little to reduce women's self-presentational concerns during the exam. However, changes in examination procedures that lower women's self-presentational concerns should reduce one source of the aversiveness of the procedure. In support of this, Williams and her colleagues showed that simply using a gown that more adequately covers the patient's body than the standard drape increases patient comfort (Williams, Park, & Kline, 1992).

People's willingness to seek medical care may be affected not only by their self-presentational concerns about physical exams such as those discussed above, but also by worries about the impressions that people will form if the fact they sought medical care becomes known. Much has been written about the stigma of seeing a psychiatrist, psychologist, or other mental health professional. In the eyes of many, just a consultation with a psychiatrist or psychologist casts doubts on the individual's stability or sanity. Certainly this fear is greater among individuals for whom seeking psychiatric care, if known by others, would jeopardize their professional or social standing. These concerns are compounded when the individual is seeking medical or psychological care for a stigmatized condition. People are often reluctant to enter treatment centers for alcohol and drug abuse, for example, because of their concerns about what people both in the treatment setting and in the outside world will think of them.

Summary

People experience social anxiety when they are motivated to make desired impressions on others but doubt that they will successfully do so. Thus, situations that increase impression motivation or decrease self-presentational efficacy heighten state social anxiety. Furthermore, people who are high in trait social anxiety (the tendency to feel socially anxious) tend to be high in impression motivation, but lack confidence that they generally make the impressions they desire.

When people feel socially anxious, they tend to behave in an avoidant, inhibited, and reticent fashion. Not only does social withdrawal reduce their anxiety, but it helps the person avoid a fullblown self-presentational failure. People who are concerned about the impressions they are making also tend to be innocuously sociable and adopt a protective self-presentation style. Unfortunately, excessive concern about others' impressions can interfere with memory and lead to choking on skilled tasks.

To protect their social images, people who are worried about their impressions may behaviorally self-handicap, setting up impediments to success to which their failures can be attributed. Alternatively, they may use self-reported handicaps to convince others that their performances were hampered by factors beyond their control and/or enhance the performance of others to whom they will be compared.

Self-presentational worries can actually be hazardous to people's health. For example, some people do not practice safe sex because they are concerned about how sexual partners will perceive them if they suggest using condoms. Self-presentational concerns can also deter people from seeking medical attention.

REFERENCES

Abbey, A., & Melby, C. (1986). The effects of nonverbal cues on gender differences in perceptions of sexual intent. *Sex Roles, 15,* 283–298.

Ackerman, B. & Schlenker, B. R. (1975, August). *Self-presentation: Attributes of the actor and audience.* Paper presented at the meeting of the American Psychological Association, Chicago.

Ainsworth, M. D. S. (1989). Attachments beyond infancy. *American Psychologist, 44,* 709–716.

Allies Dealing Sternly with Iraqis. (1991, March 4). *Winston-Salem Journal,* pp. 1, 4.

Altmann, S. A. (1967). The structure of primate communication. In S. A. Altmann (Ed.), *Social communication among primates.* Chicago: University of Chicago Press.

American Psychiatric Association (1987). *Diagnostic and statistical manual of mental disorders* (3rd ed. rev). Washington, D.C.: American Psychiatric Association.

Apsler, R. (1975). Effects of embarrassment on behavior toward others. *Journal of Personality and Social Psychology, 32,* 145–153.

Archer, R. L., & Burleson, J. A. (1980). The effects of timing and responsibility of self-disclosure on attraction. *Journal of Personality, 38,* 120–130.

Arkin, R. M. (1981). Self-presentational style. In J. T. Tedeschi (Ed.), *Impression management theory and social psychological research* (pp. 311–333). New York: Academic Press.

Arkin, R. M., Appleman, A. J., & Berger, J. M. (1980). Social anxiety, self-presentation, and the self-serving bias in causal attribution. *Journal of Personality and Social Psychology, 38,* 23–35.

Asendorpf, J. (1990). The expression of shyness and embarrassment. In W. R. Crozier (Ed.), *Shyness and embarrassment: Perspectives from social psychology* (pp. 87–118). New York: Cambridge University Press.

Austin, J. L. (1956). A plea for excuses. *Proceedings of the Aristotelian Society, 57,* 1–30.

Bagby, R. M., Gillis, J. R., & Dickens, S. (1990). Detection of dissimulation with the new generation of objective personality measures. *Behavioral Sciences and the Law, 8,* 93–102.

Bandura, A. (1973). *Aggression.* Englewood Cliffs, NJ: Prentice-Hall.

Barash, D. P. (1977). *Sociobiology and behavior.* New York: Elsevier.

Baumeister, R. F. (1982a). A self-presentational view of social phenomena. *Psychological Bulletin, 91,* 3–26.

Baumeister, R. F. (1982b). Self-esteem, self-presentation, and future interaction: A dilemma of reputation. *Journal of Personality, 50,* 29–45.

Baumeister, R. F. (1984). Choking under pressure: Self-consciousness and paradoxical effects of incentives on skilled performance. *Journal of Personality and Social Psychology, 46,* 610–620.

Baumeister, R. F. (Ed.). (1986). *Public self and private self.* New York: Springer-Verlag.

Baumeister, R. F. (1987). How the self became a problem: A psychological review of historical research. *Journal of Personality and Social Psychology, 52,* 163–176.

Baumeister, R. F. (1989). Motives and costs of self-presentation in organizations. In R. A. Giacalone & P. Rosenfeld (Eds.), *Impression management in the organization* (pp. 57–71). Hillsdale, NJ: Erlbaum.

Baumeister, R. F. (1991). *Escaping the self.* New York: Basic Books.

Baumeister, R. F., & Cairns, K. J. (1992). Repression and self-presentation: When audiences interfere with self-deceptive strategies. *Journal of Personality and Social Psychology, 62,* 851–862.

Baumeister, R. F., Cooper, J., & Skib, B. (1979). Inferior performance as a selective response to expectancy: Taking a dive to make a point. *Journal of Personality and Social Psychology, 37,* 424–432.

Baumeister, R. F., & Jones, E. E. (1978). When self-presentation is constrained by the target's knowledge: Consistency and compensation. *Journal of Personality and Social Psychology, 36,* 608–618.

Baumeister, R. F., & Leary, M. R. (1993). The need to belong: Desire for interpersonal attachments as a fundamental human motivation. Manuscript under review, Case Western Reserve University.

Baumeister, R. F., & Showers, C. J. (1986). A review of paradoxical performance effects: Choking under pressure in sports and mental tests. *European Journal of Social Psychology, 16,* 361–383.

Baumeister, R. F., & Steinhilber, A. (1984). Paradoxical effects of supportive audiences on performance under pressure: The home field advantage in sports championships. *Journal of Personality and Social Psychology, 47,* 85–93.

Baumeister, R. F., & Tice, D. M. (1990). Anxiety and social exclusion. *Journal of Social and Clinical Psychology, 9,* 165–195.

Baumeister, R. F., Tice, D. M., & Hutton, D.G. (1989a). Cognitive processes during deliberate self-presentation: How self-presenters alter and misinterpret the behavior of their interaction partners. *Journal of Experimental Social Psychology, 25,* 59–78.

Baumeister, R. F., Tice, D. M., & Hutton, D. G. (1989b). Self-presentational motivations and personality differences in self-esteem. *Journal of Personality, 57,* 547–579.

Baumeister, Roy (June 14, 1992). Personal communication.

Baumgardner, A. H. (1991). Claiming depressive symptoms as a self-handicap: A protective self-presentation strategy. *Basic and Applied Social Psychology, 12,* 97–113.

Baumgardner, A. H., Kaufman, C. M., & Levy, P. E. (1989). Regulating affect interpersonally: When low esteem leads to greater enhancement. *Journal of Personality and Social Psychology, 56*, 907–921.

Baumgardner, A. H., Lake, E. A., & Arkin, R. M. (1985). Claiming mood as a self-handicap: The influence of spoiled and unspoiled public identities. *Personality and Social Psychology Bulletin, 11*, 349–357.

Baumgardner, A. H., & Levy, P. E. (1987). Interpersonal reactions to social approval and disapproval. Unpublished manuscript, Michigan State University.

Beck, R. (1983). *Motivation: Theories and principles* (2nd ed.). Englewood Cliffs, NJ: Prentice-Hall.

Becker, W. (1976). Biasing effect of respondents' identification on responses to a social desirability scale: A warning to researchers. *Psychological Reports, 39*, 756–758.

Bednar, R. L., Wells, M. G., & Peterson, S. R. (1989). *Self-esteem: Paradoxes and innovations in clinical theory and practice*. Washington, D.C.: American Psychological Association.

Bell, S. S., Holbrook, M. B., Solomon, M. R. (1991). Combining esthetic value and social value to explain preferences for product styles with the incorporation of personality and ensemble effects, *Journal of Social Behavior and Personality, 6*, 243–274.

Bem, D. J. (1972). Self-perception theory. In L. Berkowitz (Ed.), *Advances in experimental social psychology* (Vol. 6). New York: Academic Press.

Bem, D. J., & McConnell, H. K. (1970). Testing the self-perception explanation of dissonance phenomena: On the salience of premanipulation attitudes. *Journal of Personality and Social Psychology, 14*, 23–41.

Berglas, S. (1985). Self-handicapping and self-handicappers: A cognitive/attributional model of interpersonal self-protective behavior. In R. Hogan & W. H. Jones (Eds.), *Perspectives in personality* (pp. 235–270). (Vol. 1). Greenwich, CT: JAI Press.

Berglas, S., & Jones, E. E. (1978). Drug choice as a self-handicapping strategy in response to noncontingent success. *Journal of Personality and Social Psychology, 36*, 405–417.

Berkowitz admits inventing demons (1979, Feb. 23). *Gainesville (FL) Sun*, p. 4B.

Bernhardt, P. C. (1993, June). Basking in reflected glory in politics: Losing candidates' yard signs come down. Paper presented at the meeting of the American Psychological Society, Chicago.

Berscheid, E., Graziano, W., Monson, T., & Dermer, M. (1976). Outcome dependency: Attention, attribution, and attraction. *Journal of Personality and Social Psychology, 34*, 978–989.

Biddle, B. J. (1979). *Role theory: Expectations, identities, and behavior*. New York: Academic Press.

Birtchnell, S., Whitfield, P., & Lacey, J. H. (1990). Motivational factors in women requesting augmentation and reduction mammaplasty. *Journal of Psychosomatic Research, 34*, 509–514.

Blumstein, P. W. (1973). Audience, Machiavellianism, and tactics of identity bargaining. *Sociometry, 36*, 346–365.

Bohra, K. A., & Pandy, J. (1984). Ingratiation toward different target persons: A stranger, a friend, and a boss. *Journal of Social Psychology, 122*, 217–222.

Bolwig, N. (1978). Communicative signals and social behavior of some African monkeys: A comparative study. *Primates, 19*, 61–99.

Bond, Jr., C. F. (1982). Social facilitation: A self-presentational view. *Journal of Personality and Social Psychology, 42,* 1042–1050.

Bond, Jr., C. F., & Anderson, E. L. (1987). The reluctance to transmit bad news: Private discomfort or public display? *Journal of Experimental Social Psychology, 23,* 176–187.

Bond, Jr., C. F., & Omar, A. S. (1990). Social anxiety, state dependence, and the next-in-line effect. *Journal of Experimental Social Psychology, 26,* 185–198.

Bond, M. H. (1991). Cultural influences on modes of impression management. In R. A. Giacalone & P. Rosenfeld (Eds.), *Applied impression management.* Newbury Park, CA: Sage.

Bond, M. H., & Venus, C. K. (1991). Resistance to group or personal insults in an ingroup or outgroup context. *International Journal of Psychology, 26,* 83–94.

Bowlby, J. (1969). *Attachment and loss* (Vol. 1). New York: Basic Books.

Bradley, G. W. (1978). Self-serving biases in the attribution process: A re-examination of the fact or fiction question. *Journal of Personality and Social Psychology, 36,* 56–71.

Braginsky, B., & Braginsky, D. (1967). Schizophrenic patients in the psychiatric interview: An experimental study of their effectiveness at manipulation. *Journal of Consulting Psychology, 30,* 295–300.

Braginsky, B. M., Braginsky, D. D., & Ring, K. (1969). *Methods of madness: The mental hospital as a last resort.* New York: Holt, Rinehart, and Winston.

Braginsky, D. D. (1970). Machiavellianism and manipulative interpersonal behavior in children. *Journal of Experimental Social Psychology, 6,* 77–99.

Braver, S. L., Linder, D. E., Corwin, T. T., & Cialdini, R. B. (1977). Some conditions that affect admissions of attitude change. *Journal of Experimental Social Psychology, 13,* 565–576.

Brenner, M. (1973). The next-in-line effect. *Journal of Verbal Learning and Verbal Behavior, 12,* 320–323.

Brent, E., & Granberg, D. (1982). Subjective agreement with the presidential candidates of 1976 and 1980. *Journal of Personality and Social Psychology, 42,* 393–403.

Briggs, S. R., & Cheek, J. M. (1988). On the nature of self-monitoring: Problems with assessment, problems with validity. *Journal of Personality and Social Psychology, 54,* 663–678.

Briggs, S. R., Cheek, J. M., & Buss, A. H. (1980). An analysis of the Self-Monitoring Scale. *Journal of Personality and Social Psychology, 38,* 679–686.

Brissett, D., & Edgley, C. (Eds.) (1990). *Life as theatre.* Hawthorne, NY: Walter de Gruyter.

Broadstock, M., Borland, R., & Gason, R. (1992). Effects of suntan on judgments of healthiness and attractiveness by adolescents. *Journal of Applied Social Psychology, 22,* 157–172.

Brockner, J., Rubin, J. Z., & Lang, E. (1981). Face-saving and entrapment. *Journal of Experimental Social Psychology, 17,* 68–79.

Broll, L., Gross, A., & Pilliavin, J. (1974). Effects of offered and requested help on help seeking and reactions to being helped. *Journal of Applied Social Psychology, 4,* 255–258.

Brown, B. R. (1968). The effects of need to maintain face on interpersonal bargaining. *Journal of Experimental Social Psychology, 4,* 107–122.

Brown, B. R., & Garland, H. (1971). The effects of incompetency, audience acquaintanceship, and anticipated evaluative feedback on face-saving behavior. *Journal of Experimental Social Psychology, 7,* 490–502.

Brown, J. D. (1993). Self-esteem and self-evaluations: Feeling is believing. In J. Suls (Ed.), *Psychological perspectives on the self* (Vol. 4). Hillsdale, NJ: Erlbaum.

Brownell, K. D. (1991a). Dieting and the search for the perfect body: Where physiology and culture collide. *Behavior Therapy, 22,* 1–12.

Brownell, K. D. (1991b). Personal responsibility and control over our bodies: When expectation exceeds reality. *Health Psychology, 10,* 303–310.

Bruch, M. A., Hamer, R. J., & Heimberg, R. G. (in press). Shyness and public self-consciousness: Additive or interactive relation with social interaction? *Journal of Personality.*

Bruskin Associates (1973, July). What are Americans afraid of? *The Bruskin Report: A Market Research Newsletter* (No. 53).

Bugental, D. B. (1986). Unmasking the "polite smile:" Situational and personal determinants of managed affect in adult-child interactions. *Personality and Social Psychology Bulletin, 12,* 7–16.

Burroughs, W. J., Drews, D. R., & Hallman, W. K. (1991). Predicting personality from personal possessions: A self-presentational analysis. *Journal of Social Behavior and Personality, 6,* 147–163.

Buss, A. H. (1980). *Self-consciousness and social anxiety.* San Francisco: Freeman.

Buss, A. H., & Briggs, S. (1984). Drama and the self in social interaction. *Journal of Personality and Social Psychology, 47,* 1310–1324.

Byrne, D. (1971). *The attraction paradigm.* New York: Academic Press.

Byrne, D., Ervin, C. F., & Lamberth, J. (1970). Continuity between the experimental study of attraction and real-life computer dating. *Journal of Personality and Social Psychology, 16,* 157–165.

Cahill, S. E., Distler, W., Lachowetz, C., Meaney, A., Tarallo, R., & Willard, T. (1985). Meanwhile backstage: Public bathrooms and the interaction order. *Urban Life, 14,* 33–58.

Cain, A. C. (1964). On the meaning of "playing crazy" in borderline children. *Psychiatry, 27,* 278–289.

Calder, B. J. (1977). An attribution theory of leadership. In J. Salancik & B. Staw (Eds.), *New directions in organizational behavior* (pp. 47–62). New York: St. Clair Press.

Caldwell, D. F., & O'Reilly, C. A. (1982). Responses to failure: The effects of choice and responsibility on impression management. *Academy of Management Journal, 25,* 121–136.

Camacho, L. M., & Paulhus, P. B. (1993). Social and procedural factors in brainstorming: The role of social anxiousness. Manuscript under review, University of Texas at Arlington.

Campbell, J. (1990). Self-esteem and clarity of the self-concept. *Journal of Personality and Social Psychology, 59,* 538–549.

Cantor, N., & Mischel, W. (1979). Prototypes in person perception. In L. Berkowitz (Ed.), *Advances in experimental social psychology* (Vol. 12, pp. 3–52). New York: Academic Press.

Carlson, M. (1992, September 14). All eyes on Hillary. *Time,* pp. 28–33.

Carnevale, P. J. D., Pruitt, D. G., & Britton, S. D. (1979). Looking tough: The negotiator under constituent surveillance. Personality and Social Psychology Bulletin, 5, 118–121.

Caron, M. D., Whitbourne, S. K., & Halgin, R. P. (1992). Fraudulent excuse making among college students. Teaching of Psychology, 19, 90–93.

Carson, R. C. (1969). *Interaction concepts of personality*. Chicago: Aldine.

Carver, C. S., & Scheier, M. F. (1985). Aspects of the self and control of behavior. In B. R. Schlenker (Ed.), *The self and social life* (pp. 146–174). New York: McGraw-Hill.

Casteneda, C. (1972). *Journey to Ixtlan*. New York: Pocket Books.

Catania, J. A., Coates, T. J., Stall, R., Bye, L., Kegeles, S. M., Capell, F., Henne, J., McKusick, L., Morin, S., Turner, H., & Pollack, L. (1991). Changes in condom use among homosexual men in San Francisco. *Health Psychology, 10*, 190–199.

Chaiken, S., & Pliner, P. (1987). Women, but not men, are what they eat: The effect of meal size and gender on perceived femininity and masculinity. *Personality and Social Psychology Bulletin, 13*, 166–176.

Cheek, J. M., & Buss, A. H. (1981). Shyness and sociability. *Journal of Personality and Social Psychology, 41*, 330–339.

Cherry, E. C. (1953). Some experiments on the recognition of speech, with one and with two ears. *Journal of the Acoustical Society of America, 25*, 975–979.

Chevalier-Skolnikoff, S. (1973). Facial expression of emotion in nonhuman primates. In P. Ekman (Ed.), *Darwin and facial expression* (pp. 11–89). New York: Academic Press.

Christensen, L. (1981). Positive self-presentation: A parsimonious explanation of subject motives. *The Psychological Record, 31*, 553–571.

Christie, R., & Geis, F. L. (Eds.) (1970). *Studies in Machiavellianism*. New York: Academic Press.

Cialdini, R. B. (1989). Indirect tactics of image management: Beyond basking. In R. A. Giacalone & P. Rosenfeld (Eds.), *Impression management in the organization* (pp. 45–56). Hillsdale, NJ: Erlbaum.

Cialdini, R. B., Borden, R., Thorne, A., Walker, M., Freeman, S., & Sloane, L. T. (1976). Basking in reflected glory: Three (football) field studies. *Journal of Personality and Social Psychology, 34*, 366–375.

Cialdini, R. B., & DeNicholas, M. E. (1989). Self-presentation by association. *Journal of Personality and Social Psychology, 57*, 626–631.

Cialdini, R. B., & Kenrick, D. T. (1976). Altruism as hedonism: A social development perspective on the relationship of negative mood state and helping. *Journal of Personality and Social Psychology, 34*, 907–914.

Cialdini, R. B., & Richardson, K. D. (1980). Two indirect tactics of image management: Basking and blasting. *Journal of Personality and Social Psychology, 39*, 406–415.

Clance, P. R. (1985). *The imposter phenomenon: When success makes you feel like a fake*. Toronto: Bantam.

Clinkscales, K., & Gallo, J. (1977). How teens see it. In D. J. Bogue (Ed.), *Adolescent fertility* (pp. 134–144). Chicago: University of Chicago Press.

Conger, J. A., & Kanungo, R. N. (1987). Toward a behavioral theory of charismatic leadership in organizational settings. *Academy of Management Review, 12*, 637–647.

Cooley, C. H. (1902). *Human nature and the social order*. New York: Scribner.

Coopersmith, S. (1967). *The antecedents of self-esteem*. San Francisco: W. H. Freeman.

Cosmides, L., Tooby, J., & Barkow, J. H. (1992). Introduction: Evolutionary psychology and conceptual integration. In J. H. Barkow, L. Cosmides, & J. Tooby (Eds.), *The adapted mind* (pp. 3–15). Oxford: Oxford University Press.

Countess was chained for almost 50 years (1980, Nov. 10). *Columbus (OH) Dispatch,* p. 2.

Cozzarelli, C., & Major, B. (1990). Exploring the validity of the imposter phenomenon. *Journal of Social and Clinical Psychology, 9,* 401–417.

Crandall, V. C., Crandall, V. J., & Katkovsky, W. (1965). A children's social desirability questionnaire. *Journal of Consulting Psychology, 29,* 27–36.

Crocker, J., Cornwell, B., & Major, B. (1993). The stigma of overweight: Affective consequences of attributional ambiguity. *Journal of Personality and Social Psychology, 64,* 60–70.

Crowne, D. P., & Marlowe, D. (1964). *The approval motive.* New York: Wiley.

Croyle, R. T., & Cooper, J. (1983). Dissonance arousal: Physiological evidence. *Journal of Personality and Social Psychology, 45,* 782–791.

Darby, B. W., & Schlenker, B. R. (1982). Children's reactions to apologies. *Journal of Personality and Social Psychology, 43,* 742–753.

Darby, B. W., & Schlenker, B. R. (1989). Children's reactions to transgressions: Effects of the actor's apology, reputation, and remorse. *British Journal of Social Psychology, 28,* 353–364.

Darwin, C. (1872/1955). *The expression of emotion in man and animals.* New York: The Philosophical Library.

Davison, R., & Jones, S. C. (1976). Similarity in real-life friendship pairs. *Journal of Personality and Social Psychology, 34,* 313–317.

Dean, D. G., Braito, R., Powers, E. A., & Britton, B. (1975). Cultural contradictions and sex roles revisited: A replication and a reassessment. *The Sociological Quarterly, 16,* 201–215.

Deaux, K. (1977). Sex differences. In T. Blass (Ed.), *Personality variables in social behavior.* Hillsdale, NJ: Erlbaum.

Deaux, K., & Major, B. (1987). Putting gender into context: An interactive model of gender-related behavior. *Psychological Review, 94,* 369–389.

DeGree, C. E., & Snyder, C. R. (1985). Adler's psychology (of use) today: Personal history of traumatic events as a self-handicapping strategy. *Journal of Personality and Social Psychology, 48,* 1512–1519.

de Mille, R. (1980). *The don Juan papers.* Santa Barbara: Ross-Erikson.

Denzin, N. K. (1984). *On understanding emotion.* San Francisco: Jossey-Bass.

DePaulo, B. M. (1992). Nonverbal behavior and self-presentation. *Psychological Bulletin, 111,* 203–243.

DePaulo, B. M., Epstein, J. A., & LeMay, C. S. (1990). Responses of the socially anxious to the prospect of interpersonal evaluation. *Journal of Personality, 58,* 623–640.

DePaulo, B. M., Kenny, D. A., Hoover, C., Webb, W., & Oliver, P. (1987). Accuracy of person perception: Do people know what kinds of impressions they convey? *Journal of Personality and Social Psychology, 52,* 303–313.

Derlega, V. J., Metts, S., Petronio, S., & Margulis, S. T. (1993). *Self-disclosure.* Newbury Park, CA: Sage.

Derlega, V. J., Wilson, J., & Chaiken, A. L. (1976). Friendship and disclosure reciprocity. *Journal of Personality and Social Psychology, 34,* 578–582.

Deutsch, M., & Gerard, H. (1955). Study of normative and informational influence upon individual judgment. *Journal of Abnormal and Social Psychology, 51,* 629–636.

Deutsch, F. M., & Lamberti, D. M. (1986). Does social approval increase helping? *Personality and Social Psychology Bulletin, 12,* 149–157.

Diener, E. (1980). Deindividuation: The absence of self-awareness and self-regulation in group members. In P. B. Paulus (Ed.), *The psychology of group influence.* Hillsdale, NJ: Erlbaum.

Dies, R. (1970). Need for social approval and blame assignment. *Journal of Consulting and Clinical Psychology, 35,* 311–316.

Dingler-Duhon, M., & Brown, B. B. (1987). Self-disclosure as an influence strategy: Effects of Machiavellianism, androgyny, and sex. *Sex Roles, 16,* 109–123.

Dion, K., Berscheid, E., & Walster, E. (1972). What is beautiful is good. *Journal of Personality and Social Psychology, 24,* 285–290.

Dion, K. L., Dion, K. K., & Keelan, J. P. (1990). Appearance anxiety as a dimension of social-evaluative anxiety: Exploring the ugly duckling syndrome. *Contemporary Social Psychology, 14,* 220–224.

Dlugolecki, D. W., & Schlenker, B. R. (1985, August). *Self-presentations and self-appraisals: Cognitive activity, internalization, and behavior.* Paper presented at the meeting of the American Psychological Association, Los Angeles.

Doherty, K., & Schlenker, B. R. (1991). Self-consciousness and strategic self-presentation. *Journal of Personality, 59,* 1–18.

Doherty, K., Weigold, M. F., & Schlenker, B. R. (in press). Self-serving interpretations of motives. *Personality and Social Psychology Bulletin.*

Dollard, J. (1949). Under what conditions do opinions predict behavior? *Public Opinion Quarterly, 12,* 623–632.

Domar, A. D. (1986). Psychological aspects of pelvic exams: Individual needs and physician involvement. *Women and Health, 10,* 75–89.

Duffy, M., & Goodgame, D. (1992, Aug. 24). Warrior for the status quo. *Time,* pp. 32–45.

Dunn, P. K., & Ondercin, P. (1981). Personality variables related to compulsive eating in college women. *Women and Health, 10,* 75–89.

Duval, S., & Wicklund, R. A. (1972). *A theory of objective self-awareness.* New York: Academic Press.

Edelmann, R. J. (1987). *The psychology of embarrassment.* New York: John Wiley & Sons.

Edelmann, R. J., & Iwawaki, S. (1987). Self-reported embarrassment and consequences of embarrassment in the United Kingdom and Japan. *Psychologia—An International Journal of Psychology in the Orient, 30,* 205–216.

Elliott, G. C. (1982). Self-esteem and self-presentation among the young as a function of age and gender. *Journal of Youth and Adolescence, 11,* 135–153.

Elwood, J. M., Whitehead, S. M., & Gallagher, R. P. (1989). Epidemiology of human malignant skin tumors with special reference to natural and artificial ultraviolet radiation exposures. In C. J. Conti, T. J. Slaga, & A. J. P. Klein-Szanto (Eds.), *Skin tumors: Experimental and clinical aspects* (pp. 55–84). New York: Raven.

Emerson, J. P. (1970). Nothing unusual is happening. In T. Shibutani (Ed.), *Human nature and collective behavior: Papers in honor of Herbert Blumer* (pp. 208–222). Englewood Cliffs, NJ: Prentice-Hall.

Epstein, S. (1973). The self-concept revisited: Or a theory of a theory. *American Psychologist, 28,* 404–416.

Exline, R. V., Thibaut, J., Hickey, C. B., & Gumbert, P. (1970). Visual interaction in relation to Machiavellianism and an unethical act. In Christie, R., & Geis, F. L. (Eds.) *Studies in Machiavellianism* (pp. 53–75). New York: Academic Press.

Farina, A., Allen, J. G., & Saul, B. B. (1968). The role of the stigmatized person in affecting social relationships. *Journal of Personality, 36,* 169–182.

Farina, A., Holland, C. H., & Ring, K. (1966). Role of stigma and set in interpersonal interaction. *Journal of Abnormal Psychology, 71,* 421–428.

Fazio, R. H., Effrein, E. A., & Falender, V. J. (1981). Self-perceptions following social interactions. *Journal of Personality and Social Psychology, 41,* 232–242.

Fears, T. R., & Scotto, J. (1982). Changes in skin cancer morbidity between 1971–72 and 1977–78. *Journal of the National Cancer Institute, 69,* 365–370.

Feingold, A. (1992). Good-looking people are not what we think. *Psychological Bulletin, 111,* 304–341.

Feldman, D. C., & Klich, N. R. (1991). Impression management and career strategies. In R. A. Giacalone & P. Rosenfeld (Eds.), *Applied impression management* (pp. 67–80). Newbury Park, CA: Sage.

Felson, R. B. (1978). Aggression as impression management. *Social Psychology Quarterly, 41,* 205–213.

Felson, R. B. (1982). Impression management and the escalation of aggression and violence. *Social Psychology Quarterly, 45,* 245–254.

Felson, R. B., & Tedeschi, J. T. (1993). *Aggression and violence: Social interactionist perspectives.* Washington, D.C.: American Psychological Association.

Fenigstein, A. (1979). Self-consciousness, self-attention, and social interaction. *Journal of Personality and Social Psychology, 37,* 75–86.

Fenigstein, A., Scheier, M. F., & Buss, A. H. (1975). Public and private self-consciousness: Assessment and theory. *Journal of Consulting and Clinical Psychology, 43,* 522–527.

Festinger, L. (1957). *A theory of cognitive dissonance.* Stanford, CA: Stanford University Press.

Festinger, L., & Carlsmith, J. M. (1959). Cognitive consequences of forced compliance. *Journal of Abnormal and Social Psychology, 58,* 203–210.

Festinger, L., Schachter, S., & Back, K. (1950). *Social pressures in informal groups.* New York: Harper.

Fielding, J. E., & Williams, C. A. (1991). Adolescent pregnancy in the United States: A review and recommendations for clinicians and research needs. *American Journal of Preventive Medicine, 7,* 47–52.

Finch, J. F., & Cialdini, R. B. (1989). Another indirect tactic of (self-) image management: Boosting. *Personality and Social Psychology Bulletin, 15,* 222–232.

Findlay, S. (1988, May 1). Buying the perfect body. *U.S. News and World Report,* pp. 68–75.

Fleming, J. H., Darley, J. M., Hilton, J. L., & Kojetin, B. A. (1990). Multiple audience problem: A strategic communication perspective on social perception. *Journal of Personality and Social Psychology, 58,* 593–609.

Fleming, J. H., & Rudman, L. A. (1993). Between a rock and a hard place: Self-concept regulating and communicative properties of distancing behaviors. *Journal of Personality and Social Psychology, 64,* 44–59.

Flett, G. L., Blankstein, K. R., Pliner, P., & Bator, C. (1988). Impression-management and self-deception components of appraised emotional experience. *British Journal of Social Psychology, 27*, 67–77.

Fontana, A. F., & Gessner, T. (1969). Patients' goals and the manifestation of psychopathology. *Journal of Consulting and Clinical Psychology, 33*, 247–253.

Fontana, A. F., & Klein, E. B. (1968). Self-presentation and the schizophrenic "deficit." *Journal of Consulting and Clinical Psychology, 32*, 250–256.

Forsyth, D. R. (1980). The functions of attributions. *Social Psychology Quarterly, 43*, 184–189.

Forsyth, D. R. (1987). *Social psychology*. Monterey, CA: Brooks/Cole.

Forsyth, D. R., Riess, M., & Schlenker, B. R. (1977). Impression management concerns governing reactions to a faulty decision. *Representative Research in Social Psychology, 8*, 12–22.

Forsyth, D. R., Schlenker, B. R., Leary, M. R., & McCown, N. E. (1985). Self-presentational determinants of sex differences in leadership. *Small Group Behavior, 16*, 197–210.

Frable, D. E. S., Blackstone, T., & Scherbaum, C. (1990). Marginal and mindful: Deviants in social interactions. *Journal of Personality and Social Psychology, 59*, 140–149.

Franke, R. & Leary, M. R. (1991). Disclosure of sexual orientation by lesbians and gay men: A comparison of private and public processes. *Journal of Social and Clinical Psychology, 10*, 262–269.

Freedman, R. J. (1984). Reflections on beauty as it relates to health in adolescent females. *Women and Health, 9*, 29–45.

French, J. R. P., & Raven, B. (1959). The bases of social power. In D. Cartwright (Ed.), *Studies in social power*. Ann Arbor, MI: Institute for Social Research.

Frey, D. (1978). Reactions to success and failure in public and in private conditions. *Journal of Experimental Social Psychology, 14*, 172–179.

Fridlund, A. J. (1991). The sociality of solitary smiling: Potentiation by an implicit audience. *Journal of Personality and Social Psychology, 60*, 229–240.

Frijda, N. H. (1986). *The emotions*. Cambridge: Cambridge University Press.

Froming, W. J., & Carver, C. S. (1981). Divergent influences of private and public self-consciousness in a compliance paradigm. *Journal of Research in Personality, 15*, 159–171.

Furnham, A., & Henderson, M. (1982). The good, the bad, and the mad: Response bias in self-report measures. *Personality and Individual Differences, 3*, 311–320.

Gabrenya, W. K., & Arkin, R. M. (1980). Factor structure and factor correlates of the Self-Monitoring Scale. *Personality and Social Psychology Bulletin, 6*, 13–22.

Gaes, G. G., Kalle, R. J., & Tedeschi, J. T. (1978). Impression management in the forced compliance situation: Two studies using the bogus pipeline. *Journal of Experimental Social Psychology, 14*, 493–510.

Gallup, G. G. (1977). Self-recognition in primates: A comparative approach to the bidirectional properties of consciousness. *American Psychologist, 32*, 329–338.

Geen, R. G. (1991). Social motivation. *Annual review of psychology, 42*, 377–399.

Geis, F., & Christie, R. (1970). Overview of experimental research. In Christie, R., & Geis, F. L. (Eds.) *Studies in Machiavellianism* (pp. 258–313). New York: Academic Press.

Geis, F., Weinheimer, S., & Berger, D. (1970). Playing legislature: Cool heads and hot issues. In Christie, R., & Geis, F. L. (Eds.) *Studies in Machiavellianism* (pp. 190–209). New York: Academic Press.

Geis, F. L., & Moon, T. H. (1981). Machiavellianism and deception. *Journal of Personality and Social Psychology, 41,* 766–775.

Geizer, R. S., Rarick, D. L., & Soldow, G. F. (1977). Deception and judgment accuracy: A study in person perception. *Personality and Social Psychology Bulletin,* 446–449.

Geller, J. L., Erlen, J., Kaye, N. S., & Fisher, W. H. (1990). Feigned insanity in nineteeth-century America: Tactics, trials, and truth. *Behavioral Sciences and the Law, 8,* 3–26.

Gentry, M., & Herrman, D. J. (1990). Memory contrivances in everyday life. *Personality and Social Psychology Bulletin, 16,* 241–253.

Gergen, K. J. (1965). The effects of interaction goals and personalistic feedback on the presentation of self. *Journal of Personality and Social Psychology, 1,* 413–424.

Gergen, K. J. (1968). Personal consistency and the presentation of self. In C. Gordon & K. J. Gergen (Eds.), *The self in social interaction* (Vol. 1, pp. 299–308). New York: Wiley.

Gergen, K. J., & Taylor, M. G. (1969). Social expectancy and self-presentation in a status hierarchy. *Journal of Experimental Social Psychology, 5,* 79–92.

Gergen, K. J., & Wishnov, V. B. (1965). Others' self-evaluation and interaction anticipation as determinants of self-presentation. *Journal of Personality and Social Psychology, 2,* 348–358.

Giacalone, R. A., & Rosenfeld, P. (1989). *Impression management in the organization.* Hillsdale, NJ: Erlbaum.

Giacalone, R. A., & Rosenfeld, P. (1991). *Applied impression management.* Newbury Park, CA: Sage.

Gibbons, F. X., & Gaeddert, W. P. (1984). Focus of attention and placebo utility. *Journal of Experimental Social Psychology, 20,* 159–176.

Giddon, D. B. (1983). Through the looking glasses of physicians, dentists, and patients. *Perspectives in Biology and Medicine, 26,* 451–458.

Gilbert, D. T., & Jones, E. E. (1986). Exemplification: The self-presentation of moral character. *Journal of Personality, 54,* 593–615.

Godfrey, D. K., Jones, E. E., & Lord, C. G. (1986). Self-promotion is not ingratiating. *Journal of Personality and Social Psychology, 50,* 106–115.

Goffman, E. (1955). On facework. *Psychiatry, 18,* 213–231.

Goffman, E. (1959). *The presentation of self in everyday life.* Garden City, NY: Doubleday Anchor.

Goffman, E. (1961). *Encounters.* Indianapolis: Bobbs-Merrill.

Goffman, E. (1963). *Stigma.* Englewood Cliffs, NJ: Prentice-Hall.

Goffman, E. (1967). *Interaction ritual.* Garden City, NJ: Anchor.

Goffman, E. (1971). *Relations in public.* New York: Basic Books.

Gold, R. S., Skinner, M. J., Grant, P. J., & Plummer, D. C. (1991). Situational factors and thought processes associated with unprotected intercourse in gay men. *Psychology and Health, 5,* 259–278.

Gollwitzer, P. M. (1986). Striving for specific identities: The social reality of self-symbolizing. In R. F. Baumeister (Ed.), *Public self and private self* (pp. 143–160). New York: Springer-Verlag.

Gonzales, M. H., & Meyers, S. A. (1993). "Your mother would like me": Self-presentation in the personal ads of heterosexual and homosexual men and women. *Personality and Social Psychology Bulletin, 19*, 131–142.

Gonzales, M. H., Pederson, J. H., Manning, D. J., & Wetter, D. W. (1990). Pardon my gaffe: Effects of sex, status, and consequence severity on accounts. *Journal of Personality and Social Psychology, 58*, 610–621.

Goodall, J. (1988). *In the shadow of man*. Boston: Houghton Mifflin.

Goodman, E. (1991). Employee's natural look earns her a pink slip. *Winston-Salem Journal*, July 17, p. 8.

Gordon, G. (1966). *Role theory and illness: A sociological perspective*. New Haven, CT: College and University Press.

Gould, S., & Penley, L. E. (1984). Career strategies and salary progression: A study of their relationships in a municipal bureaucracy. *Organizational Behavior and Human Performance, 34*, 244–265.

Gove, W. R., Hughes, M., & Geerken, M. R. (1980). Playing dumb: A form of impression management with undesirable side effects. *Social Psychology Quarterly, 43*, 89–102.

Graham, J. W., Gentry, K. W., & Green, J. (1981). The self-presentational nature of emotional expression: Some evidence. *Personality and Social Psychology Bulletin, 7*, 467–474.

Grammer, K. (1990). Strangers meet: Laughter and nonverbal signs of interest in opposite-sex encounters. *Journal of Nonverbal Behavior, 14*, 209–236.

Greenberg, J., & Pyszczynski, T. (1985). Compensatory self-inflation: A response to the threat to self-regard of public failure. *Journal of Personality and Social Psychology, 49*, 273–280.

Greenfield, M. (1992). Rediscovering "real people." *Newsweek*, January 20, p. 62.

Gregorich, S. E., Kemple, K., & Leary, M. R. (1986). Fear of negative evaluation and reactions to information regarding others' performances. *Representative Research in Social Psychology, 16*, 15–27.

Gross, A., & Latané, B. (1974). Receiving help, reciprocation, and interpersonal attraction. *Journal of Applied Social Psychology, 4*, 220–223.

Hall, P. M. (1979). The presidency and impression management. In N. K. Denzin (Ed.), *Studies in symbolic interaction* (Vol. 2, pp. 283–305). Greenwich, CT: JAI Press.

Hanna, J. (1989, September 25). Sexual abandon: The condom is unpopular on campus. *Maclean's*, p. 48.

Hardy, C. J., Hall, E. G., & Prestholdt, P. H. (1986). The mediational role of social influence in the perception of exertion. *Journal of Sport Psychology, 8*, 88–104.

Harré, R., & Lamb, R. (1986). *The dictionary of personality and social psychology*. Cambridge, MA: The MIT Press.

Harris, R. N., & Snyder, C. R. (1986). The role of uncertain self-esteem in self-handicapping. *Journal of Personality and Social Psychology, 51*, 451–458.

Hart, E. A., Leary, M. R., & Rejeski, W. J. (1989). The measurement of social physique anxiety. *Journal of Sport and Exercise Psychology, 11*, 94–104.

Hass, R. G. (1981). Presentational strategies and the social expression of attitudes: Impression management within limits. In J. T. Tedeschi (Ed.), *Impression management theory and social psychological research* (pp. 127–146). New York: Academic Press.

Hayes, D., & Ross, C. E. (1987). Concern with appearance, health beliefs, and eating habits. *Journal of Health and Social Behavior, 28*, 120–130.

Heider, F. (1958). *The psychology of interpersonal relations.* New York: Wiley.

Heise, D. (1989). Effects of emotion displays on social identification. *Social Psychology Quarterly, 52,* 10–21.

Hendricks, M., & Brickman, P. (1974). Effects of status and knowledgeability of audience on self-presentation. *Sociometry, 37,* 440–449.

Henley, N. (1977). *Body politics: Power, sex, and nonverbal communication.* Englewood Cliffs, NJ: Prentice-Hall.

Herold, E. S. (1981). Contraceptive embarrassment and contraceptive behavior among young single women. *Journal of Youth and Adolescence, 10,* 233–242.

Hill, M. G., Weary, G., & Williams, J. (1986). Depression: A self-presentation formulation. In R. F. Baumeister (Ed.), *Public self and private self* (pp. 213–240). New York: Springer-Verlag.

Hogan, R., & Jones, W. H. (1983). A role theoretical model of criminal conduct. In W. S. Laufer & J. M. Days (Eds.), *Personality theory, moral development, and criminal behavior.* Boston: Lexington.

Hope, D. A., & Heimberg, R. G. (1988). Public and private self-consciousness and social phobia. *Journal of Personality Assessment, 52,* 626–639.

Horowitz, R., & Schwartz, G. (1974). Honor, normative ambiguity, and gang violence. *American Sociological Review, 39,* 238–251.

House, W. C. (1980). Effects of knowledge that attributions will be observed by others. *Journal of Research in Personality, 14,* 528–545.

Hull, J. (1981). A self-awareness model of the causes and effects of alcohol consumption. *Journal of Abnormal Psychology, 90,* 586–600.

Jackson, S. A., & Marsh, H. W. (1986). Athletic or antisocial? The female sport experience. *Journal of Sport Psychology, 8,* 198–211.

Janis, I. (1982). *Victims of groupthink* (2nd ed.). Boston: Houghton-Mifflin.

Jaynes, J. (1976). *The origin of consciousness in the breakdown of the bicameral mind.* Boston: Houghton-Mifflin.

Jellison, J. M., & Gentry, K. W. (1978). A self-presentation interpretation of the seeking of social approval. *Personality and Social Psychology Bulletin, 4,* 227–230.

Johnson, R., Conlee, M., & Tesser, A. (1974). Effects of similarity of fate on bad news transmissions: A reexamination. *Journal of Personality and Social Psychology, 29,* 644–648.

Jones, E. E. (1964). *Ingratiation.* New York: Appleton-Century-Crofts.

Jones, E. E. (1990). *Interpersonal perception.* New York: W. H. Freeman.

Jones, E. E., & Baumeister, R. F. (1976). The self-monitor looks at the ingratiator. *Journal of Personality, 44,* 654–674.

Jones, E. E., & Berglas, S. (1978). Control of attributions about the self through self-handicapping strategies: The appeal of alcohol and the role of underachievement. *Personality and Social Psychology Bulletin, 4,* 200–206.

Jones, E. E., Berglas, S., Rhodewalt, F., & Skelton, J. R. (1981). Effects of strategic self-presentation on subsequent self-esteem. *Journal of Personality and Social Psychology, 41,* 407–421.

Jones, E. E., Brenner, K. J., & Knight, J. G. (1990). When failure elevates self-esteem. *Personality and Social Psychology Bulletin, 16,* 200–209.

Jones, E. E., Farina, A., Hastorf, A. H., Markus, H., Miller, D. T., & Scott, R. A. (1984). *Social stigma: The psychology of marked relationships.* New York: W. H. Freeman.

Jones, E. E., Gergen, K. J., Gumpert, P., & Thibaut, J. W. (1965). Some conditions affecting the use of ingratiation to influence performance evaluation. *Journal of Personality and Social Psychology, 1,* 613–625.

Jones, E. E., Gergen, K. J., & Jones, R. G. (1963). Tactics of ingratiation among leaders and subordinates in a status hierarchy. *Psychological Monographs, 77*(3, Whole No. 566).

Jones, E. E., & Gordon, E. M. (1972). Timing of self-disclosure and its effects on personal attraction. *Journal of Personality and Social Psychology, 24,* 358–365.

Jones, E. E., & Pittman, T. S. (1982). Toward a general theory of strategic self-presentation. In J. Suls (Ed.), *Psychological perspectives on the self* (Vol. 1, pp. 231–262). Hillsdale, NJ: Erlbaum.

Jones, E. E., & Wortman, C. (1973). *Ingratiation: An attributional approach.* Morristown, NJ: General Learning Press.

Jones, J. L., & Leary, M. R. (1994). Effects of appearance-based admonitions against sun exposure on tanning intentions in young adults. *Health Psychology, 13,* 86–90.

Jones, S. C., & Tager, R. (1972). Exposure to others, need for social approval, and reactions to agreement and disagreement from others. *Journal of Social Psychology, 86,* 111–120.

Jones, W. H., Nickel, T. W., & Schmidt, A. (1979). Machiavellianism and self-disclosure. *Journal of Psychology, 102,* 33–41.

Kandel, D. B. (1978). Similarity in real-life adolescent friendship pairs. *Journal of Personality and Social Psychology, 36,* 306–312.

Karau, S. J., & Williams, K. D. (1993). Social loafing: A meta-analytic review and theoretical integration. *Journal of Personality and Social Psychology, 65,* 681–706.

Katzman, M. A., & Wolchik, S. A. (1984). Bulimia and binge eating in college women: A comparison of personality and behavioral characteristics. *Journal of Consulting and Clinical Psychology, 52,* 423–428.

Kauffman, B. E., & Anderson, N. R. (1992, August). "And so's your mother!": Current experiences of teasing and embarrassment among children and adolescents. Paper presented at the meeting of the American Psychological Association, Washington, D.C.

Kelly, F. S., Farina, A., & Mosher, D. L. (1971). Ability of schizophrenic women to create a favorable or unfavorable impression on an interviewer. *Journal of Consulting and Clinical Psychology, 36,* 404–409.

Kelly, A. E., McKillop, K. J., & Neimeyer, G. J. (1991). Effects of counselor as audience on internalization of depressed and nondepressed self-presentations. *Journal of Counseling Psychology, 38,* 126–132.

Kiesler, D. J. (1983). The 1982 interpersonal circle: A taxonomy for complementarity in human transactions. *Psychological Review, 90,* 185–214.

Kimble, C. E., & Zehr, H. D. (1982). Self-consciousness, information load, self-presentation, and memory in a social situation. *Journal of Social Psychology, 118,* 39–46.

Klapp, O. E. (1964). *Symbolic leaders.* Chicago: Aldine-Atherton.

Kleck, R. E., & Strenta, A. (1980). Perceptions of the impact of negatively valued physical characteristics on social interaction. *Journal of Personality and Social Psychology, 39,* 861–873.

Kolditz, T. A., & Arkin, R. M. (1982). An impression management interpretation of the self-handicapping strategy. *Journal of Personality and Social Psychology, 43,* 492–502.
Komarovsky, M. (1950). Cultural contradictions and sex roles. *American Journal of Sociology, 52,* 184–189.
Korda, M. (1976). *Power.* New York: Ballatine Books.
Kowalski, R. M. (1992). Nonverbal behaviors and perceptions of sexual intentions: Effects of sexual connotativeness, verbal response, and rape outcome. *Basic and Applied Social Psychology, 13,* 427–445.
Kowalski, R. M. (1993). Inferring sexual interest from behavioral cues: Effects of gender and sexual-relevant attitudes. *Sex Roles, 29,* 13–31.
Kowalski, R. M., & Chapple, T. (1993). Effects of the social stigma of menstruation on impression-motivation: Facilitator or inhibitor? Paper presented at the meeting of the Southeastern Psychological Association, Atlanta.
Kowalski, R. M., & Leary, M. R. (1990). Strategic self-presentation and the avoidance of aversive events: Antecedents and consequences of self-enhancement and self-depreciation. *Journal of Experimental Social Psychology, 26,* 322–336.

Lamphere, R., & Leary, M. R. (1988, April). *Resolution of a principled-pragmatic self-presentational dilemma.* Paper presented at the meeting of the Southeastern Psychological Association, New Orleans.
Lamphere, R. A., & Leary, M. R. (1990). Private and public self-processes: A return to James' constituents of the self. *Personality and Social Psychology Bulletin, 16,* 717–725.
Latané, B., & Darley, J. M. (1970). *The unresponsive bystander: Why doesn't he help?* New York: Appleton-Century-Crofts.
Laux, L., & Weber, H. (1991). Presentation of self in coping with anger and anxiety: An intentional approach. *Anxiety Research, 3,* 233–255.
Leary, M. R. (1980). *Testing a social psychological model of shyness.* Unpublished doctoral dissertation, University of Florida.
Leary, M. R. (1983a). A brief version of the Fear of Negative Evaluation Scale. *Personality and Social Psychology Bulletin, 9,* 371–376.
Leary, M. R. (1983b). Social anxiousness: The construct and its measurement. *Journal of Personality Assessment, 47,* 66–75.
Leary, M. R. (1983c). *Understanding social anxiety.* Beverly Hills, CA: Sage.
Leary, M. R. (1986). The impact of interactional impediments on social anxiety and self-presentation. *Journal of Experimental Social Psychology, 22,* 122–135.
Leary, M. R. (1989). Self-presentational processes in leadership emergence and effectiveness. In R. A. Giacalone & P. Rosenfield (Ed.), *Impression management in the organization.* Hillsdale, NJ: Erlbaum.
Leary, M. R. (1990a). Responses to social exclusion: Social anxiety, jealousy, loneliness, depression, and low self-esteem. *Journal of Social and Clinical Psychology, 9,* 221–229.
Leary, M. R. (1990b). Social anxiety, shyness, and related constructs. In J. Robinson, P. Shaver, & L. Wrightsman (Eds.), *Measures of personality and social psychological attitudes* (pp. 161–194). New York: Academic Press.

Leary, M. R. (1992). Self-presentational processes in exercise and sport. *Journal of Sport and Exercise Psychology, 14,* 339–351.

Leary, M. R. (1993). The interplay of private self-processes and interpersonal factors in self-presentation. In J. Suls (Ed.), *Psychological perspectives on the self* (Vol. 4). Hillsdale, NJ: Erlbaum.

Leary, M. R., Barnes, B. D., & Griebel, C. (1986). Cognitive, affective, and attributional effects of potential threats to self-esteem. *Journal of Social and Clinical Psychology, 4,* 461–474.

Leary, M. R., Britt, T. W., Cutlip, W. D., & Templeton, J. L. (1992). Social blushing. *Psychological Bulletin, 112,* 446–460.

Leary, M. R., & Downs, D. L. (in press). Interpersonal functions of the self-esteem motive: The self-esteem system as a sociometer. In M. Kernis (Ed.), *Efficacy, agency, and self-esteem.* New York: Plenum.

Leary, M. R., & Forsyth, D. R. (1987). Attributions of responsibility for collective endeavors. In C. Hendrick (Ed.), *Group processes* (pp. 167–188). Newbury Park, CA: Sage.

Leary, M. R., & Jones, J. L. (1993). The social psychology of tanning and sunscreen use: Self-presentational variables as a predictor of health risk. *Journal of Applied Social Psychology, 23,* 1390–1406.

Leary, M. R., Knight, P. D., & Barnes, B. D. (1986). Ethical ideologies of the Machiavellian. *Personality and Social Psychology Bulletin, 12,* 75–80.

Leary, M. R., Knight, P. D., & Johnson, K. A. (1987). Social anxiety and dyadic conversation: A verbal response analysis. *Journal of Social and Clinical Psychology, 5,* 34–50.

Leary, M. R., & Kowalski, R. M. (1990). Impression management: A literature review and two-factor model. *Psychological Bulletin, 107,* 34–47.

Leary, M. R., & Kowalski, R. M. (1993). The Interaction Anxiousness Scale: Construct and criterion-related validity. *Journal of Personality Assessment, 61,* 136–146.

Leary, M. R., & Kowalski, R. M. (in press). The self-presentation model of social anxiety/phobia. In R. Heimberg, M. Liebowitz, D. Hope, & F. Schneier (Eds.), *Social phobia: Diagnosis, assessment, and treatment.* New York: Guilford.

Leary, M. R., Kowalski, R. M., & Bergen, D. J. (1988). Interpersonal information acquisition and confidence in first encounters. *Personality and Social Psychology Bulletin, 14,* 68–77.

Leary, M. R., Kowalski, R. M., & Campbell, C. (1988). Self-presentational concerns and social anxiety: The role of generalized impression expectancies. *Journal of Research in Personality, 22,* 308–321.

Leary, M. R., & Meadows, S. (1991). Predictors, elicitors, and concomitants of social blushing. *Journal of Personality and Social Psychology, 60,* 254–262.

Leary, M. R., & Miller, R. S. (1986). *Social psychology and dysfunctional behavior.* New York: Springer-Verlag.

Leary, M. R., Nezlek, J., Downs, D., Radford-Davenport, J., Martin, J., & McMullen, A. (1994). Self-presentation in everyday encounters: Effects of target familiarity and gender composition. *Journal of Personality and Social Psychology.*

Leary, M. R., Rejeski, W. J., Britt, T. W., & Smith, G. (1993). *Physiological differences between embarrassment and social anxiety.* Manuscript under review, Wake Forest University.

Leary, M. R., Robertson, R. B., Barnes, B. D., & Miller, R. S. (1986). Self-presentations of small group leaders: Effects of role requirements and leadership orientation. *Journal of Personality and Social Psychology, 51,* 742–748.

Leary, M. R., & Schlenker, B. R. (1980). Self-presentation in a task-oriented leadership situation. *Representative Research in Social Psychology, 11,* 152–158.

Leary, M. R., & Shepperd, J. A. (1986). Behavioral self-handicaps versus self-reported handicaps: A conceptual note. *Journal of Personality and Social Psychology, 51,* 1265–1268.

Leary, M. R., Tchividjian, L. R., & Kraxberger, B. E. (1994). Self-presentation can be hazardous to your health: Impression management and health risk. Manuscript under review, Wake Forest University.

Lefebvre, L. M. (1975). Encoding and decoding of ingratiation in modes of smiling and gaze. *British Journal of Social and Clinical Psychology, 14,* 33–42.

Lennox, R. D., & Wolfe, R. N. (1984). Revision of the self-monitoring scale. *Journal of Personality and Social Psychology, 46,* 1349–1364.

Lerman, C., Rimer, B., Trock, B., Balshem, A., & Engstrom, P. F. (1990). Factors associated with repeat adherence to breast cancer screening. *Preventive Medicine, 19,* 279–290.

Lewis, M., Sullivan, M. W., Stanger, C., & Weiss, M. (1989). Self development and self-conscious emotions. *Child Development, 60,* 146–156.

Linderman, G. F. (1987). *Embattled courage.* New York: Free Press.

Lindskold, S., & Propst, L. R. (1981). Deindividuation, self-awareness, and impression management. In J. T. Tedeschi (Ed.), *Impression management theory and social psychological research* (pp. 201–222). New York: Academic Press.

Lord, C. G., Saenz, D. D., & Godfrey, D. K. (1987). Effects of perceived scrutiny on participant memory for social interaction. *Journal of Experimental Social Psychology, 23,* 498–517.

Lott, D. E., & Sommer, R. (1967). Seating arrangements and status. *Journal of Personality and Social Psychology, 7,* 90–95.

Ludwig, A. M., & Farrelly, F. (1967). The weapons of insanity. *American Journal of Psychotherapy, 21,* 737–749.

Machiavelli, N. (1513/1966). *The prince and selected discourses.* New York: Bantam Books.

Maddux, J. E., Norton, L. W., & Leary, M. R. (1988). Cognitive components of social anxiety: An investigation of the integration of self-presentation theory and self-efficacy theory. *Journal of Social and Clinical Psychology, 6,* 180–190.

Manis, M., Cornell, S. D., & Moore, J. C. (1974). Transmission of attitude-relevant information through a communication change. *Journal of Personality and Social Psychology, 30,* 81–94.

Manning, A. (1972). *An introduction to animal behavior* (2nd ed.). Reading, MA: Addison-Wesley.

Markus, H., & Nurius, P. (1986). Possible selves. *American Psychologist, 41,* 954–969.

Martens, R., & Landers, D. M. (1972). Evaluation potential as a determinant of coaction effects. *Journal of Experimental Social Psychology, 8,* 347–359.

McGovern, L. P. (1976). Dispositional social anxiety and helping behavior under three conditions of threat. *Journal of Personality, 44,* 84–97.

McGraw, K. M. (1990). Avoiding blame: An experimental investigation of political excuses and justifications. *British Journal of Political Science, 20*, 119–142.

McGraw, K. M. (1991). Managing blame: An experimental test of the effects of political accounts. *American Political Science Review, 4*, 1133–1157.

McGraw, K. M., Timpone, R., & Bruck, G. (in press). Justifying controversial political decisions: Home style in the laboratory. *Political Behavior*.

McKillop, Jr., K. J., Berzonsky, M. D., & Schlenker, B. R. (1992). The impact of self-presentations on self-beliefs: Effects of social identity and self-presentational context. *Journal of Personality, 60*, 789–808.

Mead, G. H. (1934). *Mind, self, and society*. Chicago: University of Chicago Press.

Meleshko, K. G. A., & Alden, L. (1993). Anxiety and self-disclosure: Toward a motivational model. *Journal of Personality and Social Psychology, 64*, 1000–1009.

Milham, J., & Kellogg, R. W. (1980). Need for social approval: Impression management or self-deception? *Journal of Research in Personality, 14*, 445–457.

Miller, A. G. (1970). Role of physical attractiveness in person perception. *Psychonomic Science, 19*, 241–243.

Miller, A. G., Ashton, W. A., McHoskey, J. W., & Gimbel, J. (1990). What price attractiveness? Stereotype and risk factors in adolescence. *Journal of Applied Social Psychology, 20*, 1272–1300.

Miller, L. C., & Cox, C. L. (1982). For appearances' sake: Public self-consciousness and make-up use. *Personality and Social Psychology Bulletin, 8*, 748–751.

Miller, R. E. (1975). Nonverbal expressions of aggression and submission in social groups of primates. In P. Pliner, L. Krames, & T. Alloway (Eds.), *Nonverbal communication of aggression*. New York: Plenum.

Miller, R. S. (1986). Embarrassment: Causes and consequences. In W. H. Jones, J. M. Cheek, S. R. Briggs (Eds.), *Shyness: Perspectives on research and treatment* (pp. 295–311). New York: Plenum.

Miller, R. S. (1992). The nature and severity of self-reported embarrassing circumstances. *Personality and Social Psychology Bulletin, 18*, 190–198.

Miller, R. S., & Leary, M. R. (1992). Social sources and interactive functions of emotion: The case of embarrassment. In M. S. Clark (Ed.), *Emotion and social behavior* (pp. 202–221). Newbury Park, CA: Sage.

Miller, R. S., & Schlenker, B. R. (1985). Egotism in group members: Public and private attributions of responsibility for group performance. *Social Psychology Quarterly, 48*, 85–89.

Miller, T. M., Linke, J. G., & Linke, R. A. (1980). Survey on body image, weight, and diet of college students. *Journal of American Dietetic Association, 77*, 561–566.

Millstein, S. G., Adler, N. E., & Irwin, Jr., C. E. (1984). Sources of anxiety about pelvic examinations among adolescent females. *Journal of Adolescent Health Care, 5*, 105–111.

Modigliani, A. (1971). Embarrassment, facework, and eye contact: Testing a theory of embarrassment. *Journal of Personality and Social Psychology, 17*, 15–24.

Mori, D., Chaiken, S., & Pliner, P. (1987). "Eating lightly" and the self-presentation of femininity. *Journal of Personality and Social Psychology, 53*, 693–702.

Muehlenhard, C. L., & Hollabaugh, L. C. (1988). Do women sometimes say no when they mean yes? The prevalence and correlates of women's token resistence to sex. *Journal of Personality and Social Psychology, 54,* 872–879.

Nasser, M. (1988). Eating disorders: The cultural dimension. *Social Psychiatry and Psychiatric Epidemiology, 23,* 184–187.

Natale, M., Entin, E., & Jaffe, J. (1979). Vocal interruptions in dyadic communication as a function of speech and social anxiety. *Journal of Personality and Social Psychology, 37,* 865–878.

Native son? Two states claim Jackson (1991, Aug. 24). *Winston-Salem Journal,* p. 2.

Nisbett, R. E., & Wilson, T. D. (1977). Telling more than we can know: Verbal reports on mental processes. *Psychological Review, 84,* 231–259.

Ogilvie, D. M. (1987). The undesired self: A neglected variable in personality research. *Journal of Personality and Social Psychology, 52,* 379–385.

Orne, M. (1962). On the social psychology of the psychological experiment. *American Psychologist, 17,* 776–783.

Ornstein, S. (1989). Impression management through office design. In R. A. Giacalone & P. Rosenfeld (Eds.), *Impression management in the organization* (pp. 411–426). Hillsdale, NJ: Erlbaum.

Overheard. (1991, May 6). *Newsweek,* p. 21.

Page, M. M. (1981). Demand compliance in laboratory experiments. In J. T. Tedeschi (Ed.), *Impression management theory and social psychological research* (pp. 57–82). New York: Academic Press.

Palmer, D. L., & Kalin, R. (1985). Dogmatic responses to belief dissimilarity in the "bogus stranger" paradigm. *Journal of Personality and Social Psychology, 48,* 171–179.

Palmer, R. J., Welker, R. B., & Giacalone, R. (in press). The context of anticipated performance evaluation, self-presentational motivation, and performance effort. *Basic and Applied Social Psychology.*

Pandey, J. (1981). A note on social power through ingratiation among workers. *Journal of Occupational Psychology, 54,* 65–67.

Pandey, J. (1986). Sociocultural perspectives on ingratiation. In B. Maher (Ed.), *Progress in experimental personality research* (Vol. 14, pp. 205–229). New York: Academic Press.

Pandy, J., & Rastagi, R. (1979). Machiavellianism and ingratiation. *Journal of Social Psychology, 108,* 221–225.

Pardon My Blooper (1972). Phonograph recording.

Parrott, W. G., & Smith, S. F. (1991). Embarrassment: Actual vs. typical cases, classical vs. prototypical representations. *Cognition and Emotion, 5,* 467–488.

Parsons, T. (1951). *The social system.* Glencoe, IL: Free Press.

Patterson, M. L. (1987). Presentational and affect-management functions of nonverbal involvement. *Journal of Nonverbal Behavior, 11,* 110–122.

Paulhus, D. L. (1984). Two-component models of socially desirable responding. *Journal of Personality and Social Psychology, 46,* 598–609.

Paulhus, D. L. (1991). Measurement and control of response bias. In J. Robinson, P. Shaver, & L. Wrightsman (Eds.), *Measures of personality and social psychological attitudes* (pp. 17–59). San Diego: Academic Press.

Pendleton, M. G., & Batson, C. D. (1979). Self-presentation and the door-in-the-face technique for inducing compliance. *Personality and Social Psychology Bulletin, 5,* 77–81.

Pennebaker, J. W. (1990). *Opening up: The healing power of confiding in others*. New York: William Morrow & Co.

Periscope (1993), *Newsweek*, Oct. 18, p. 6.

Petronio, S., & Martin, J. N. (1986). Ramifications of revealing private information: A gender gap. *Journal of Clinical Psychology, 42*, 499–506.

Pilkonis, P. A. (1977). The behavioral consequences of shyness. *Journal of Personality, 45*, 596–611.

Pin, E. J., & Turndorf, J. (1990). Staging one's ideal self. In D. Brissett & C. Edgley (Eds.), *Life as theatre* (pp. 163–181). Hawthorne, NY: Aldine de Gruyter.

Pliner, P., & Chaiken, S. (1990). Eating, social motives, and self-presentation in women and men. *Journal of Experimental Social Psychology, 26*, 240–254.

Pliner, P., Chaiken, S., & Flett, G. L. (1990). Gender differences in concern with body weight and physical appearance over the life span. *Personality and Social Psychology Bulletin, 16*, 263–273.

Pozo, C., Carver, C. S., Wellens, A. R., & Scheier, M. F. (1991). Social anxiety and social perception: Construing others' reactions to the self. *Personality and Social Psychology Bulletin, 17*, 355–362.

Pyszczynski, T., & Greenberg, J. (1983). Determinants of reduction in intended effort as a strategy for coping with anticipated failure. *Journal of Research in Personality, 17*, 412–422.

Quinn, S. (1992, December 28). Beware of Washington. *Newsweek*, (pp. 26, 28).

Radelet, M. L., & Roberts, L. M. (1983). Parole interviews of sex offenders: The role of impression management. *Urban Life, 12*, 140–161.

Reis, H. T., & Gruzen, J. (1976). On mediating equity, equality, and self-interest: The role of self-presentation in social exchange. *Journal of Experimental Social Psychology, 12*, 487–503.

Reiss, M. (1982). Seating preferences as impression management: A literature review and theoretical integration. *Communication, 11*, 85–113.

Reiss, M., Kalle, R. J., & Tedeschi, J. T. (1981). Bogus pipeline attitude assessment, impression management, and misattribution in induced compliance settings. *Journal of Social Psychology, 115*, 247–258.

Reiss, M., & Rosenfeld, P. (1980). Seating preferences as nonverbal communication: A self-presentational analysis. *Journal of Applied Communication Research, 8*, 22–30.

Rejeski, W. J., & Lowe, C. A. (1980). Nonverbal expression of effort as causally relevant information. *Personality and Social Psychology Bulletin, 6*, 436–440.

Rezek, P. J., & Leary, M. R. (1991). Evaluation apprehension, hypochondriasis, and the strategic use of symptoms. *Basic and Applied Social Psychology, 11*, 233–242.

Rhodewalt, F. (1986). Self-presentation and the phenomenal self: On the stability and malleability of self-conceptions. In R. F. Baumeister (Ed.), *Public self and private self* (pp. 117–142). New York: Springer-Verlag.

Rhodewalt, F., & Agustsdottir, S. (1986). Effects of self-presentation on the phenomenal self. *Journal of Personality and Social Psychology, 50*, 47–55.

Rhodewalt, F., & Davison, Jr., J. (1986). Self-handicapping and subsequent performance: Role of outcome valence and attributional certainty. *Basic and Applied Social Psychology, 7*, 307–322.

Rhodewalt, F., Saltzman, A. T., & Wittmer, J. (1984). Self-handicapping among competitive athletes: The role of practice in self-esteem protection. *Basic and Applied Social Psychology, 5,* 197–210.

Riordan, C. A. (1989). Images of corporate success. In R. A. Giacalone & P. Rosenfeld (Eds.), *Impression management in the organization* (pp. 87–103). Hillsdale, NJ: Erlbaum.

Rodin, M., Price, J., Sanchez, F., & McElligot, S. (1989). Derogation, exclusion, and unfair treatment of persons with social flaws: Controllability of stigma and the attribution of prejudice. *Personality and Social Psychology Bulletin, 15,* 439–451.

Rosen, S., Cochran, W., & Musser, L. M. (1990). Reactions to a match versus mismatch between an applicant's self-presentational style and work reputation. *Basic and Appied Social Psychology, 11,* 117–129.

Rosen, S., & Tesser, A. (1970). On the reluctance to communicate undesirable information: The MUM effect. *Sociometry, 33,* 81–94.

Rosenfeld, H. M. (1966). Approval-seeking and approval-inducing functions of verbal and nonverbal responses in the dyad. *Journal of Personality and Social Psychology, 4,* 597–605.

Rosenfeld, L. B., & Bowen, G. L. (1991). Marital disclosure and marital satisfaction: Direct-effect versus interaction-effect models. *Western Journal of Speech Communication, 55,* 69–84.

Rosenfeld, P., Giacalone, R. A., & Tedeschi, J. T. (1984). Cognitive dissonance and impression management explanations for effort justification. *Personality and Social Psychology Bulletin, 10,* 394–401.

Rosenfeld, P., Melburg, V., & Tedeschi, J. T. (1981). Forgetting as an impression management strategy in the forced compliance situation. *Journal of Social Psychology, 114,* 69–74.

Roth, D. L., Harris, R. N., & Snyder, C. R. (1988). An individual differences measure of attributive and repudiative tactics of favorable self-presentation. *Journal of Social and Clinical Psychology, 6,* 159–170.

Roth, D. L., Snyder, C. R., & Pace, L. M. (1986). Dimensions of favorable self-presentation. *Journal of Personality and Social Psychology, 51,* 867–874.

Russo, N. F. (1966). Connotations of seating arrangements. *Cornell Journal of Social Relations, 2,* 37–44.

Rx for the Veep (1991, May 20). *Newsweek,* p. 22.

Sadalla, E. K., Linder, D. E., & Jenkins, B. A. (1988). Sport preference: A self-presentational analysis. *Journal of Sport and Exercise Psychology, 10,* 214–222.

Sadow, L., & Suslick, A. (1961). Simulation of a previous psychotic state. *Archives of General Psychiatry, 4,* 452–458.

Sanders, G. S. (1984). Self-presentation and drive in social facilitation. *Journal of Experimental Social Psychology, 20,* 312–322.

Sansom, C. D., MacInerney, J., Oliver, V., & Wakefield, J. (1975). Differential response to recall in a cervical screening programme. *British Journal of Preventative and Societal Medicine, 29,* 40–47.

Satow, K. (1975). Social approval and helping. *Journal of Experimental Social Psychology, 11,* 501–509.

Sattler, J. M. (1966). Embarrassment and blushing: A theoretical review. *Journal of Social Psychology, 69,* 117–133.

Schachter, S. (1951). Deviation, rejection, and communication. *Journal of Abnormal and Social Psychology, 46,* 190–207.

Schachter, S. (1959). *The psychology of affiliation.* Stanford, CA: Stanford University Press.

Schlenker, B. R. (1975). Self-presentation: Managing the impression of consistency when reality interferes with self-enhancement. *Journal of Personality and Social Psychology, 32,* 1030–1037.

Schlenker, B. R. (1980). *Impression management: The self-concept, social identity, and interpersonal relations.* Monterey, CA: Brooks/Cole.

Schlenker, B. R. (1982). Translating actions into attitudes: An identity-analytic approach to the explanation of social conduct. In L. Berkowitz (Ed.), *Advances in experimental social psychology* (Vol. 15, pp. 193–246).

Schlenker, B. R. (1985). Identity and self-identification. In B. R. Schlenker (Ed.), *The self and social life* (pp. 65–99). New York: McGraw-Hill.

Schlenker, B. R. (1986). Self-identification: Toward an integration of the private and public self. In R. F. Baumeister (Ed.), *Public self and private self* (pp. 21–62). New York: Springer-Verlag.

Schlenker, B. R., & Darby, B. W. (1981). The use of apologies in social predicaments. *Social Psychology Quarterly, 44,* 271–278.

Schlenker, B. R., Forsyth, D. R., Leary, M. R., & Miller, R. S. (1980). A self-presentational analysis of the effects of incentives on attitude change following counterattitudinal behavior. *Journal of Personality and Social Psychology, 39,* 553–577.

Schlenker, B. R., & Leary, M. R. (1982a). Audiences' reactions to self-enhancing, self-denigrating, and accurate self-presentations. *Journal of Experimental Social Psychology, 18,* 89–104.

Schlenker, B. R., & Leary, M. R. (1982b). Social anxiety and self-presentation: A conceptualization and model. *Psychological Bulletin, 92,* 641–669.

Schlenker, B. R., & Miller, R. S. (1977). Egotism in groups: Self-serving bias or logical information processing. *Journal of Personality and Social Psychology, 35,* 755–764.

Schlenker, B. R., Miller, R. S., & Leary, M. R. (1983). Self-presentation as a function of self-monitoring and the validity and quality of past performance. *Representative Research in Social Psychology, 13,* 2–14.

Schlenker, B. R., & Weigold, M. F. (1992). Interpersonal processes involving impression regulation and management. *Annual review of psychology, 43,* 133–168.

Schlenker, B. R., Weigold, M. F., & Doherty, K. (1991). Coping with accountability: Self-identification and evaluative reckonings. In C. R. Snyder & D. R. Forsyth (Eds.), *Handbook of social and clinical psychology* (pp. 96–115). New York: Pergammon.

Schlenker, B. R., Weigold, M. F., & Hallam, J. R. (1990). Self-serving attributions in social context: Effects of self-esteem and social pressure. *Journal of Personality and Social Psychology, 58,* 855–863.

Schneider, D. J. (1969). Tactical self-presentation after success and failure. *Journal of Personality and Social Psychology, 13,* 262–268.

Schneider, D. J. (1981). Tactical self-presentations: Toward a broader conception. In J. T. Tedeschi (Ed.), *Impression management theory and social psychological research* (pp. 23–40). New York: Academic Press.

Schneider, D. J., & Eustis, A. C. (1972). Effects of ingratiation motivation, target positiveness, and revealingness on self-presentation. *Journal of Personality and Social Psychology, 22,* 149–155.

Schneider, D. J., & Turkat, D. (1975). Self-presentation following success and failure: Defensive self-esteem models. *Journal of Personality, 43,* 127–135.

Schneider, W., & Shiffrin, R. M. (1977). Controlled and automatic human information processing: I. Detection, search, and attention. *Psychological Review, 84,* 1–66.

Schwartz, S., & Gottlieb, A. (1976). Bystander reactions to a violent theft: Crime in Jerusalem. *Journal of Personality and Social Psychology, 34,* 1188–1199.

Schwartz, S., & Gottlieb, A. (1980). Bystander anonymity and reactions to emergencies. *Journal of Personality and Social Psychology, 39,* 418–430.

Schwartz, S. M., & Bilsky, W. (1987). Toward a universal psychological structure of human values. *Journal of Personality and Social Psychology, 53,* 550–562.

Scott, M. B., & Lyman, S. (1968). Accounts. *American Sociological Review, 33,* 46–62.

Segrin, C., & Dillard, J. P. (1992). The interactional theory of depression: A meta-analysis of the research literature. *Journal of Social and Clinical Psychology, 11,* 43–70.

Semin, G. R., & Manstead, A. S. R. (1982). The social implications of embarrassment displays and restitution behavior. *European Journal of Social Psychology, 12,* 367–377.

Sexually Transmitted Diseases Up (1993, April 1). *Winston-Salem Journal,* p. 20.

Shaffer, D. R., Smith, J. E., & Tomarelli, M. (1982). Self-monitoring as a determinant of self-disclosure reciprocity during the acquaintance process. *Journal of Personality and Social Psychology 43,* 163–175.

Shaw, M. E., & Wagner, P. J. (1975). Role selection in the service of self-presentation. *Memory and Cognition, 3,* 481–484.

Sheppard, B. H., & Vidmar, N. (1980). Adversary pretrial procedures and testimonial evidence: Effects of lawyer's role and Machiavellianism. *Journal of Personality and Social Psychology, 39,* 320–332.

Shepperd, J. A., & Arkin, R. M. (1989). Self-handicapping: The moderating roles of public self-consciousness and task importance. *Personality and Social Psychology Bulletin, 15,* 252–265.

Shepperd, J. A., & Arkin, R. M. (1990). Shyness and self-presentation. In W. R. Crozier (Ed.), *Shyness and embarrassment: Perspectives from social psychology* (pp. 286–314). Cambridge: Cambridge University Press.

Shepperd, J. A., & Arkin, R. M. (1991). Behavioral other-enhancement: Strategically obscuring the link between performance and evaluation. *Journal of Personality and Social Psychology, 60,* 79–88.

Sherman, M., Trief, P., & Sprafkin, R. (1975). Impression management in the psychiatric interview: Quality, style, and individual differences. *Journal of Consulting and Clinical Psychology, 43,* 867–871.

Shrauger, J. S., & Schoeneman, T. J. (1979). Symbolic interactionist view of self-concept: Through the looking glass darkly. *Psychological Bulletin, 86,* 549–573.

Sicoly, F., & Ross, M. (1977). Facilitation of ego-biased attributions by means of self-serving observer feedback. *Journal of Personality and Social Psychology, 35,* 734–741.

Siegel, L. (1993, March 29). When stress is high, workers fake illnesses, play hookey. *Winston-Salem Journal*, p. 16.

Sigall, H., Aronson, E., & Van Hoose, T. (1970). The cooperative subject: Myth or reality. *Journal of Experimental Social Psychology, 6,* 1–10.

Silver, M., Sabini, J., & Parrott, W. G. (1987). Embarrassment: A dramaturgic approach. *Journal for the Theory of Social Behavior, 17,* 47–61.

Smith, T. W., Snyder, C. R., & Handelsman, M. M. (1982). On the self-serving function of an academic wooden leg: Test anxiety as a self-handicapping strategy. *Journal of Personality and Social Psychology, 42,* 314–321.

Smith, T. W., Snyder, C. R., & Perkins, S. C. (1983). The self-serving function of hypochondriacal complaints: Physical symptoms as self-handicapping strategies. *Journal of Personality and Social Psychology, 44,* 787–797.

Snell, Jr., W. E. (1989). Willingness to self-disclose to female and male friends as a function of social anxiety and gender. *Personality and Social Psychology Bulletin, 15,* 113–125.

Snyder, C. R., Higgins, R. L., & Stucky, R. J. (1983). *Excuses: Masquerades in search of grace*. New York: Wiley-Interscience.

Synder, C. R., Lassegard, M., Ford, C. E. (1986). Distancing after group success and failure: Basking in reflected glory and cutting off reflected failure. *Journal of Personality and Social Psychology, 51,* 382–388.

Snyder, C. R., & Smith, T. W. (1986). On being "shy like a fox": A self-handicapping analysis. In W. H. Jones, J. M. Cheek, & S. R. Briggs (Eds.), *A sourcebook on shyness: Research and treatment* (pp. 161–172). New York: Plenum.

Snyder, C. R., Smith, T. W., Augelli, R. W., & Ingram, R. E. (1985). On the self-serving function of social anxiety: Shyness as a self-handicapping strategy. *Journal of Personality and Social Psychology, 48,* 970–980.

Snyder, M. (1974). Self-monitoring of expressive behavior. *Journal of Personality and Social Psychology, 30,* 526–537.

Snyder, M. (1987). *Public appearances/private realities: The psychology of self-monitoring*. New York: W. H. Freeman.

Snyder, M., & Copeland, J. (1989). Self-monitoring processes in organizational settings. In R. A. Giacalone & P. Rosenfeld (Eds.), *Impression management in the organization* (pp. 7–19). Hillsdale, NJ: Erlbaum.

Snyder, M., & Gangestad, S. (1986). On the nature of self-monitoring: Matters of assessment, matters of validity. *Journal of Personality and Social Psychology, 51,* 125–139.

Snyder, M. L., Smoller, B., Strenta, A., & Frankel, A. (1981). A comparison of egotism, negativity, and learned helplessness as explanations of poor performance after unsolvable problems. *Journal of Personality and Social Psychology, 40,* 24–30.

Solomon, M. R., & Schopler, J. (1982). Self-consciousness and clothing. *Personality and Social Psychology Bulletin, 8,* 508–514.

Sommers, S. (1984). Reported emotions and conventions of emotionality among college students. *Journal of Personality and Social Psychology, 46,* 207–215.

Spivey, E., & Leary, M. R. (1990). *Working against the odds: Self-enhancing tactics in a self-presentational dilemma*. Paper presented at the meeting of the Southeastern Psychological Association, Atlanta.

Steele, C. M. (1988). The psychology of self-affirmation: Sustaining the integrity of the self. In L. Berkowitz (Ed.), *Advances in experimental social psychology* (Vol. 21, pp. 261–302). San Diego, CA: Academic Press.

Stein, D. M. (1991). The prevalence of bulimia: A review of empirical research. *Journal of Nutrition Education, 23,* 205–213.

Stiles, W. B. (1987). "I have to talk to somebody." A fever model of self-disclosure. In V. J. Derlega & J. H. Berg (Eds.), *Self-disclosure: Theory, research, and therapy* (pp. 257–282). New York: Plenum.

Stiles, W. B., Shuster, P. L., & Harrigan, J. A. (1992). Disclosure and anxiety: A test of the fever model. *Journal of Personality and Social Psychology, 63,* 980–988.

Stires, L. D., & Jones, E. E. (1969). Modesty vs. self-enhancement as alternative forms of ingratiation. *Journal of Experimental Social Psychology, 5,* 172–188.

Stone, E. F. (1989). Self-presentation biases in organizational research. In R. A. Giacalone & P. Rosenfeld (Eds.), *Impression management in the organization* (pp. 189–202). Hillsdale, NJ: Erlbaum.

Strong and steady: Bush wants to project an image of control. (1991, Jan. 28). *Newsweek,* p. 34.

Swann, Jr., W. B. (1983). Self-verification: Bringing social reality into harmony with the self. In J. Suls & A. G. Greenwald (Eds.), *Social psychological perspectives on the self* (Vol. 2, pp. 33–66). Hillsdale, NJ: Erlbaum.

Swann, W. B., Jr. (1987). Identity negotiation: Where two roads meet. *Journal of Personality and Social Psychology, 53,* 1038–1051.

Swann, W. B., Jr., Griffin, J. J., Predmore, S. C., & Gaines, B. (1987). The cognitive-affective crossfire: When self-consistency confronts self-enhancement. *Journal of Personality and Social Psychology, 52,* 881–889.

Swann, Jr., W. B., Pelham, B. W., & Krull, D. S. (1989). Agreeable fancy or disagreeable truth: Reconciling self-enhancement with self-verification. *Journal of Personality and Social Psychology, 57,* 782–791.

Tedeschi, J. T. (March 11, 1992). Personal communication.

Tedeschi, J. T., & Norman, N. (1985). Social power, self-presentation, and the self. In B. R. Schlenker (Ed.), *The self and social life* (pp. 293–322). New York: McGraw-Hill.

Tedeschi, J. T., & Riordan, C. A. (1981). Impression management and prosocial behavior following transgression. In J. T. Tedeschi, *Impression management theory and social psychological research* (pp. 223–244). New York: Academic Press.

Tedeschi, J. T., & Rosenfeld, P. (1981). Impression management theory and the forced compliance situation. In J. T. Tedeschi, *Impression management theory and social psychological research* (pp. 147–180). New York: Academic Press.

Tedeschi, J. T., Schlenker, B. R., & Bonoma, T. V. (1971). Cognitive dissonance: Private ratiocination or public spectacle? *American Psychologist, 26,* 685–695.

Tedeschi, J. T., Smith, R. B. III, & Brown, R. C. (1974). A reinterpretation of research on aggression. *Psychological Bulletin, 81,* 540–563.

Tesser, A., & Moore, J. (1986). On the convergence of public and private aspects of self. In R. F. Baumeister (Ed.), *Public self and private self* (pp. 99–116). New York: Springer-Verlag.

Tesser, A., Rosen, A., & Batchelor, T. (1972). On the reluctance to communicate bad news (the MUM effect): A role play extension. *Journal of Personality, 40,* 88–103.

Tessler, R., & Schwartz, S. (1972). Help-seeking, self-esteem, and achievement motivation: An attributional analysis. *Journal of Personality and Social Psychology, 21*, 318–326.

Tetlock, P. E. (1985). Toward an intuitive politician model of attribution processes. In B. R. Schlenker (Ed.), *The self and social life* (pp. 203–234). New York: McGraw Hill.

Tetlock, P. E., & Manstead, A. S. R. (1985). Impression management vs. intrapsychic explanations in social psychology: A useful dichotomy? *Psychological Review, 92*, 59–77.

The Quayle handicap. (1991, May 20). *Newsweek*, pp. 20–24.

The Random House Dictionary (1972). New York: Random House.

Tice, D. M. (1992). Self-concept change and self-presentation: The looking glass self is also a magnifying glass. *Journal of Personality and Social Psychology, 63*, 435–451.

Tice, D. M. (1993). The social motivations of people with low self-esteem. In R. F. Baumeister (Ed.), *Self-esteem: The puzzle of low self-regard*. New York: Plenum.

Tice, D. M., & Baumeister, R. F. (1990). Self-esteem, self-handicapping, and self-presentation. The strategy of inadequate practice. *Journal of Personality, 58*, 443–464.

Toby, E. L., & Tunnell, G. (1981). Predicting our impressions on others: Effects of public self-consciousness and acting, a self-monitoring subscale. *Personality and Social Psychology Bulletin, 7*, 661–669.

Toch, H. (1992). *Violent men*. Washington, D.C.: American Psychological Association.

Tucker, J. A., Vuckinich, R. E., & Sobell, M. B. (1981). Alcohol consumption as a self-handicapping strategy. *Journal of Abnormal Psychology, 90*, 220–230.

Turner, R. E., & Edgley, C. (1976). Death as theatre: A dramaturgical analysis of the American funeral. *Sociology and Social Research, 60*, 377–392.

Turner, R. H. (1990). Role taking: Process versus conformity. In D. Brissett & C. Edgley (Eds.), *Life as theatre: A dramaturgical source book*. Hawthorne, NY: Aldine de Gruyter.

Upshaw, H. S., & Yates, L. A. (1968). Self-persuasion, social approval, and task success as determinants of self-esteem following impression management. *Journal of Experimental Social Psychology, 4*, 143–152.

Vallacher, R. R., Wegner, D. M., & Frederick, J. (1987). The presentation of self through action identification. *Social Cognition, 5*, 301–322.

VanderVelde, C. D. (1985). Body images of oneself and of others: Developmental and clinical significance. *The American Journal of Psychiatry, 142*, 526–531.

van Hooff, J. (1972). A comparative approach to the phylogeny of laughter and smiling. In R. A. Hinde (Ed.), *Non-verbal communication* (pp. 209–241). Cambridge: Cambridge University Press.

Wall, Jr., J. A. (1991). Impression management in negotiations. In R. A. Giacalone & P. Rosenfeld (Eds.), *Applied impression management* (pp. 133–156). Newbury Park, CA: Sage.

Walters, J. R., & Seyfarth, R. M. (1987). Conflict and cooperation. In B. B. Smuts, D. L., Cheney, R. M. Seyfarth, R. W. Wrangham, & T. T. Struhsaker (Eds.), *Primate societies*. Chicago: University of Chicago Press.

Watson, C. G. (1972). Roles of impression management in the interview, self-report, and cognitive behavior of schizophrenics. *Journal of Consulting and Clinical Psychology, 38*, 452–456.

Watson, C. G. (1973). Conspicuous psychotic behavior as a manipulative tool. *Journal of Clinical Psychology, 29*, 3–7.

Watson, C. G. (1975). Impression management ability in psychiatric hospital samples and normals. *Journal of Consulting and Clinical Psychology, 43,* 540–545.

Watson, D., & Friend, R. (1969). Measurement of social-evaluative anxiety. *Journal of Consulting and Clinical Psychology, 33,* 448–457.

Weary, G., & Arkin, R. M. (1981). Attributional self-presentation and the regulation of self-evaluation. In J. H. Harvey, W. Ickes, R. F. Kidd (Eds.), *New directions in attribution research* (Vol. 3). Hillsdale, NJ: Erlbaum.

Weary, G., & Williams, J. P. (1990). Depressive self-presentation: Beyond self-handicapping. *Journal of Personality and Social Psychology, 58,* 892–898.

Wegner, D. M., & Giuliano, T. (1982). The forms of social awareness. In W. Ickes & E. S. Knowles (Eds.), *Personality, roles, and social behavior* (pp. 165–198). New York: Springer-Verlag.

Weideger, P. (1976). *Menstruation and menopause.* New York: Alfred A. Knopf.

Weinberg, M. S. (1968). Embarrassment: Its variable and invariable aspects. *Social Forces, 46,* 382–388.

Weinstein, H. M., & Richman, A. (1984). The group treatment of bulimia. *Journal of American College Health, 32,* 208–215.

Weissman, H. N. (1990). Distortions and deceptions in self presentation: Effects of protracted litigation in personal injury cases. *Behavioral Sciences and the Law, 8,* 67–74.

Wheeler, L., Reis, H., & Nezlek, J. (1983). Loneliness and social interaction. *Journal of Personality and Social Psychology, 45,* 943–953.

Wheeless, V. E. (1984). Communication apprehension and trust as predictors of willingness to discuss gynecological health topics. *Communication Research Reports, 1,* 117–121.

Wicklund, R. A., & Gollwitzer, P. M. (1982). *Symbolic self-completion.* Hillsdale, NJ: Erlbaum.

Wilcox, R., & Krasnoff, A. (1967). Influence of test-taking attitudes on personality inventory scores. *Journal of Consulting Psychology, 31,* 188–194.

Williams, J. E., Saiz, J. L., & Munick, M. (1991). *Scaling the Adjective Check List for psychological importance* (Tech. Rep. No. 1). Winston-Salem, NC: Wake Forest University, Department of Psychology.

Williams, J. G., Park, L. I., & Kline, J. (1992). Reducing distress associated with pelvic examinations: A stimulus control intervention. *Women and Health, 19,* 107–115.

Williams, K. D., Harkins, S., & Latané, B. (1981). Identifiability as a deterrent to social loafing: Two cheering experiments. *Journal of Personality and Social Psychology, 40,* 303–311.

Williams, K. D., Nida, S. A., Baca, L. D., & Latane, B. (1989). Social loafing and swimming: Effects of identifiability on individual and relay performance of intercollegiate swimmers. *Basic and Applied Social Psychology, 10,* 73–81.

Wine, J. D. (1971). Test anxiety and direction of attention. *Psychological Bulletin, 76,* 92–104.

Worringham, C. L., & Messick, D. M. (1983). Social facilitation of running: An unobtrusive study. *Journal of Social Psychology, 121,* 23–29.

Zanna, M. P., & Pack, S. J. (1975). On the self-fulfilling nature of apparent sex differences in behavior. *Journal of Experimental Social Psychology, 11,* 583–591.

Zimbardo, P. G. (1977). *Shyness.* New York: Jove.

INDEX

LaVergne, TN USA
09 December 2010

208046LV00004B/5/A

9 780813 330044